MW0 1413601

General George S. Patton, Jr.

MAN UNDER MARS

BY

JAMES WELLARD

WITH ILLUSTRATIONS
AND MAPS

NEW YORK
DODD, MEAD & COMPANY
1946

Copyright, 1946,
By JAMES WELLARD

ALL RIGHTS RESERVED
NO PART OF THIS BOOK MAY BE REPRODUCED IN ANY FORM
WITHOUT PERMISSION IN WRITING FROM THE PUBLISHER

PRINTED IN THE UNITED STATES OF AMERICA

DEDICATION

TO THE OFFICERS, ENLISTED MEN, AND WAR CORRESPONDENTS WHO WERE MY COMRADES DURING FOUR YEARS OF WAR IN ENGLAND, NORTH AFRICA, SICILY, ITALY, FRANCE, LUXEMBURG, BELGIUM, HOLLAND, AND GERMANY

PREFACE

THIS book is not an official biography of General George Smith Patton, Jr.; it is an interpretative study of an American who typifies in his career and personality a phase of history which has just ended with the last of what we may come to know as the "Gunpowder Wars."

So far, Patton has been written about almost exclusively under the title of "Old Blood and Guts," though no one associated with him or his armies ordinarily calls him by that name. The impression given by newspaper and magazine accounts is of a brilliant and impetuous general who makes war as exciting and colorful a spectacle as an epic in glorious technicolor.

Whatever Patton did, he seems to have had a label slapped on him. The labels are many, including among the more complimentary, Buck Rogers, Flash Gordon, The Man from Mars, The Green Hornet, Iron Pants, and, of course, Old Blood and Guts. After the "slapping" incident in Sicily, he was known as "the man 50,000 G.I.s were waiting to shoot." After the Third Army's victories in Europe, he was re-labelled Hero. Before long he can, in the nature of things, expect to be called Fascist and Warmonger.

Who, then, is this Patton who is booed one day and applauded the next by a hundred million of his fellow countrymen? In this book I have tried to tell, by relating the whole story of the man, his exploits, and his beliefs. I have tried to show that Patton is not a man covered over with many contradictory labels, but a soldier whose life has been devoted to a single idea which he has elevated into a faith. That idea, or faith, is a passionate love of war, which becomes, in Patton, a martyr's urge to die on the battlefield.

It is hard for civilians in a modern democratic society to understand this self-sacrificial love of war, for the warrior class which held such ideas is now almost extinct. But war is what Patton believes in; and it is this belief which explains why he was once called Hero, why he pommeled a sick soldier, why he raced across Europe, why he attacked the Siegfried Line in the depth of winter, why he crossed the Rhine without firing a shot, why he came home a Conqueror, why he told a Sunday-school class there would always be wars, and why he showed covert sympathy with Nazis in Occupied Germany.

If Patton was merely the exponent of the gospel of expert killing, he would be a more fitting subject for a military historian than for me. But his personality and ideas fell with tremendous impact on millions of Americans who fought in the last of the "Gunpowder Wars"; and I felt that in telling his story I could tell, in part, their story, too.

So I have attempted to describe Patton as I saw him against the background of great events, when I was serving as a war correspondent with his armies in Tunisia, Sicily, and Europe, from November, 1942, to May, 1945. What I saw and experienced helped me to understand not only Patton, but also the men who fought with him, and the war they fought, and the significance of that war to him and to them. Because I was a civilian, I saw many aspects of war which the professional soldier either does not notice or disregards; and I saw especially that while war has its sad splendor which Patton has glorified into a creed, it has a physical and spiritual ugliness which transcends even the beauty of brave men doing brave deeds.

And so when I came to examine the life and times of Patton, I tried to find in the circumstances of his origin and environment an explanation for the prayer he addresses to a Deity he calls "God of Battle," a prayer which says: "To slay, God make us wise." My inquiries took me as far back as another Patton who lived a hundred years ago, Brigadier-General George Smith Patton, who died a hero's death on the field of battle at Winchester, September 9, 1864.

This, then, is where the book begins; and it ends almost a century later, June, 1945.

In writing this first book-length biography of Patton, I had a great deal of material based on his exploits as commander of our European armies, but little or nothing on the previous phases of his life. The short newspaper and magazine accounts which have appeared in the last three years were full of picturesque episodes and quotations; but they all seemed, to me at least, rather hearty and hasty attempts to justify a successful general to a dubious public. I found, for instance, a whole series of oft-repeated stories which had a vaguely apocryphal sound. There was the story of the twenty-six polo ponies which Patton was reputed to have taken to his first camp in Texas, after he graduated as a second lieutenant from West Point. I mentioned this story to Mrs. Beatrice Patton, the general's wife, and received an indignant denial: "We never had twenty-six ponies."

I realized, then, in order to get an accurate account of Patton's early life, I would have to consult people rather than records. I, therefore, applied to Mrs. Patton, who graciously received me, and gave me the data I needed, even though her experiences with interviewers had not been happy ones; for the information she gave them, she said, was often distorted or misused. Nonetheless, she was kind enough to go over the part of the manuscript I had finished, correcting certain errors of fact, and to give me material for the earlier chapters.

I wish to thank Mrs. Patton for her invaluable help, at the same time pointing out that she is in no way responsible for any of the views about her husband which I have put forward; but, on the contrary, she is in strong disagreement with many of the conclusions I have drawn. But I believe my facts are accurate, and the twenty-six polo ponies, together with a number of other "tall tales," are, thanks to her guidance, now struck from the record.

I also had the opportunity of talking with men who knew Patton before and during the First World War, and from them I obtained certain information which is incorporated into this book. All of it is not favorable to Patton; but I was not writing either a panegyric or an obituary; only a factual account with a personal interpretation of those facts. Admirers of the General may disagree with my interpretation on the grounds that I have overemphasized the less favorable aspects of his character. His friends at West Point will hotly dispute the statement that he was unpopular at the Academy, or that he was called a "quilloid," though this information was forthcoming from a fellow cadet of the same class as Patton. Others may object to my account of Patton's role in the Mexican and First World Wars; but here again I have drawn my own conclusions from the accounts of his contemporaries.

On the other hand, some readers may see in this study of

a victorious general and brilliant field commander a justification of a warlike man and his philosophy. I reply that I have given Patton credit on the basis of military facts which are indisputable; and certainly I had no intention of rooting for another war, having just finished four years of this last one.

In conclusion, I wish to thank the Public Relations Officers of the War Department for making available a tremendous file on Patton; Mr. Edward Dodd, Jr., for his encouragement to write this book; and my wife, Mary, who has helped me throughout in gathering and collating material and being my "gentle reader."

New York, October, 1945.

NOTE

JUST as this book was going to press news came of General Patton's fatal accident in Germany. A brief factual Epilogue has been added, detailing the final events of Patton's career from the time of his return to Europe until his death at Heidelberg December 21, 1945.

CONTENTS

	INTRODUCTION: CONCERNING BLOOD AND GUTS ...	1
I	"GEORGE I"-"GEORGE III," 1836-1885	19
II	"SIEGEL-COOPER COWBOY"	33
III	PATTON DONS HIS SHINING CASQUE	45
IV	CASABLANCA—"A NICE FIGHT"	51
V	BIRTH OF AN ARMY	71
VI	"BORN AT SEA, BAPTIZED IN BLOOD ..."	105
VII	THE SLAP HEARD ROUND THE WORLD	125
VIII	THE GETHSEMANE OF THE HEDGEROWS	134
IX	THE COVERED WAGON WAR	149
X	THE FALAISE GAP	162
XI	EISENHOWER MAKES HIS DECISION	167
XII	THE TANKS STOP	175
XIII	GERMANY DECLARES A NEW WAR	182
XIV	THE BATTLE OF THE TUNNELS	195
XV	ASSAULT ON THE SAAR	200
XVI	PATTON'S GOOSE—AND THE SIEGFRIED LINE	218
XVII	"I'LL TAKE VON RUNDSTEDT AND SHOVE HIM ..."	227
XVIII	"WHERE IS 'BLOODY' PATTON?"	244
XIX	DEATH OF A NATION	254
XX	TO VALHALLA VIA SUNSET BOULEVARD	270
	EPILOGUE	275

INTRODUCTION

CONCERNING BLOOD AND GUTS ...

I

WAR, says General George Smith Patton, Jr., is the supreme test of man, in which he rises to heights never approached in any other activity.

This, then, is the creed which has determined George Smith Patton's thoughts and actions during the sixty years of his life, earning for him at the end of it the titles of General of the United States Army, Commander of the Seventh and Third United States Armies, Conqueror of Metz, Most Honourable Order of the Bath, Buck Rogers, Flash Gordon, The Man from Mars, The Green Hornet, Iron Pants, and Old Blood and Guts.

This is the creed, and symbols of that creed are the pistol and the tank: the pistol because it is the weapon which bridges the gap between the era of armor and the gunpowder age; and the tank because it is the machine which links the medieval with the modern warrior. Pistol and tank symbolize for Patton the fusion of the romantic and the mechanical arts of war.

Part of the creed is the uniform, the martial garb which distinguishes the soldier from the civilian. Hence the suits of mail which he himself makes and wears at fancy dress parties; hence the Robin Hood uniform with white buttons on a green tunic, black stripes down the trouser legs, and a golden helmet, which he designed for himself as a tank commander; and hence the buskin in which he ultimately presented himself to the American people as a Conquering Hero—in full general's dress, resplendent, not with four, but with twenty-four stars.

Such a man, with such a creed, obviously belongs to a warrior caste, now extinct in modern democratic society. For though this is a century of wars, it is not a century of warriors. It is a political century, and soldiers do not now rule the world. They alone do not make wars, start or end them, win or lose them. In the interplay of political, economic, and social factors which shape our world, the professional soldier is an insignificant piece, who is moved, like a pawn, ahead of the kings, queens, and bishops of the international chess game.

But though professional soldiers do not make wars, General George S. Patton, Jr., with his creed of blood and guts, his pistol and his tank, has become a kind of symbol not only of this, but of all traditional or romantic wars. The development of the atomic explosive and the rocket makes it now certain that future wars will not be fought with the traditional means and romantic methods of this recent conflict; that armies and navies, guns and tanks, blood and guts, are already obsolescent and belong, with the charges of light brigades, to the pages of history. Yet we can still study Patton, his philosophy and his career, as symbolic of an historical phase; and we can read in his story the story of millions of Americans who fought in the last of the traditional wars, which has just ended and is still fresh in the memories of each of us.

George S. Patton was not necessarily the greatest of the American generals who commanded armies or groups of armies in this war. He had little to do with the larger planning of victory. He is emotionally unsuited to grasp the higher mathematics of modern war. Mathematics has always been his academic stumbling block. Nor is he temperamentally suited to the strategy of crushing the enemy by weight. He prefers personal encounters, which he calls blood; and personal courage, which he pronounces guts. So he remains a brilliant field commander, combining the qualities of army general with those of company sergeant-major, with a highly developed skill in the art of killing.

Significantly, his chosen weapon, the pistol, is an anachronism in the arsenal of modern war. The pistol is the least lethal of all the tubes and barrels through which men eject explosive missiles; and compared with the rocket, belongs to the crossbow era of warfare. And even the tank is relatively unimportant compared with a score of newer devices which were used in this War, or are being prepared for the next. In this last War, the main problem confronting the Allies on all fronts was the problem of crossing oceans, seas, and rivers, and landing their armies on hostile shores. It could be contended that we might have won the European war without tanks, as we won the Asiatic War; but we could have won neither without the LCT (Landing Craft Tanks), or LCI (Landing Craft Infantry), or "ducks" (amphibious trucks), or crocodiles (amphibious troop carriers), floating piers, floating oilpipe lines, waterproof jeeps, or any one of many engineering devices which enabled our armies to undertake amphibious operations.

In comparison with these new accouterments of war, the tank was a second-line weapon, which only became significant once these newer weapons had, as it were, made victory already a certainty. In both the Sicilian and European campaigns, our air forces first, and our amphibious machines next, cracked the enemy's inner and perimetral defenses before the first tank rolled ashore. In Sicily, that process had been so thorough that jeeps, half-tracks, and trucks carrying infantry were able to complete the reduction of the island as effectively as tanks. In Normandy, once the air forces, artillery, and infantry had done their preparatory work, and torn the German defenses apart, any mobile force, whether tanks or trucks, was able to race right across France, meeting scarcely any organized resistance. In fact, many of the Third Army infantry divisions, entrucked and motorized, fought their way almost to the German frontiers without the aid of armored divisions.

Still, the pistol and the tank, of all the multifarious machines of modern war, symbolize Patton's particular military genius. That genius was such that out of the impersonality of mechanized war, with its new gadgets, scientists, physicists, engineers, strategists, technical advisers, and general staffs, emerges the figure of George S. Patton as a prototype of the last traditional war. More than any other general, he symbolizes the violence of battle; and more than any other is his story the story of Americans at war between 1941 and 1945.

2

What special strategic or tactical genius, then, did Patton have to be thus distinguished among American commanders?

The Third Army's Saar offensive in the winter of 1944 provides, in part, the answer.

In November, 1944, Patton received orders to attack the Saar. The general strategy of this campaign had already been worked out months before in a series of conferences between Eisenhower and his chiefs of staff. It was these planners who assessed the objects, cost, and desirability of the plan; and who drew the thick arrows on the large-scale maps which, months later, were to become the intricate movements of hundreds of small units.

In modern war, no one general is wholly responsible for the planning of an attack. The procedure is extremely complex, passing all the way down the military hierarchy, from the Supreme Commander to some unnamed sergeant who eventually leads his squad into action. I have often thought how difficult—indeed, impossible—it is to apportion the credit for victory to individuals, whether they carry a star on their shoulders or simply a stripe on their sleeves.

In the case of the Saar offensive, the large strategy had, as I said, already been decided upon by the Supreme Command even before Patton's Third Army had landed on the beaches of Normandy. Long before the time came to execute the plan, it had been passed over to General Bradley, as commander of the 12th Army Group, which comprised the Ninth, First, and Third U. S. Armies. Bradley and his advisers studied the plan in more detail, weighing it in relation to the role of the three American armies on the central sector of the Western Front; and breaking down the thick arrows on the large-scale maps into finer symbols on particularized war charts.

Next, Bradley turned over the assignment to Patton, as commander of the Army which was to make the actual attack. The purpose of the Supreme Command in launching the offensive was explained; and it will be seen later in this book how at this time, in the winter of 1944, the Allies changed their whole European strategy from the quick "knock-out" theory to a policy of first destroying Germany's entire war industry. The attack on the Saar, therefore, was not Patton's idea, but the concept of the Supreme Command.

So, under orders from Bradley, the group commander—who was, in turn, under orders from Eisenhower, Supreme Commander—Patton summoned his army and air force chiefs to a conference at his headquarters in Nancy. The general plan of attack which resulted from this conference was again the work of a dozen specialists. The air advisers provided most of the data concerning terrain, weather, and extent of air support. The intelligence officers gave the estimated enemy strength and dispositions. The artillery officers predicted the extent and effect of the artillery support. The personnel department reported on the state of the troops, the strength of our battle units, and the figures concerning replacements. The quartermaster provided vital figures concerning supplies and the number of trucks available for moving those supplies. All of it was essential information; and only after it had been collated and interpreted, could Patton outline the general strategy which would govern the Saar offensive.

Next, with the framework of his plan thus developed, Patton turned the problem over to the commanders of the divisions which were to make the actual attacks. Within divisional headquarters the procedure was repeated, large arrows were attenuated into small dagger-like symbols, big units were subdivided into regiments, battalions, and companies.

And so, after months of planning by a chain of officers who reached from the front line in Lorraine to the Pentagon Building in Washington, Thomas Smith, rifleman, was moved as inexorably as a pawn in a chess game.

Whether Rifleman Smith was moved successfully depended primarily, in the Saar offensive, on two strategic decisions which Patton alone, as commander of the Army, could make: the first decision was where to launch the attack, the second was what troops to employ in making it.

Patton's choice of place was largely determined by a temperamental trait which has always motivated his own personal conduct. When Patton jumps a hurdle, he invariably chooses the highest place to urge his horse across. He is constantly attempting the impossible. So his "strategy of place" in this war reflected his temperament. Wherever he found terrain which, because of thickly-wooded mountain slopes or a flooded river, looked impassable, that was where Patton decided to attack. It was an extremely sound and successful policy, and became in practice the strategy of attacking where the enemy least expected it.

He used this "strategy of the unexpected" consummately in the second attack on Metz. To reduce Metz, Patton decided to by-pass the fortress by crossing the Moselle where the flooded river looked unfordable. That was where the 90th Infantry Division crossed to the north of the town, while the 5th, at a similar apparently unfordable point, crossed to the south. To deceive the German defenders of the citadel, Patton made a feinting frontal assault with the 95th Division. The plan succeeded brilliantly. The impregnable fortress was reduced by a vast pincer operation which closed round and behind Metz while the Germans were busy with the frontal assault. Metz was a nice example of Patton's famed dictum: "Grab your enemy by the nose, and kick him in the behind."

He was to repeat these tactics throughout the Saar offensive. The Third Army was always attacking "impossible" places, across rivers in flood, through swamps, and finally, right into the heart of the Siegfried Line. Yet wherever the assault seemed likeliest to be most costly, it was made with the fewest casualties.

This daring exploitation of terrain is Patton's first claim to greatness as a field commander. His second is an equally daring use of his troops.

All commanders have to calculate the human factor as part of their strategy. In fact, strategy is an equation between the place chosen for the attack and the type of troops chosen to make it. Within limits, the human factor involved is not incalculable. Military statisticians can predict the percentage of casualties in a given engagement. But the higher mathematics of death are more complex than that. The factor of human capability is the quintessence of the thing. How many men in a company, for instance, will advance up a hill under fire, after they have crossed a river in their rubber boats? How many will simply lie down on the far bank in a hole, and pretend to be a casualty, so that they can have a better chance to survive, in the feeling that they have already taken one chance too many in the grim gamble with life itself? How many of the original company will rise from the ground to storm the hill? And will they be enough for success?

In calculating these contingencies and incorporating them into his plan, Patton always reckoned on the capacity of American troops to do the emotionally, as well as the physically impossible. Herein he again showed his strange genius as a field commander. He knew with sure intuition what each of the divisions under his command could do—what lengths of courage they would go to, not from faith, as the German or Russian soldier, but from training, experience, and that vague unit loyalty which was a substitute for faith in the American Army.

And so when Patton prepared his series of attacks on the Saar, he showed his intuition for "plain soldiering" in the allocation of certain divisions for certain tasks; and he was never wrong, except in Tunisia, where he miscalculated the capabilities of a still inexperienced American force. But later, he accurately assessed the "human factor" even in the new divisions which came under his command, and actually sent a green unit, the 98th Division—which had never been in battle—to cross the Saar River on the Luxemburg border, right under the guns of Siegfried forts dug into the overhanging hills. The division made the crossing and took its objectives, even more skilfully than the veteran 5th, which was one of the Third Army's elite divisions.

So Patton made his plans for the attack on the Saar; and once they had been made, he took a personal hand in seeing them carried out, changing from Army to divisional commander, and from divisional commander to the leader of the smaller units. They said he himself swam the Saar River at the time the 98th crossed. He did not. But, because he was so ubiquitous, he was always on the scene when an attack was launched, and not a company went down to its assignment without his knowing about it and going with it in spirit.

Patton's genius as a field commander was, in brief, the genius of a general who fought his battles with the strategy of the "impossible." The terrain he chose to attack across, the feats of arms he expected of his men, and the speed with which he moved, all seemed at the time impossible. To other generals whose instincts were more humane, such strategy and tactics *were* impossible. But Patton's violent passion for war enabled him to subject his soldiers continually to that "supreme test in which man rises to heights never approached in any other activity."

Fortunately for Patton, the American soldiers passed the test, bringing him with their life's blood the many prizes of victory.

3

Patton's bellicosity is more than an adolescent passion for flying banners, charging horses, and the clash of armor. It is a mature and studied partiality for blood and gore. All his thinking, all his actions, and all his words, are consistent with his creed that blood must flow and guts be spilled to the end that he may be justified in the eyes of God and men.

He has expressed his views often in formal public pronouncements, in the harsher lingo of the barrack square, and even in the soft language of poetry.

The world has heard the first of these expressions of his faith. "War is the supreme test of man," he said as far back as 1936.

"In my opinion there will be another war, because there have always been wars," he told a Sunday-school class of children only a few months ago.

Thus his public pronouncements. Unfortunately, his more candid and more representative sentiments cannot always be given verbatim, because of the conventions of print. But Patton believes that "Goddamit, you can't run an army without profanity," and when he addresses the soldiery, his favorite words are "bastard," "son of a bitch," and four-lettered Anglo-Saxon monosyllables describing the fundamental processes of procreation and bowel movements. But it is on such occasions, when a gathering of soldiers stand before his reviewing stand, that he expresses most forcefully his true faith; and not in such relatively polite dicta as get printed in the magazines, like "Retreat is as cowardly as it is fatal"; and "A pint of sweat will save a gallon of blood"; and "Americans do not surrender."

On a blue-and-white day in June, 1944, he stood on a reviewing stand in the green countryside of Western England, looking out over a solid mass of khaki-clad men who had come from America to fight and die in France. A band had just finished playing "The March of the Armored Force," written by Mrs. Patton. The chaplain had ended his brief invocation, asking divine guidance for the Third Army which was shortly to leave for the continent. Then Major-General Cook introduced Lieutenant-General Simpson, whose Ninth Army was still in America.

"We are here," said General Simpson, "to listen to the words of a great man. . . ."

The great man rose and strode to the microphone. His audience rose from their places on the ground, and stood to attention.

"Be seated," said General Patton.

Then, to the men who were his soldiers, chosen by fate as the instruments of his will, he expounded his simple creed of blood and guts in simple and unmistakable phrases. He said:

"Men, this stuff we hear about America wanting to stay out of the war, not wanting to fight, is a lot of bull. Americans love to fight—traditionally. All real Americans love the sting and clash of battle. When you were kids, you all admired the champion marble player, the fastest runner, the big league ball players, the toughest boxers. . . .

You are not all going to die. Only two per cent of you

here, in a major battle, would die. Death must not be feared. Every man is frightened, at first, in battle. If he says he isn't, he's a goddam liar. . . .

All through your army career you men have bitched about what you call this chicken-crap drilling. That is all for a purpose. . . .

An army is a team. Lives, sleeps, eats, fights, as a team. This individual heroic stuff is a lot of crap. The bilious bastards who write that sort of stuff for *The Saturday Evening Post* don't know any more about real battle than they do about ———. . . .

We have the best food, the finest equipment, the best spirit, the best men in the world. Why, by God, I actually pity those poor sons of bitches we're going up against. By God, I do. . . .

Every dam' last man has a job to do. Even the chaplain is important, for if we get killed and he isn't there to bury us, we'll all go to hell . . . We don't want yellow cowards in this army. They should be killed off like flies. If not, they will go home after the war, and breed more cowards. The brave men will breed more brave men. Kill off the dam' cowards, and we'll have a nation of brave men. . . .

I'm not supposed to be commanding this Army—I'm not even supposed to be in England. Let the first bastards to find out be the goddam Germans. Some day I want them to rise up on their hind legs and howl, 'Jesus Christ, it's the goddam Third Army and that son of a bitch Patton again.' . . .

We want to get the hell over there. We want to get over there and clean up the goddam thing—and then we'll have to take a little jaunt against the purple-pissin' Japanese, before the Marines get all the goddam credit . . .

Keep moving. We'll win this war, but we'll only win it by fighting and by showing our guts. . . .

CONCERNING BLOOD AND GUTS ... 13

There's one great thing that you men can say when it's all over, and you're home once more. You can thank God that twenty years from now, when you're sitting by the fireside with your grandson on your knee and he asks what you did in the war, you won't have to shift him to the other knee, cough, and say, 'I shoveled crap in Louisiana.' "

4

General Patton also writes poetry. Though these poems lack the Elizabethan lushness of that oration bawled across the still English landscape in June, 1944, they express in a far more subtle and revealing manner the muted desires of his inner self.

Patton has written poetry all his life. His early work is merely a reiteration of the themes and jingles of the third-rate rhymesters. In his later compositions, notably in two poems he has seen fit to print, he tries to express, with considerable poetic feeling but inadequate skill, the quintessence of his faith. One of these poems is called "A Soldier's Burial," and was printed in the *Chicago Sun* of August 1, 1943. It reads:

> Not midst the chanting of the requiem hymn,
> Nor with the solemn ritual of prayer,
> 'Neath misty shadows from the oriel glass,
> And dreamy perfume of the incensed air,
> Was he interred.
>
> But in the subtle stillness after fight,
> And in the half-light, between the night and day,
> We dragged his body all besmeared with blood,
> And dropped it, clodlike, back into the clay.

> Yet who shall say that he was not content,
> Or missed the priest or drone of chanting choir,
> He, who had heard all day the battle hymn,
> Sung on all sides by a thousand throats of fire?
>
> What painted glass can lovelier shadows cast
> Than those of starlit skies shall ever shed?
> While mingled with their light, Red Battle's sun
> Completes in magic colors o'er our dead,
> The flag for which they died.

The poetic instinct in these verses is strong, though the general feeling and form of the poem have both been subconsciously borrowed from Gray's *Elegy*. Yet we can detect something in Patton's poetry which is seldom apparent in his prose—and particularly in his bombastic utterances meant for what he considers the untutored soldiery. We can discern a dichotomy in his own nature—some inner yearning for a beauty which has nothing to do with "blood and guts." We note the poet's absorption with the more obvious manifestations of such beauty: the requiem hymn, the solemn ritual of prayer, misty shadows, dreamy perfume, painted glass, and starlit skies. It is as though he is about to surrender himself to the soft and lovely beatitudes of peace, when suddenly he recalls that he is not a poet at all, but a warrior, concerned not with the delicate aesthetic sensations of misty shadows from the oriel glass, or still lovelier shadows cast by painted windows, but with bodies "all besmeared with blood." In that concept of the dead and mutilated soldier, Patton, the lover of war, brutally asserts himself over Patton, the lover of life. But the impression remains that the soldier who has so consistently preached the nihilism of war, with its horror and suffering and futility, secretly yearns for the beatitude of peace, with its beauty, serenity, and meaningfulness.

This is a rare aspect of George S. Patton, Jr. But when we hear of him weeping at the bedside of one wounded soldier and a moment later slapping another, we should remember this dichotomy of his nature. The "soft" side of that nature he has gone to great lengths to conceal; and in the second of his published poems, he has hidden it altogether under a forthright statement of his faith. This poem is the "God of Battles," which somehow got itself printed in a woman's magazine, the *Woman's Home Companion*. It reads:

> From pride and foolish confidence,
> From every weakening creed,
> From the dread fear of fearing,
> Protect us, Lord, and lead.
>
> Great God, who through the ages
> Has braced the bloodstained hand,
> As Saturn, Jove, or Wodin,
> Hast led our warrior band,
>
> Again we seek Thy council,
> But not in cringing guise;
> We whine not for Thy mercy—
> To slay: God make us wise.
>
> For slaves who shun the issue
> We do not ask Thy aid.
> To Thee we trust our spirits,
> Our bodies unafraid.

> From doubt and fearsome boding,
> Still Thou our spirits guard;
> Make strong our souls to conquer,
> Give us the victory, Lord.

In this poem Patton renounces all concern with the mystical yearnings of peace and beauty, and with the God of requiem hymns, oriel glasses, and painted windows. His God is now a bloody-minded deity whose function it is to assist the strong to vanquish the weak; and his creed is the brutal creed of killing efficiently.

5

It has not been difficult for a man of Patton's physique and temperament to pay homage to a god of battles and to perfect the art of killing. Even that aspect of his nature which is glimpsed in the "Oriel Glass" poem found expression in war. For war has its manifold beauty and cloaks the men who are about to enter its lists with a sad splendor which they never have in civilian life.

You cannot help but be struck in wartime by this aesthetic transformation of the normal civilian into the helmeted soldier. It is poignantly apparent on the faces of a line of infantrymen marching down to a river which they must cross under fire. They march by in silence. Their faces wear no expression. Their eyes are dull and remote. Their bodies are bowed under the weight of equipment. Their clothes are soiled, their boots unshined. But as they pass by along some hillside or through some dark grove, they shine with a strange splendor; and you realize that every one of them is beautiful. The profound quietness of their faces is beautiful, so are their occasional words. Their round, ugly helmets, their soiled uniforms and wide boots, their rifles, their machine gun parts, their bazookas, their little sacks of personal belongings, the cigarettes dangling in their mouths, are all tremendously beautiful, as they pass by, one behind another, to the river which they think will be the last river they will cross.

War, then, is beautiful. Especially the combat soldier is beautiful; and at the front, you suddenly are aware that you never see an ugly man, though they all may seem ugly and coarse in the cities where they congregate between battles. So, too, the background of war is beautiful: the tents, trees, rain, mud, the groups of men who just stand about, their postures indefinably graceful, these things and their uniforms and their faces now part of their character and their thinking. The gravity of every man's mien, the way they look at each other, the sudden and rare smiles, the exchange of cigarettes, are all harmonious and aesthetic, and all become experiences which have a profound significance not known in cities.

So war has its beauty and emotion; and the explanation of Patton's love for it is partly this awareness of its beauty, to which he opens wide his eyes, while shutting out the horrible spiritual and physical ugliness of it. For Patton, the beauty atones for the agony. Discipline, loyalty, and courage are held to be prizes worth the price of regimentation, self-abnegation, and terror. Heroism justifies annihilation. A soldier's medal justifies a mother's anguish.

It is a nihilistic philosophy for which the world has paid in indescribable suffering for the glorification of those who hold it. The American soldier wanted no part of such a philosophy, or such beauty, or such glorification. His attitude was summed up by a wounded Ranger who lay on a cot in southern Tunisia, when Patton was commander of the Second Corps which was attacking Rommel's flank; he turned on his bed and said:

"Blood and guts! We supply the blood and he supplies the guts. To hell with that."

CHAPTER I

"GEORGE I"-"GEORGE III," 1836-1885

I

GENERAL GEORGE SMITH PATTON, JR., was born on November 11, 1885, but his story begins fifty years before with another Patton, also George Smith, and also a general. Grandfather Patton was the first of what is now a military hierarchy. The Patton father was also a military man for a time, although his martial experience was restricted to the Virginia Military Institute and to battles fought in the imagination around the family hearth. The present Patton is, therefore, the third of the line; and the young Patton, also George Smith, now a cadet at West Point, is actually Patton the Fourth. Indeed, this boy began by calling himself "George the Fourth," but the family felt the title began to sound pretentious, so he is known as "George III."

General Patton I, then, set the pattern of the family career and philosophy one hundred years ago, and was the prototype of four generations of warlike men. He was the "perfect warrior" in the romantic tradition, and his story is, in microcosm, the story of Patton, Commander-in-Chief of the largest army in American history.

Patton I was a member of the Virginian minor aristocracy. He graduated from V.M.I., and since there were then no armies or wars to speak of, he settled down to practice law in the little township of Kanawha, in Virginia. But even in Kanawha, in 1856, a Patton could hear the distant sound of fife and drum; and nobody in the whole South was more eager for a call to arms than "Captain" George S. Patton, lawyer.

The call came a year or so later, when a big, black-bearded fanatic called John Brown made a raid on Harpers Ferry and suddenly split America into two nations. For "Captain" Patton, the Civil War began on November 14, 1859. On that day he organized the first Confederate "Army," a company of small-town businessmen and farmers banded together as a regiment called "The Kanawha Riflemen."

At first, it was an "army" without uniforms, weapons, or training. With true military intuition, the self-appointed captain first designed a uniform, so that "The Kanawha Riflemen" were not a mob of coatless, tobacco-chewing, small-town citizens, but soldiers in appearance and bearing. "Captain" Patton himself created the uniform, as his grandson was to do almost a hundred years later for the tank corps. Both grandfather and grandson, it seems, had a partiality for epaulets, gold braid, and flamboyant headgear, suggestive of the musical comedy soldier rather than the foxhole fighting man. Thus the Kanawha Riflemen were to appear on the parade ground one spring morning in long, dark green coats, with epaulets of gold braid, shoulder capes, tight-fitting trousers with black stripes down the side, buttons of gold stamped with the Virginian coat of arms, and, on their heads, wide black hats with ostrich feathers dangling from the brims.

Eighty years later, the grandson was to try his hand at military dress design, and to show that he, too, loved green, black, and gold. For the tank corps, the present Patton created a tight-fitting green uniform, with black stripes down the sides of the trousers and white instead of gold buttons on the tunics. The gold was used to burnish the general's helmet. Ostrich feathers were not available in 1940.

The first thing, then, in creating an "army" and in imbuing a warlike spirit, was to clothe ordinary, peaceful men in an extraordinary, martial dress. The next thing was to change them from ordinary, peaceful civilians into disciplined, bellicose fighting men. This "Captain" Patton accomplished by daily marching to and fro, up and down the streets of Kanawha, with his Riflemen in military formations, their capes swinging from the shoulders, their ostrich feathers dangling from their hats. The "Captain" was known as a "martinet for discipline." Here, too, we see how history repeats itself, even though historians try not to by varying their expression of the same theme. The present Patton is termed not a "martinet for discipline" but "an old disciplinary so-and-so." But it is the same thing.

For arms, the Kanawha Riflemen had shotguns and muskets; but we can be sure their "Captain" had a revolver stuck into his ornate belt.

Instead of war, they had ceaseless drills, marchings about, military bands, and visits to county fairs. They were in great demands at fairs all over Virginia and the neighboring states, and were inevitably admired by the women and sneered at by the men, who dubbed them "The Kid Glove Company."

Two years later, in 1861, Captain Patton had the opportunity he had dreamed of. He lead his Riflemen, no longer in capes and ostrich plumes, to battle. In more sober garb, they fought one of the first battles of the Civil War, on a wooden bridge across Scovey's Creek, on July 17, 1861.

The leader of the Kanawha Riflemen behaved exactly in accordance with the Patton tradition. While his men were on foot, he was upraised on horseback. While they fired muskets, he wielded a sword. When they retreated, he advanced. When they grew silent and dispirited, he shouted and urged them forward. When the enemy balls fell short of the prone Riflemen, he got himself struck by a spent ball which knocked him off his horse. Such a demonstration of heroism could not fail. The bridge was held at the loss of one Rifleman, and the company was lead back to Charleston to receive the homage of pretty ladies waving from balconies.

Thus Patton I fought his war, rising from Captain to Colonel to Brigadier-General by the time he was twenty-eight. He fought it high on horseback, waving a sword, shouting at the top of his voice, and finally falling on the field of battle at Winchester, on September 9, 1864, one of a Confederate force of 12,000 brave men, routed in the nature of things by an opposing force of 40,000. Brigadier-General George S. Patton thus disappears into history, a plumed man on a horse, standing in his saddle in the middle of the street up which the routed Confederate troops were fleeing, waving his sword, rallying his men, until a bullet silenced him forever.

2

Such a man was the first Patton, who gave the clan a name and a tradition. And destiny arranged it so that another remarkable American, equally characteristic of his locale and time, should be the maternal grandfather of our hero. This was Benjamin Davis Wilson, who gave his name to a county and an observatory in California. Benjamin Davis

Wilson had emigrated to California, in 1837, as a little boy, when that state was still Mexican and most emigrants renounced their American for Mexican citizenship and a resultant grant of rich farming land. According to the Pattons, Wilson retained his citizenship and bought most of the vast estates which he subsequently owned. Part of his property was the San Pasqual Ranch, on which the present General Patton was born. But Wilson was more than a landowner. He trekked the Oregon Trail, hunted Indians, became "alcalde" of Los Angeles, and profited from the exploitation of the vast territory, selling ten thousand acres of land to the newly planned city of Pasadena without affecting the extent of his own holdings.

It was the daughter of "Don Benito" Wilson who married the son of General Patton, and gave birth, in 1885, to a son who was to fuse, in one personality and career, the qualities of soldier, swordsman, and patriot, with the qualities of explorer, Indian hunter, and rancher.

With such ancestors and in such circumstances, it was inevitable that Patton, as infant, boy, youth, and man, should be given a life with predestined direction. His father, though a peaceful and successful lawyer, holding the office of district attorney for Los Angeles, had inherited the military tradition. The gene of heroism was in his blood, and the military way had marked his life as a graduate of the Virginia Military Institute and the son of a Civil War general. But in that lush period of peace, his wars were confined to the fireside hours, when he read his son the *Iliad* and *Odyssey* and related tales of that sword-bearing grandfather who had died in the saddle. Thus did Hector and Achilles and the captain of the Kanawha Riflemen become the paragons of the boy Patton's virtue; and the heroic the principle of his life. From the age of seven, when he claims to have performed his first military maneuver by dragging a chicken round the house nine times in imitation of Patroclus dragging Hector's body round the walls of Troy, Patton saw the world as a battleground over which men in armor and men on horseback marched or rode to death and glory. The impact of this early reading on his mind is still observable today. Patton has always loved to make suits of mail (from wire scourers filched from the kitchen, says Mrs. Patton), and instinctively clothes himself in armor for fancy dress parties. In a place of honor at his Massachusetts home stands an array of perfectly modeled knights on horseback and afoot, bought in the Burlington Arcade in London many years ago, and played with regularly by the General and any children visiting the house.

The young Patton had more than antique tales and dead chickens to turn his mind to the life of the horse and the sword. He had his grandfather's vast estates to ride over, and the choice of a hundred ponies to mount. The legend has grown up that he was an accomplished polo player at the age of eleven. This is untrue, for polo was not known in the West in 1896. But Patton's godfather, an Englishman who had emigrated to California, presented the boy with the first English saddle to appear on the Pacific Coast; and in this saddle Patton perfected his horsemanship, which has always been above reproach.

He went to school in Pasadena and for one year to the Virginia Military Institute, when he won an appointment to West Point, by competitive examination. So far, his scholastic attainments were not high; but he was not interested only in horses, sailing, football, and running. He was, because of his strength and grace, a tremendous athlete, but he was equally interested in the scholarship of war. His reading of military history had already begun, and he was working hard at the basic knowledge required for the career of a professional soldier. His English was good, though limited to an appreciation of the more jingoistic of the poets. He has always written a certain brand of poetry himself, and has always loved poetry. I asked Mrs. Patton which poets in particular. She said "Kipling," thought a little while, and added "Shakespeare."

Patton's intellectual attainments, then, were fair, except in two subjects—mathematics and spelling. His inability to compute and spell were to become real liabilities later on.

But his accomplishments, physical and mental, were nothing unusual at all, and were not more than to bring the young Patton fame as a college athlete before passing into the oblivion of a small-town legal career. But he had something else much more important to success: he had a dream of glory and he had the ambition to strive for that dream. He regarded himself, in fact, as a man under a star.

Both the dream and the ambition are understandable in a boy who had such men as a Civil War general and a California millionaire rancher as his grandparents. But it was only natural that they were not immediately understandable to the young warrior's companions, at school in Pasadena, at the Virginia Military Institute, and later at West Point. For the young Patton's inner convictions appear to have made him a stiff-necked and arrogant youth, who found it difficult to attain the same sense of harmony and belonging which he had inwardly with the world outside of his books, family, and dreams. His fellows were prepared to concede his athletic prowess but not his matter-of-fact boast that he was going to be a great soldier, or the first general from his class at West Point. His boasting did not make him popular or sympathetic to his equally self-confident companions, who observed that whereas George S. Patton, Jr., as he called himself in deference to his father, could run faster and ride better than they, he could not compute or spell as well. This inability to make friends became more pronounced as Patton passed from boyhood to adolescence, and from adolescence to manhood. For whereas boys will accept, albeit grudgingly, standards of physical prowess, men have alternative values, and do not pay homage to proficiency in horsemanship and foot-racing, except in those countries where force is esteemed higher than intelligence. The record shows that Patton was unpopular during his schooldays; and for a youth who envisaged himself as the Great American Hero, unpopularity was all the more an incentive to excel.

So, by the time Patton won an appointment to West Point, in 1904, the inflexible and lonely course of his life had been charted, and he was to follow it to the end. His dream was to be realized. He was to become an American Hero, riding through thronged streets of great cities, acclaimed by many thousand times more admirers than had ever welcomed his grandfather back to Charleston. So he gained the generalship, the medals, and the glory, but he was never to make many friends. He still attracts rather the sycophant than the equal companion of his thoughts and feelings, which was very evident among the men who surrounded him at his various headquarters.

In 1904, then, George S. Patton, Jr., now nineteen years old, arrived at the Academy, a tall, handsome, strong youth, who managed by his athletic distinction, his arrogance, and his boasting, to intimidate many of his fellows and to alienate the others. He announced clearly his ambitions: he intended to get his major A as a footballer; he intended to win the highest honor the Academy could offer; and he intended to be the first general from his class.

He achieved none of these ambitions. He never made his A in football, because while he was on the squad, he was always getting a bone broken or fractured, and had his nose broken three times. Perhaps his misfortunes were due to his size and thinness, as Mrs. Patton suggests; or perhaps they were caused by heavier men who disliked Patton Junior. But injuries always kept him from playing on the team proper.

He did achieve the second highest honor, when he became class adjutant. He was not the first or the second general from his class. Lieutenant-General Delos C. Emmons, a considerably more obscure figure than Patton, was the first cadet of the 1909 class to wear a general's star on his shoulder.

At all events, the announcement of his ambitions and his manner of working for them were not calculated to endear him to his fellow students. He seems to have had no special friends at West Point, and, rather, was called by the opprobious term of "quilloid," which is defined in West Point jargon as a "cadet who is ready to curry favor by skinning other cadets." His intellectual attainments were far from distinguished. He knew a great deal of military history, and could recite jingles by Rudyard Kipling; but the other students got all the military history they wanted in class, and most of them knew as many Kipling jingles as Patton did. His manner of learning was the uninspired method of the too-ambitious student, namely, memorizing by rote his copious notes. Indeed, his scholastic ability was below average, and he took five instead of the customary four years to graduate.

Yet he was officially an exemplary cadet, showing none of the normal adolescent tendencies to break the rules and to escape occasionally from the monotony of institutional life. In fact, in five years he appears to have broken the regulations only once, when he went without a pass to Highland Point with Joe Carberry, a fellow athlete, and ran like a hare to escape detention when the officer of the day, Lieutenant Joseph Stilwell (now Lieutenant-General) spotted him.

Apart from this lapse, Patton's conduct was officially exemplary, as was to be expected from a "quilloid," a sergeant-major of his corps, a member of the fencing, rifle, riding, and track teams, and an aspirant for class adjutant. He passed out of West Point with high distinction, no doubt considering that any price he had paid in loneliness and unpopularity was well worth it.

3

A year out of West Point, now a commissioned second lieutenant in the United States Army, Patton was to marry a woman who, with love and devotion through the years to come, was to compensate for the penalties of ambition. Beatrice Ayer, whom Patton met in California, was the daughter of a New England family which had Yankee wealth, tradition, and prestige comparable with the Patton Southern aristocracy. The Ayer family, says Mrs. Patton, has been in New England "since 1600 and something." Here they had built up the American Woolen Company. These Ayers and the Pattons were friends, and the fusion of the Yankee and Virginia aristocracy seemed a fitting and expedient expression of such friendship. The marriage was consecrated near Beatrice Ayer's home, at Beverly Farms Church, Massachusetts, in 1910. Three children were born: a daughter Beatrice, in 1911; Ruth Ellen, in 1915; and George Smith III, in 1923.

Beatrice Ayer would not have seemed, by circumstances and upbringing, to be the ideal mate for a man of Patton's temperament. Even their physical appearance is sharply contrasting. He is over six feet tall; she is not much more than five. He is forceful and muscular in manner; she is gentle and soft. She was New England and intellectual; he was Wild West and unacademic. The difference is still marked. Beatrice Ayer's education had been typical, with the emphasis on literature, languages, music, and maidenly deportment. For some years, her family spoke French together. She went to a "select" private school, or to two such schools; one run by a Miss Carroll, the other by a Miss Heskill. School was from 9:00 A.M to 1:30 P.M. This was all the formal education Mrs. Patton says she received; and she adds, "I'm not really educated at all." After grooming by the Misses Carroll and Heskill, Beatrice Ayer "came out," took the customary tours in Europe, and visited with friends.

Thus hers was a very different world from her future husband's world of war, sport, the army camp, and barrackroom literature and language. It is unlikely she had ever heard such words as "guts," "goddamit," and "son of a bitch," and other similar words the General uses in casual conversation which are not printed in full, but with lines between the first and last letters, a convention Mrs. Patton abhors, to the extent of abjuring me either to spell out the "cuss words" in full or in parlor synonym. The deep adaptability of her nature and the completeness of her transformation are shown in her simple attitude towards her husband's profanity.

"I never notice his cussing," she says, "except when I realize it is shocking a guest."

And she explains that it is only "soldier talk," in much the same manner as a mother excuses a child's misuse of a word.

If there ever was any conflict between their two personalities and philosophies, it was quickly resolved by Beatrice's wifely acceptance of her husband's conduct, language, and idiosyncrasies. Both the mother and the children have always accepted the head of the household without question. He is the *paterfamilias* in the ancient Roman manner. He is lord and master, and can do no wrong. Even the father's sudden rages directed towards his children—towards one of his daughters who hesitated at a hurdle, for instance—are accepted as natural phenomena, like a summer storm, which there is no point in disputing.

Mrs. Patton herself tells the steps of her progression from New England girl to army officer's wife in an address on army etiquette she gave to a gathering of women.

"I was not born in the Army but joined it from civil life and made my first visit to an Army post six weeks before my wedding. Everyone was giving us parties—or so it seemed to me—and the ladies of the post were trying to get me primed on Army etiquette. After my third evening I tried to give my true love his freedom. He was quite upset about it, and demanded the reason.

"'You're ambitious. Why don't you marry some nice

Army girl who knows all the ropes?' I told him. 'I'll never make a success of it.' "

"But he persuaded me."

Within a few years the New England maiden had become an "Army Wife." The morning after she and her husband reported at their first post, she found an Order of the Day posted in her mail box. It said: "The sun will rise at 5:05 A.M. and will set at 6:30 P.M. By order of W. S. Pickett, Colonel, Nth Infantry, Commanding."

This army, she said to herself, must mean something. Even the sun conforms.

And Mrs. Patton has conformed, unquestioningly and happily. She and the children learned to ride horses cavalryman style, to talk Army lingo, to hear profanity without wincing, and to raise their glasses for a toast and say "How" in the regular Army style, knowing that when they gave the old Indian greeting they were members of a clan.

She even learned how to quiet her maternal fears for the sake of her husband, and did not demur when he announced his intention of sailing to an army post in Hawaii in a third-hand yacht, which meant a four-thousand-mile voyage across the world's most violent ocean. This boat was the *Arcturus,* and it had as crew, Patton, his wife, a Swedish sailor, and the eight-year-old George III. The yacht had an inboard motor, but Patton filled the gas tanks with water, except for a hundred gallons of oil, and they sailed almost every mile of the voyage. Later, they were to sail back to California, spending seven days hove to in a storm. Mrs. Patton is a racing yachtswoman, and her ambition is to win the Women's Sailing Championship of America. Her husband, she says, is a "blue water man."

As Beatrice Patton accepted the hazards of the passage to Hawaii, so she has accepted everything her husband thinks, does, and says. She even listens to him in a department of life where she obviously excels him—in literature. Throughout the writing of her successful novel, "Blood of a Shark," which took seven years to complete, she heeded her husband's editorial criticism. His knowledge of French, however, was not adequate for him to comment on her "Legendes Hawaiiennes," which was published in Paris in its original French. The general, she explains, speaks "International French," with unwarranted use of the infinitive.

Mrs. Patton is a musician and composer, too, and here her husband's influence is paramount, though he is completely unmusical. But the wife's composition, "The March of the Armored Force," which she composed in pianoforte score, with instructions to the arranger for full band orchestration, is pure Patton. It starts with the firing by the bandmaster of two pistols, after which come three blasts on a tank siren, followed by trumpets, drums, oboes, piccolos, tubas, and a plentiful assortment of brass. Mrs. Patton, who seldom allows herself to be humorous where her husband is concerned, admits that "they say the introductory pistol shots are to notify the General they are going to play my march."

CHAPTER II

"SIEGEL-COOPER COWBOY"

I

IN 1912, Lieutenant Patton's career proper began with an unusual opportunity for personal glory. The Olympic Games were being held that year in Stockholm, Sweden, and in June a number of American athletes set sail to take part. Patton was among them, one of several army officers who were to compete in the Pentathlon, in which ancient contest a man demonstrated his skill in the five classical military accomplishments of foot-racing, swimming, fencing, horsemanship, and target shooting. No other contest could so well have suited the young lieutenant's personality, training, and physical prowess. He loved all five skills and excelled in all of them.

The American party sailed on a privately chartered liner the *Finland,* hired for the occasion from the Red Star Line by an ex-officer of the Marines, Colonel Robert M. Thompson. The ship was large enough to accommodate the wives and families of the athletes, and Patton was accompanied by his wife, his father, mother, and sister, Miss Anne Patton.

Stockholm, in 1912, was a perfect setting for the Olympics. That year was a bountiful epoch in European history. The Old World had enjoyed a long period of peace, and seemed politically and economically stable. Non-tyrannical monarchs were firmly seated on their thrones; liberal governments maintained order and democracy in their nations. There was time, then, for leisure and recreation, literature, music, and sport. And Stockholm, in June, was a lovely, sun-flecked city, bedecked with flags, thronged with rich and distinguished visitors, and imbued, from the clear mornings to the starry nights, with the spirit of an international carnival.

Patton was then twenty-seven, already a member of American military aristocracy and a lordling in his looks, bearing, and manner, with the dash and color Europeans expected of Americans. The Swedes, of all people, worship sport and idolize the sportsman; and the tall, fair American Pentathlon contestant was their model of a man. He was more popular than he had ever been among his compatriots at school and college; he was tremendously admired, fêted, entertained, and introduced to the King.

Of the American Pentathlon entrants, Patton was the only one to survive the preliminary contests, and thus became our official representative. The first trial of skill was pistol shooting. The day before the actual contest, Patton broke the world record with a perfect score. He seemed to be a certainty for this competition. But on the day itself he was extremely nervous, missing the target altogether with some shots, and coming twenty-first out of forty-three entrants. Stories that he hit the bull's-eye twenty-three times out of twenty-four, with the twenty-fourth shot passing right through a previous bullet hole are flattering but untrue. Actually, he made a very poor showing in pistol shooting, which affected his final placing in the Pentathlon.

On the second day, the swimming contest, he came third. On the third day, fencing, he was first. On the fourth and fifth days, for cross-country running and riding, he was placed third in both races.

His placing in the complete Pentathlon was fourth out of forty-three. He was beaten by three Swedes: Lillihock, Asbrink, and Delaval.

The autumnal brown pages of the *New York Times* of July 12, 1912, give a brief picture of Patton as competitor in the 4,000-meter cross-country race:

"Lieutenant Patton, a tall, slim man, took the regulation sprinter's start. He got away more like a runner than most of the starters—and the crowd cheered him! Patton had a lead of twenty yards in front of Asbrink (Sweden), but lost ground in the last fifty yards, and finished tenth, falling almost fainting onto the grass. Several men went to his assistance, and rubbed his legs and arms, and in a few minutes he walked off, holding a friend's arm."

Somehow, that race sounds characteristically Patton.

"After it was all over, and Sweden had won, the whole assembly of 25,000 people rose and sang the Swedish National Anthem," continues the *Times*. "American competitors gave an American yell, followed by 'Sweden' three times, after which the Swedes applauded Lieutenant Patton."

After Stockholm, the two Pattons took a trip down to France, making their way in a little open two-seater car to Saumur, a hundred miles east of Nantes. Saumur was the Headquarters of the French saber and "epée" schools, which Patton now wished to study. He returned to Saumur the next year, on a scholarship, and formally studied saber methods, with Beatrice Patton translating all the sword manuals, which he was later to incorporate into his military work entitled "Saber Methods."

Patton's study of the saber and sword were not to have a very profound effect on either military history or his own career; and perhaps nothing illustrates the change in our world so much as the American Army's decision to send an officer to Saumur, in 1913, to study French fencing methods, and its decision to experiment with an atomic bomb thirty years later. But Patton's visits to France were not concerned only with sabers. He and his wife, in their car, reconnoitered the entire Breton and Normandy countryside, spending many an hour around St. Lo, where Patton worked out imaginary battles which were later to materialize into the decisive struggles of this last war. Patton was fighting battles on every hillside in those days, ancient battles he had read about in history books and new battles he wrote in his own mind.

Mrs. Patton recalls their journeyings quite clearly. She now has an embossed chest in her home which they bought at the Lion d'Or in St. Lo. And she recalls a French baby she held in her arms, who was later to become Captain Houdemon, liaison officer for the French 2nd Armored Division to General Patton's Third Army Headquarters.

2

In March, 1916, now back in America and stationed at Fort Bliss, Texas, Patton heard for the first time the ominous music of guns and drums being played by men at war and not men on the parade ground. The Mexican War had begun. This war, dryly called the Punitive Expedition, was begun and fought ostensibly to punish a super-bandit, Pancho Villa, who was a jackal nipping at the American eagle's tail. It was the last war of the Wild West variety, a cavalryman's and scout's war, fought in a setting of mountains, plains, and deserts. It was a war for men on horseback, for men of great physical endurance and personal courage. It was, above all, a war for a first lieutenant with a good horse, a strong physique, a brace of pistols, and a desire for personal glory.

The Punitive Expedition, seen through the lenses of history, was a melodramatic and quasi-comic affray, involving as its principal character a tremendous bandit whom only the West could have produced in America a half a century ago, and a type which disappeared from English history with Robin Hood. The bandit was Pancho Villa, whose name itself typifies the bewhiskered and kerchiefed Bad Man of the Border.

Arrayed against this picaresque villain, before the war was ended, was almost the entire fighting strength of the United States. In the early days of March, 1916, General Pershing, commander of the American forces, had two infantry regiments, two cavalry regiments, a battery of field artillery, and an air squadron with which to teach Pancho and his assortment of bandits a lesson. By January, 1917, he had a potential force of 175,000 troops, consisting of sixty-five regiments of infantry, twenty-five of cavalry, and various artillery units and so-called "air squadrons," not to mention the National Guard, which had been called out in the emergency in nearly every state in the Union. The regular Mexican forces, who had been nibbling away at our scattered units, were naturally overawed by this show of strength—especially by the artillery batteries—and peace was formally signed in January, 1917. But it was never signed with Pancho, and Pancho was never overawed. In fact, he was never caught, and presumably died a good old man is some far hacienda. He must have died scornful of both American promises and threats, for he had been promised American support by General Scott, the Indian hunter, whereas our state department preferred to back Carranza. And he had certainly been threatened with dire punishment by the American jingoist press. The threats, like the promises, faded in the hot sunshine of the Mexican interior, where hundreds of American soldiers, parched with thirst and short of provisions, saw nobody to punish but a few miserable Indians.

But the young Patton was not concerned with the politics of war. He was then, and always, only concerned with war. And so he was to play an excellent character role in this "epic in glorious technicolor," dashing about on his fiery steed, shooting off his brace of pistols, and waving his sword as though directed by Cecil B. de Mille himself. First, he became "aide-de-camp" to General Pershing, by what his fellow officers of the time term "a modest insistence on his own excellence." With this office, where he anticipated his exploits would be most likely to be observed by the people who recommended promotion, he proceeded to conduct himself in a manner which won for him the title of "Siegel-Cooper Cowboy." This was the second of his numerous soubriquets, "quilloid" apparently being the first. Patton, like his cowboy counterpart, wore a brace of pistols, and they were always going in and out of their holsters in approved Hollywood fashion. Nothing that moved, from snakes on the ground to birds in the air, was safe from this one-man artillery barrage; they tell one story of how Patton, hearing a grunting noise outside his tent, rushed out, firing rapidly from both hips, and yelling, "There goes my enemy!" The enemy was a pig, which happened to be wandering by. It now lay squealing on the path, "riddled with bullets."

But Patton burned to shoot men, not pigs, and his chance came at Lake Itascate, when, with a detachment of eight men in two Dodge cars, he approached the Rubio Ranch, looking for fodder for the headquarters company's horses. As the Americans approached the ranch, they were fired on. Patton and his men quickly scattered, and began shooting from behind rocks and trees, while the bandits in the ranchhouse shot back from behind doors and windows in the classical Hopalong Cassidy style. Everyone must have been getting tired of this, and no one more so than Patton, who proceeded to advance alone on the house, need it be said "with his guns blazing." Indeed, they blazed so fast, that he found himself with empty chambers and up against a wall, while the bandits peppered away with rifles and missed, as bandits always do on these occasions—in fiction anyhow. Meanwhile, Patton reloaded and was soon blazing away again, shooting one bandit and his horse—yes, "from under him." He also shot another bandit before the battle was over, and with this pair, Julio Cardanes and Juan Garza by name, he returned to headquarters, the corpses tied on the cars' bumpers. Garza's spurs are now ornaments, along with a cannon from the Kasba at Port Lyautey, French Morocco, and sundry other trophies, in the Patton's Hamilton home.

3

As a reward for his services in the Mexican campaign, Lieutenant Patton was put in command of General Pershing's Headquarters troops, which were then being prepared for the European War. In this task, the ardent stickler for discipline was able to employ his capabilities as quondam sergeant-major. On May 28, 1917, he sailed with his snappy outfit to England; and two weeks later marched through the streets of London to the ancient Tower, where foreign troops were being billeted for the first time since the Norman Conquest.

Next came France, and a war as different from the Wild West skirmishes of Mexico as sober methods are from tank warfare. But for Patton it was still war, and more than ever an opportunity for the realization of his dreams. Perhaps no other American who fought in that first World War exploited his opportunity with such fervor. In the course of a single year, he rose from first lieutenant to full colonel, introduced the tank into the American Army, organized tank schools, trained tank corps, lead tank squadrons into battle, risked his life and got wounded, received three decorations, covered himself in glory, and returned home as a Hero.

Patton's record in World War I is truly phenomenal. We find him in the initial days of the AEF in France a constant companion of the American Commander-in-Chief, accompanying Pershing on his rounds from his Headquarters at Chaumont in Eastern France to French and British Headquarters, with innumerable routine and courtesy calls en route.

That was the summer of 1917. In the fall, when the American Army was in a position to join in the hostilities, Patton was chosen as the first American officer to study the new "secret" weapon, called the tank. He was sent to the French Tank School at Champs Lieu for that purpose. Within a month he had mastered the theory and practice of armored warfare sufficiently to set up the first American light tank school at Langres, seventy miles southwest of Nancy, which was to be the Third Army's Headquarters twenty-seven years later. Simultaneously he organized and directed the 302nd Tank Training Center at Bourg; and, now with the rank of captain, became the leading and practically only American authority on armor in war. In fact, at this time Captain Patton was the American tank. Later, Beatrice Patton was to become American tank expert Number Two, making innumerable cardboard models of light tanks, and riding in the full-scale machines at army test grounds. She relates that on one occasion, when the reviewing officers declined to take a ride in a new tank, her husband said coolly, "Mrs. Patton, then, will ride as a passenger in the test."

"I sat on the lap of a very large sergeant," says Mrs. Patton, "with his arms around me. It was really a most enjoyable ride. And the officers said they were satisfied with the test."

During the winter of 1917-1918, when the opposing armies bogged down in the indescribable mud and chaos of trench warfare, Patton, a major overnight, trained the first American tank corps, and by spring, reported he was ready for the field.

In May, 1918, he was sent to take a closer look at his assignment, and was present when the French threw in their tanks to counterattack on the Montdidier-Noyon sector. Patton tried to cover the entire front in those days, rushing about and nearly getting his head sliced off on one occasion in an automobile accident. They took him to a hospital holding his own cut throat.

Somewhere between watching the French offensive at Montdidier and getting his throat cut, he found time to study and graduate from the General Staff College at Langres. By August, 1918, the orders came for his 304th Brigade Tank Corps to move into the line on the St. Mihiel sector. Patton set off in advance to make a personal reconnaissance of the terrain.

St. Mihiel was on the Verdun front, and Patton's tanks fought two days here, when they were suddenly switched to the more critical Argonne-Meuse sector fifty miles to the west, near Reims. All this rich vineyard country, where Frenchmen and Americans died by the tens of thousands during the battles of 1917 and 1918, was swept through in a matter of days the second time Patton fought here, as commander of the Third Army.

On September 26, 1918, Captain Patton fought his first battle, as leader of the 304th Tank Brigade. As his lumbering, creaking tanks with their high silhouettes clattered forward across a green country made desert by the traffic of high explosive, Patton knew that his hour had come. He probably felt just as his grandfather had felt at Scovey Creek, and he seems to have behaved in much the same manner, even to the waving of his saber. Now a world war which involved millions of men among whom he had been just a digit became his personal war. There were, of course, his comrades in other tanks and as infantrymen; and there were also thousands of Germans, crouching in their long, neat trenches, or sitting at the embrasures of their blockhouses. But for Major (as he had now become) Patton, it was his tank and his saber against the world.

From all accounts, the engagement actually did take on the appearance of a one-man charge; for while Major Patton was advancing, his supporting infantry were moving rapidly in every direction but forward; and soon he found himself uttering war cries and waving his saber to an audience of Germans snugly placed behind machine guns.

It would be interesting to know what were Major Patton's feelings at that moment when he found himself charging the German Army, looking vaguely like Ben Hur in a chariot. It is likely he was not so afraid as chagrined that his glorious hour had suddenly become a lonely experience, in which neither friend nor foe seemed particularly interested. Everything about the man now resulted in two reactions: War Cries and Rallying. He felt the need to fill the air with martial yells like "Come on, you yellow-bellied bastards! Get up, and let's go!" So he war cried and rallied, reorganizing enough of the demoralized infantry to cover the advance of his tank, leading them forward until most of them were killed by the relentless hammering of machine guns and a neat semicircle of shrapnel around his midriff cut short his path to glory. He retained consciousness long enough to organize some sort of formation of his sector, and then the day was done.

On the same day, September 26, the war was over for Major Patton, and two months later was over for everybody. The perforations in Patton's epidermis were not serious, for he was released from hospital a month later, by this time a full colonel in the Tank Corps and recipient of the longed-for medals: the Distinguished Service Cross "for extraordinary heroism in action, near Cheppy, France, September 26, 1918"; the Distinguished Service Medal "for exceptional, meritorious, and distinguished services . . . in his organization and direction of the Tank Center at the Army schools at Langres"; and the Purple Heart.

It was a phenomenal record for a year of battle: from first lieutenant to colonel; on battlefronts from Cambrai to

Montdidier-Noyon to St. Mihiel to the Argonne; from student at a French tank school to organizer of the first American tank training center to trainer of two tank brigades to commander of a tank corps; from a combined armored and infantry attack to a one-man charge; from holder of a "Show" medal presented by the King of Sweden for his participation in the Stockholm Olympic Games to recipient of three battle decorations.

Patton could hardly bear to see the end of a war which gave him such opportunities for promotion, decorations, and heroic experiences. He mused that it was only one more step from a colonel to a general. It was only one more offensive from commander of corps to commander of an army, one more battle from a Distinguished Service Cross to a Legion of Merit. He could hardly bear to have such opportunities suddenly snatched from his grasp.

He showed this in his manner towards his command after the Armistice, and in his attitude towards war during the long years of peace which followed. Towards his men, he remained an officer on the field of battle, stern and uncompromising. Though he could no longer lead them to death or glory, he could—and did—still send them to make rock roads where no roads were needed. He did not relax his discipline one iota, but rather erected barbed-wire compounds in which to imprison offenders. The men of the First World War tank corps I have talked with have no love at all for Colonel Patton.

Nor had Patton's experience changed his philosophy, except to deepen his love of war. He came out of his year of battle with a new zeal for killing, thinking of the future only in terms of other wars and greater chances for personal glory.

CHAPTER III

PATTON DONS HIS SHINING CASQUE

I

COLONEL PATTON came back to the United States in March, 1919, when America had already forgotten the war, which scarcely touched the nation and left only the slightest of scars. But soon the grievous wounds and chronic sickness of Europe were profoundly to affect the United States, first in the form of revulsion for war, then in a pacifism so negative it preached a gospel of not even fighting to uphold the right and the instruments of peace. Whereas democratic peoples now clamored for the dissolution of armies and navies, they made no counter demands for the strengthening of such organizations as the League of Nations or the International Court of Justice.

In such an atmosphere, the professional soldier was relegated to his compound, the army camp, where he was isolated rather like an Indian on a reservation. And in such an atmosphere Patton's voice was not heeded, even when he raised it, which he was only able to do within the limits of the various camps where he was to be stationed—Maryland, Virginia, Kansas, Hawaii, Texas, and Washington, D. C.

But for the regular army man, the Army is the nation, the camp is the world, the hut is home. Patton found many compensations in such surroundings. He was a hero, in temporary retirement. And watching the events of the time, he could reasonably anticipate another war well within his lifetime.

While waiting, Patton continued to devote himself to the martial life in its peacetime forms. There were military exercises, training, study, examinations. There were fancy uniforms to don, camp parties to attend, martial sports to pursue—in general, the bustling, self-contained existence of the army camp.

Beatrice Patton and the children were an integral part of this life. They, too, participated in the horse shows, the sports, the hunting and sailing expeditions, the parties, the circuses, the social calls, and the life of army camps which included assignments to Riley, Leavenworth, Boston, Hawaii, Washington War College, Myer, Hawaii a second time, Riley again, Clark, and Benning. Occasionally Patton busied himself with some private pursuit, like the construction of model boats, of which two superlative examples stand under glass in his Hamilton home; or the fabrication of suits of mail from odds and ends of chains and kitchen scourers. Once Mrs. Patton took two of the children to tour the battlefields of France, without her husband. She was also working on her novel, "Blood of the Shark," from 1928 to 1935, and competing in the National Women's Sailing Championship, in which she managed to become runner-up. The two girls, Beatrice and Ruth Ellen, married Army officers. The son, George Smith III, duly went to the Virginia Military Institute and West Point.

It was a happy and harmonious life for a soldier, or civilian, in those not too-piping times of peace between 1920 and 1940. But Patton never forgot that he was a man under a star; and he never doubted that destiny would favor him with another war. And for this he was constantly preparing himself. He selected the tank as the chosen instrument of his destiny, for "an army without tanks is like a lobster without claws. Tanks are the claws which penetrate and envelop and pinch."

2

When war came to America, Patton was one of a handful out of 130,000,000 people who was prepared to do something. A few hundred thousand professional soldiers had some kind of training. A few thousand of these had some actual battle experience. Only a few hundred had some concept of war, and some positive ideas on how to fight it successfully.

Patton had the training, the experience, and the ideas. His special idea was the tank and its use. He had chosen his instrument for war shrewdly, for at this period in military history, the tank was supreme, and was considered by professional and layman alike as the cardinal weapon in modern strategy.

Further, the tank was bound to have a special appeal to the American mind. For while it was a machine for war, it was nonetheless a machine, with an engine and wheels and the stink of fumes—hence something American genius excelled in. In addition, it symbolized the new strategy, which was based on the simple concept of crushing your enemy by the weight of machines.

And so it came about that the romantic predilection of Patton for tanks coincided with the mechanical predilection of the nation in general for this machine. Patton, of course, loved the tank not as an engineering marvel, but as a weapon with which the individual soldier could joust and ride down his enemy, as the knights of old did on armor-flanked horses.

To him, squadrons of tanks lurching and exploding across the landscape were as beautiful as a brigade of charging cavalry. To the layman, meanwhile, the same spectacle imparted a sense of power. With machines so numerous, swift, and compelling, the enemy was bound to be crushed. Patton and his tanks gave the American public the necessary bolster in morale to start fighting with nothing but the rudiments of military equipment.

Thus Patton began to symbolize early in the war what General Montgomery symbolized to the British—the Man of the Hour, the man with the experience and the idea to set our feet on the road to victory. Like Montgomery, Patton had a flair for personal publicity, and his flamboyant personality was perfectly suited to a flamboyant press. He immediately became a "national figure" during two spectacular military maneuvers in the fall of 1941, when tens of thousands of troops marched all over Louisiana and the Carolinas; and Patton's troops in particular caused tremendous confusion among the bewildered citizens and tied up traffic in every small town for hundreds of miles. Nobody knew anything about war in those days, and nobody cared. So the maneuvers had the appearance of a carnival, which provided the newspaper reporters with much good copy. Best copy of all was the new Major-General Patton, whose personality, appearance, and behavior happened to coincide exactly with what readers of adventure stories, slick magazines, and comic strips envisaged a general should be like. A man who was called variously Buck Rogers, Flash Gordon, Six-gun Patton, The Green Hornet, The Man from Mars, Iron Pants, Gorgeous Georgie, and Old Blood and Guts, was bound to fire the imagination of even a pacifistic populace, and make them anticipate the war with enjoyment.

U. S. Signal Corps Photo

PATTON IN A MOTOR LAUNCH IN AUSTRIA. THE THIRD ARMY'S AMPHIBIOUS OPERATIONS IN SICILY, FRANCE, AND GERMANY WERE SOME OF THE MOST IMPOSSIBLE OF PATTON'S ACHIEVEMENTS

PATTON SHOWS THE FORM IN HORSEMANSHIP THAT HELPED TO WIN HIM THIRD PLACE IN THE PENTATHLON AT THE STOCKHOLM OLYMPICS OF 1912

Photo by E. Morgan Savage, Boston

Photo by E. Morgan Savage, Boston

PATTON AND HIS FAMILY—GEORGE III, MRS. PATTON, RUTH ELLEN, AND BEATRICE—ARE EXCELLENT AND ENTHUSIASTIC RIDERS

U. S. Signal Corps Photo

IN THE LOUISIANA MANEUVERS OF 1941, WHEN THIS PICTURE WAS TAKEN, PATTON'S MILITARY SEVERITY STARTED TO TURN CIVILIANS INTO SOLDIERS

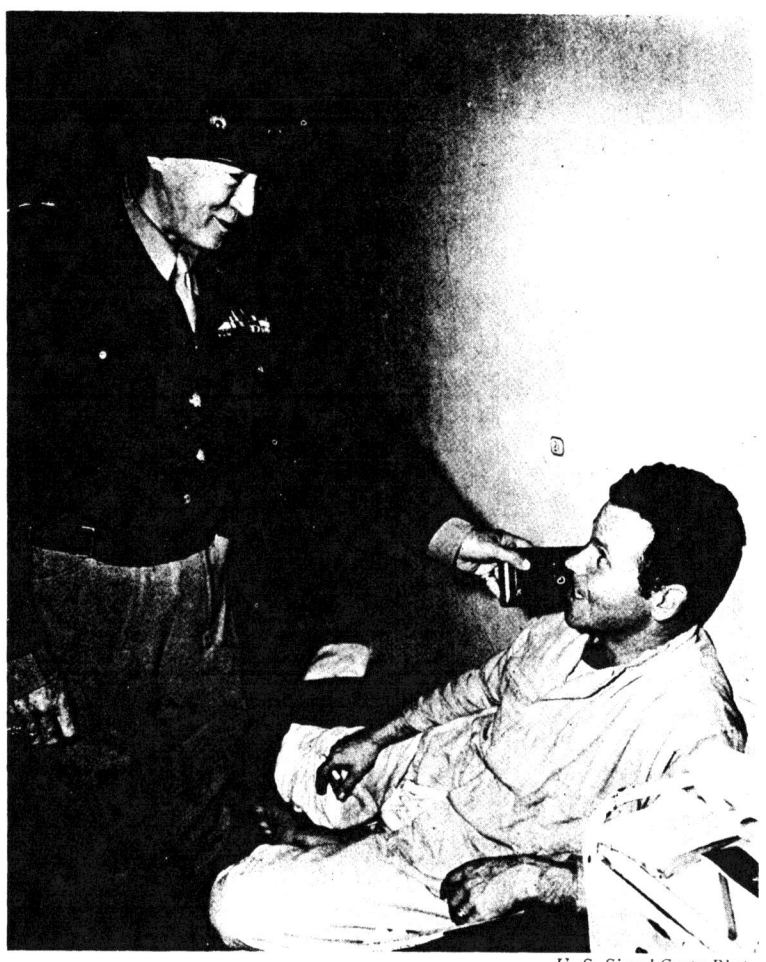

U. S. Signal Corps Photo

THE NOTORIOUS SLAPPING INCIDENT GREW OUT OF PATTON'S CUSTOM OF VISITING THE WOUNDED IN BASE HOSPITALS. TO THE PHYSICALLY WOUNDED HE WAS ALWAYS SYMPATHETIC

U. S. Signal Corps Photo

PATTON DISCUSSING TACTICS WITH GENERAL ROOSEVELT IN SICILY.
HE WEARS THE HELMET HE HELPED DESIGN AND THE UBIQUITOUS
PISTOLS

PATTON CONFERS WITH GENERAL BRADLEY, HIS SUPERIOR, AND GENERAL MONTGOMERY, IN FRANCE, JULY, 1944

U. S. Signal Corps Photo

U. S. Signal Corps Photo

BEMEDALLED PATTON IS SHOWN WITH GENERAL ZAHWATAEFF OF THE RUSSIAN ARMY AFTER THE THIRD ARMY HAD RACED ACROSS GERMANY TO CZECHOSLOVAKIA

That was not all to delight those who sat in trains reading about war. There was the story of the uniform the New Man had designed, which made war sound even more like a carnival than the Louisiana Maneuvers. It was a uniform for tankmen, bottle-green in color, with white buttons on the tunic and black stripes down the trousers, and, for the Chief Man, a golden helmet. It sounded a bit like something borrowed from the wardrobe of the Metropolitan Opera; and proved to be too fanciful for the War Department.

The accounts of the simulated battles were also amusing. They told of Patton's outfit, the 2nd Armored Division, beating and battering its way all over the countryside, knocking down trees and wooden shacks, capturing generals, making tremendous flanking attacks around New Orleans via Baltimore, and getting themselves wiped out to the last man. All this racing around was done to the accompaniment of tank sirens and Major-General Patton's war cries. "Goddam it, keep moving!" was his Order of the Day. And this, too, fitted the times.

So the public was amused and stimulated by the spectacle of a general in a golden helmet, standing up in a tank turret with his jaw thrust out like a boxer, or leaping to the road to direct traffic, yelling "Goddamit, I don't trust anybody!" Or summing up the art of war in understandable, if unprintable English, like "Always grab your enemy by the nose, and kick him in the arse." The public was amused and ready to applaud. The War Department was not so amused, and there was some discussion in high places whether General George S. Patton, Jr., was playing the game of war according to the textbook rules.

Fortunately for the future of American arms, the War Department is not governed by the dictates of an aristocratic and Blimpish clique; Patton's flamboyance, unorthodoxy, profanity, and like personal idiosyncrasies were excused in the knowledge that behind them was a field commander of potential genius and a soldier with experience and imagination. In March, 1942, the War Department announced that the U. S. Army would undertake a large-scale training program to prepare troops for action in the desert or in an airborne attack on enemy positions. The site chosen for the program was Indio, California, in the desert country west of the Colorado River. Eight thousand officers and men, commanded by Major-General Patton, were to constitute the development force.

"Knowing General Patton as I do," Mr. Stimson said, "I believe he will approximate actual desert warfare conditions as well as he is able, with consideration for innocent citizens in the neighborhood."

And so onto the stage of the world at war marched a man in a golden helmet. He was to hold the limelight as one of the principal players for the next three years. The curtain was about to go up on the first American act of the drama. The scene was Casablanca; the time November, 1942.

CHAPTER IV

CASABLANCA—"A NICE FIGHT"

I

In October, 1942, several thousand officers, army nurses, and enlisted men were summoned to the assembly hall at Fort Bragg, North Carolina, to hear an address by Major-General George S. Patton.

Normally, soldiers do not care for orations by commanding generals, or by the congressmen who occasionally visit them, or by chaplains, professional patriots, lecturers, civic leaders, or by anyone at all. But usually before some historic event, and always before a campaign, the occasion calls for sundry rhetorical references to country, flag, home, and God. Such speeches do not rank among the world's great oratory; and because security in modern war imposes silence until the last moment, generals often find themselves exhorting not the men who are about to plunge into battle, but a group of staff officers who have often helped write the speech themselves.

But whatever desultory interest the civilian newspaper reader may have in some general's pronouncement that his plans are made, God is on his side, and he will shortly be knocking hell out of the enemy, the ordinary soldier, being a quizzical youth with a somewhat cynical attitude towards the work he is engaged in, either does not hear or flatly disregards his general's exhortations.

Such an attitude was characteristic of the group of young

Americans who gathered at Fort Bragg that October evening. These were not Crusaders banded together in faith for which they were willing to fight and die. They were there because war had been declared on the United States by three Fascist nations; because enlistment was compulsory, because training was unavoidable, and because orders were inviolable.

Nonetheless, these unwilling soldiers rather looked forward to the personal appearance of Major-General George S. Patton. Most of them had already seen or heard this man who brought to war a certain super-heroic touch, not unfamiliar to readers of comic strips. They called this man the "Green Hornet" or "Flash Gordon," but actually he resembled rather a six-dimensional sergeant-major. His large stature, operatic uniforms, cold eyes, squeaky voice, and lush profanity; his energy, intensity, and fervor were incredible, strange and fearsome. As individuals, these civilian officers and men now gathered at Fort Bragg, kept as far away from this cosmic sergeant-major as they did from an urgent fire-engine, which the general most resembled in noise and speed as he moved among them. But as a group, they were intrigued. They said among themselves, "You never know what the guy will say next." Many remembered his famous first lines: "When you stick your hand into a bunch of goo that a moment before was your best friend's face . . ."

So when the Major-General strode onto the platform at Fort Bragg, there was a hush and an expectation. The General did not disappoint his audience in his dress or bearing, as he stood with his chest stuck out and his belly held in, and glanced pugnaciously and balefully over his troops.

What he said on that occasion, that historic occasion before these American troops left to engage the enemy on a foreign field for their first time, is not recorded except in the minds of those who heard the speech. General Patton's speeches are not printed verbatim in newspapers, because, like this one, they ran somewhat as follows:

"Well, they've given us a job to do. A tough job, a man-sized job. We can go on our bended knees, every one of us, and thank God the chance has been given us to serve our country."

So far it was admirable, and it was said in a quiet, almost reverent manner, though whether it carried conviction to the men who heard it, each could only answer to himself. Certainly it was not what they had come to hear or what they expected. But as the General's figure and voice rose higher, and as his pale eyes glared and his round mouth gaped, the men knew that their commander was changing from a general to a sergeant-major, from Jekyll to Hyde. "I can't tell you where we're going. But it will be where we can do the most good. And where we can do the most good is where we can fight those damn Germans or those yellow-bellied Eyetalians. And when we do, by God, we're going to go right in and kill the dirty bastards. We won't just shoot the sonsabitches. We're going to cut out their living guts—and use them to grease the treads of our tanks. We're going to murder those lousy Hun bastards by the bushel. . . ."

The audience, particularly the army nurses, got more that evening than they wanted. It is a peculiarity of Patton that he does not censor his language in the presence of women; and usually women slip away, as they did on this occasion, in the midst of his harangue. The army nurses got out as

Patton was dilating on the satisfaction of kicking bastards in the puss, and the need for guts, and the need for more guts, and the danger of soft ideas promulgated by people who "have to squat to p—," and the final exhortation always to grab your enemy by the nose and kick him in the a—.

In due course, the address of the Commanding General of the Western Task Force was printed in the newspapers. "General George S. Patton gave his troops an inspiring slogan for their forthcoming campaign," said the news items. "He told them, 'We shall attack and attack until we are exhausted; and then we shall attack again.'"

While the newspaper readers politely slid their eyes across this latest example of military rhetoric, the men and women who had heard the General's speech discussed it with indignation sometimes amounting to horror, and continued to discuss it during their last nights on American soil, and the many nights they spent from October 24 to November 10 as they sailed across the Atlantic, watching the convoys which had come out of Newport News and New York and Boston assemble into a gigantic armada of over one hundred ships, steaming south by day and east by night, until mountains loomed on the horizon, and rumor gave way to fact, and the word was given that this was a Western Task Force which was to invade the French Moroccan coast of Africa.

Of all those 60,000 men in those hundred ships, perhaps Patton alone was least concerned with "cutting out guts" and "kicking enemies in the arse." General Patton was studying the charts of the coast ahead, and reading, in his spare moments, the "Koran." He was thinking that a knowledge of the Mohammedan Bible would be useful; and he was later hurtfully surprised when the Arabs were as indifferent to it as the average soldier is to the history of the siege of Troy.

2

On the night of November 8, Patton's Western Task Force, consisting of some three divisions, landed on the French Moroccan coast in the most hazardous of our three separate North African operations. The beaches where Patton had to land were part of the "Iron Coast." Here the sea approaches were mined with coruscated reefs and the shores were pounded continually by fifty-foot swells, which had rolled half-way across the world. There were, in fact, almost no sandy beaches, but only reefs, rocks, coral, and surf. Secret reports from French Army agents stated that the sea was calm enough for a quiet beach landing only twelve days in the year.

For two days before Patton's armada arrived off the assault points, the beaches were pounded by gigantic seas. But by the time the convoys stood in battle formation and the landing craft sped to the shore, the ocean was calm as a summer evening. For this favor, Patton publicly thanked the Almighty in the awed tones with which soldiers are wont to address the Supreme Commander of the Universe. Privately he said, "I'm the Lord's favorite disciple. Those goddam Frenchmen had every light burning when we sailed up to the coast. And the sea was as flat as a hotcake."

The primary objective of the West Coast landings was the capture of the key port of Casablanca, which was to become an essential supply base in the North African campaign. For months beforehand, American and French agents, working through Mr. Robert Murphy, the American consul-general in North Africa, had smoothed the way for our coming as far as was possible politically. Many young French-speaking Americans had disappeared into the African continent during the preceding summer months. Many comings and goings had taken place, and many secret meetings. But French Morocco was, in general, solidly pro-Vichy and bitterly anti-Anglo-Saxon; and it was correctly anticipated that our landings there would be contested, especially by the large units of the French Navy and Marines stationed in and around Casablanca.

And this is what happened, almost precisely as the agents had predicted. The French Colonial Army under white officers potentially sympathetic to the Allied cause made only a token resistance. The French Navy and Marines fought vigorously and even fanatically.

In anticipation of such resistance, the Supreme Allied Command had placed its most promising field commander at the head of some three divisions, numbering 37,000 well-trained but untried troops. In addition, Patton had the guns and the dive bombers of an American naval flotilla, commanded by Rear-Admiral H. K. Hewitt. Attached to the ground forces was the 12th Air Support Group, lead by Brigadier-General John K. Cannon.

Patton's plan for the reduction of French Morocco was neat and bold. He proposed to make a three-pronged landing along the "Iron Coast," attacking Casablanca frontally and from both sides.

In the center was the 3rd Infantry Division, commanded by Major-General Jonathan W. Anderson, which landed against stiff opposition at Fedhala, just north of the large white city of Casablanca.

Ninety miles to the north of General Anderson's troops,

the 60th Combat Team of the 9th Infantry, under the command of Brigadier-General Lucian K. Truscott, went ashore against comparable opposition in front of Port Lyautey.

A hundred and fifty miles to the south of Casablanca, the 2nd Armored Division, commanded by Major-General Ernest N. Harman, landed at Safi, with negligible resistance, and with the 47th Combat Team of the 9th Infantry in support.

The Casablanca and Port Lyautey landings were, for a while, both critical. At Casablanca, the French Navy sallied forth to fight a desperate sea battle with Admiral Hewitt's warships. The battle between French destroyers, submarines, and the guns of the already crippled battleship *Jean Bart,* and the American cruisers, destroyers, and navy dive bombers went on for twenty-four hours, until, of the French flotilla of eight destroyers which attacked us, seven were sunk and the eighth damaged. General Patton, aboard the U. S. flagship, *Augusta,* was caught up in a naval battle in which he had little interest in view of developments on shore, and was not able to land until D plus 1, November 9.

On land itself, the 3rd Division got safely ashore, but was definitely stopped by French batteries of 138 and 75 guns sited on Point Blondin and around Casablanca.

On the northern front, at Port Lyautey, the 9th Infantry was simultaneously receiving its baptism of fire in an attack on the Thirteenth Century Moorish fort called Kasba Mehdia, which commanded the exposed finger of land where they had gone ashore. It became necessary—in spite of the heroic mission of two officers, Colonel Deman Craw and Major Pierpoint M. Hamilton, who volunteered to pass through the enemy's lines and negotiate a surrender— to storm the Kasba in an action beloved of Hollywood scenario writers, but highly repugnant to the untried officers and men who were ordered to make it. But Major Hamilton was killed by French machine gun bullets and Colonel Craw was captured and detained by the French Colonel Petit, commander of the 1st Regiment of Morocco Rifles; and so the assault went in, up from the beaches, across the landspit, over a creek, and up to the battlements of the fort itself. Men who had never been in battle before, stormed the walls of the Kasba, hurled hand-grenades into the courtyard of the fort, and drove bayonets through the bellies of Frenchmen. The Kasba Mehdia was finally reduced by blowing in the gates with pointblank fire from a self-propelled 105 cannon, at that time a "secret weapon." Another secret weapon, the "bazooka," was also used for the first time in this assault. After the reduction of the fort, the French surrendered.

On the extreme southern front, at Safi, the 2nd Armored landed with nothing more than snipers' fire to impede them. By dawn of the next day, Harmon's tanks had raced one hundred miles to the north, ready to begin the attack on Casablanca.

In the midst of the naval and land battles, General Patton came ashore in an assault landing craft; and as he neared Red Beach Two, he resembled a hunter harking to the distant baying of hounds, except that the music on this November morning was the percussion of battle. As the rifle fire inland grew sharper, Patton exclaimed:

"Christ, I wish I were a second lieutenant again."

It was a beatific moment for this warlike man, as he leaped onto the beach. Everything he had been hoping for during twenty or more years of peace had come true. In the humid air hung the black smoke of burning places and the white dust which obfuscates the landscape of war. In the air sang the noises of war, the crack of rifles, the whirr of machine guns and the grunt of cannon. There were planes in the sky, screaming with the torture of combat. Everything was violent, so that to stay alive, a man had to look all around, at the earth and the sea and the sky. Across the ground men ran or fell or crouched. They swore and grunted. The sweat shone on their faces. Their backs were bowed. It was loud and dust-ridden and confused. It was war.

Patton immediately assumed the role he liked best, that of the general on the field of battle. He walked up and down Red Beach calmly and quietly; and seeing him, men who had been crouching behind what cover they could find, began to stand up and handle the boxes of ammunition and food which had been dumped on the beach. Patton set up a temporary headquarters, received the reports of liaison officers, gave commands, and organized communications, so that gradually the thing began to take shape and direction.

For a while it had nothing of the kind. The French were still resisting. Transports had been sunk by naval and shore batteries. Landing craft had grounded on coral reefs instead of sandy bays. Assault boats had been fifteen miles out in their landfall and had run into French destroyers. Advance parties of the 3rd Infantry, moving on Casablanca from Fedhala, had been ambushed and almost wiped out.

From out of the confusion, now that Patton was ashore, swiftly emerged order—a proper order of battle, a plan, a new disposition of troops, liaison, and communications. What had been, in the initial assault, the fearful confusion of a beach landing, with individual acts of heroism neutralized by the fears of inexperienced soldiers, now became a professional battle, professionally directed.

The first task was to organize the beach parties to get supplies ashore. When Patton landed, he found the soldier stevedores hesitating between the dangers of battle and the job of unloading the assault craft. Under his cold eye, they shut out the noise and chaos of the fighting, and moved back and forth from the water's edge to the dumps inshore.

The next task was to press home the attack on Casablanca. The 3rd Infantry was held by two obstacles. A shore battery of four determined 75s on Cape Blondin was still firing on the beaches; and our advance parties were too close for our warships to silence this battery.

Climbing aboard a light tank, Patton himself organized an attack on the Cape Fedhala battery, which he decided must be taken by storm. It was taken by the first battalion of the 3rd Infantry at 3:00 P.M. on D plus 1.

With the Fedhala battery silenced, Patton was ready to begin an all-out assault on Casablanca itself. Navy guns and planes were to shell and bomb the town. The 3rd Infantry was to attack from the north. The 2nd Armored was to be rushed up from Safi, 150 miles to the south. Wireless massages from the 2nd said they had already marched one hundred miles north, and were now at the fortified crossroads town of Mazagan, midway along the Safi-Casablanca road.

All this time negotiations were under way for the capitulation of the French. Patton had been advised that negotiation was possible with certain French officers. He had been ordered to avoid casualties on either side and to spare Casablanca from bombardment, if possible. So American officers and French officers, under flags of truce, journeyed back and forth between the lines. Colonel John P. Ratay and Colonel W. H. Wilbur passed through the French lines on November 10, with Patton's last offer of an armistice. By now it was apparent that the French ground forces with their few batteries of 75s and their ten-ton Renault tanks were willing to cease fire. But the French Navy and the Marines were obsessed with the idea of "L'honneur," and seemed determined to continue the unequal fight, even though the small French fleet was sunk or damaged and the crippled battleship *Jean Bart* had been hit ten times by 16-inch naval guns, aerial torpedoes, and bombs. Yet she was still firing from her forward batteries. Casablanca had not fallen, and the battle was not over.

Patton, therefore, made plans to attack the city from all sides on the morning of November 11. During the night, however, the French Commander-in-Chief, General August Nogues, came to Patton's headquarters at Fedhala, and arranged for the armistice. Forty minutes before the Casablanca assault was timed to begin, the French laid down their arms, and the three-day campaign was ended.

Patton was happy. November 11 was his birthday, and at the Victory Banquet in the Hotel Miramar, recently vacated by the Axis Armistice Commission, he stood up and proposed a toast. It was short and simple. "To my success!" He radioed General Eisenhower that his mission had been accomplished and Casablanca was ours. Later, to his wife, he described the campaign as "a nice fight." He took over the Shell Building in Casablanca as his headquarters, and summoned a staff conference. Now was the time to study what had happened, to dispense praise and blame. Now was the time for one of those speeches which his subordinates discussed with indignation for days to come. Before an assembly of his officers, Patton strode into the room, sat down at a table, looked round, his eyes cold, his small mouth rounded, and said quietly:

"Gentlemen, you have done well. Mistakes were made. We should not have fallen into ambushes. Some of the troops are too slow. Too many of them want to sit on their arses and stick their heads in holes. But the operation was on the whole successful. I want to say my job and your job is not over. We have thousands of miles of territory to take care of, including the Spanish border. I'm going to do something about that. So you must work hard, every one of you. I won't have my staff sitting around their damn offices, chewing the fat. I have no use for a staff officer who doesn't know which end of an M-1 to put against his shoulder. Get out in the field and see what is the real problem. I don't want a lot of officers who get varicose veins and waffle-tails from sitting in chairs all day. That is all, gentlemen."

3

Towards the vanquished French Patton's attitude was a model of West Point diplomacy. In the first place, they had fought well and valiantly. They were, therefore, good soldiers, and were embraced by his affections. Secondly, Patton knew that his mission was as much diplomatic as military. The immediate military objective had been attained. Casablanca and a 300-mile strip of the African Atlantic seaboard had been secured. But the secondary objectives had still to be realized. Two and a half divisions was a tiny force to hold the West Coast of Africa, the thousand miles of mountains between Casablanca and Algiers, the Spanish border, and the threat of German intervention. Patton knew that the Allies, particularly the American State Department, had undertaken the North African

Campaign with the diplomacy of expediency; we had made an indirect deal with the Vichy French, and were shortly to compromise with Admiral Darlan, Pierre Boisson, Governor-General of French Equatorial Africa, and General Nogues, Governor-General of French Morocco.

Patton is no politician. Like all professional soldiers and sailors, he remains aloof from politics. But he has a keen "strategic" understanding of high diplomacy. And in the diplomacy of North Africa, none was more suitable than the professional soldier. North Africa was only made possible by professional soldiers—Eisenhower, Clark, Patton, and Giraud. Behind the simple, yet honest façade of these men, were sheltered a host of petty professional politicians, it is true. And the political history of North Africa was distinguished by dark undertones which the outside world never heard.*

Patton's approach to the intricacies of French colonial politics was a soldier's direct approach. He regarded his mission as wholly a military one. Casablanca had to be seized and made safe as a supply port to help feed the Tunisian forces. The vast and mountainous interior behind the coastal plains had to be made safe for the convoys to cross the Atlas mountains to Algeria. The Spanish border had to be watched; and beyond the border itself, the Spanish peninsula which was then, and throughout the war, a Nazi outpost.

So Patton reacted simply to what he saw as a simple problem. First, it was essential to gain the good will of the vanquished French and of the vast, amorphous Arab population whom the French controlled. For Patton saw these Moroccans not as a subject people but as a potential guerilla force which could harass the trans-Africa supply lines.

* See Kenneth Crawford's study of this subject.

Second, it was essential to hasten into the interior to patrol the continental highways over the Atlas mountains to Oran and Algiers.

Third, it was essential to stick a clenched fist in the face of the Franco military to the north, in Spanish Morocco.

Patton's method of gaining French and Arab good will was easy for a man of his temperament, since it only necessitated the emphasis of a melodramatic role which he had played so often in his fifty-seven years that it was now an integral part of his nature.

The first step, as always, was to make a speech, full of grandiose sentiments and resounding phrases for which the French have much greater regard than the Americans, who have no regard for them at all. So Patton issued a statement, which appeared in the local press, changed overnight from sound Vichy propaganda sheets to pamphlets dedicated to the cause of victory, democracy, and "la belle France." In print, Patton deplored the "nice fight" as "fratricidal strife." He commended the "—— Frenchmen" as "gallant soldiers." Of the slippery politician Nogues, who had been the most efficient of the colonial governors in carrying out the Germans' edicts (to which he had added a few anti-Semitic decrees of his own), Patton thundered:

"I wish to express how much I appreciate his full collaboration. His knowledge of the country and the confidence he enjoys from the Sultan have already been made known to us. Working together in a friendly way, I am sure we will be able to solve the numerous problems resulting from our common action."

Still in the role of a Roman emperor-general, Patton said: "The happy conclusion of these unfortunate events gives us great satisfaction, for we want political as well as economic normalcy to return as soon as possible."

And the General informed the youthful and bemused Sultan that the American army had no wish to infringe on his authority in any way. He did not add, of course, his private sentiments that the Sultan had no authority to infringe on; and the American army did not give "a good goddam" for him in any case.

The next step was to get into his buskin. The G.I. uniform in which he had come ashore at Fedhala was taken off. The full dress uniform, with all the medals and all the pistols, was put on. On his head was placed the sacred helmet with its two bright stars, because, though the American helmet is a hideous and ponderous headgear, and was now as redundant in the sun-washed streets of Casablanca as jingling spurs, it has for Patton the aura of ancient war—Greek and Roman wars, and the wars of Crusaders and golden-helmeted Hussars.

In this garb, which sat on the General's manly figure as snugly as a pair of boxing gloves on a pugilist's fists, Patton called to pay his respects to the plenipotentiaries of the French Moroccan world. Patton called first, in accordance with protocol, on the Governor-General of Morocco, General Nogues. Nogues was still a Vichy man, like almost the entire body of French administrators of the Moroccan protectorate. They had the imperialistic interests of France at heart—and such interests were potentially hostile to the Anglo-Saxon intruders as much as they were to the Axis invaders.

Patton's task, then, was the tricky diplomatic one of reassuring Nogues and the group he represented that the Allies came not as conquerors of this rich colonial territory, but as friends of France. For this reason the Western Task

Force was almost wholly an American force. West Africa was no place at the time for either the British or the Free French.

For the first two months nothing was changed in the existing French administration of the territory. All French officers and troops retained their positions and their arms. The outright Vichy appointees were left alone, though these men underwent a rapid change of heart; and in due course followed an unreal period when Vichy men such as Nogues, and Pierre Boisson, Governor-General of French Equatorial Africa, and Marcel Peyrouton, Governor-General of Algiers, and Yves Chatel, governor of the city of Algiers, all came forward as patriotic Frenchmen, with hand on heart. M. Yves Chatel, speaking on the Moroccan radio, gave a fine performance in this histrionic role of the repentant traitor. He said, with his forked tongue in his cheek: "Do everything possible to aid the Allies. It is no time to discuss whether we are fighting for the restoration of the France of Richelieu or the France of the Revolution. The liberation of France is a union of both these parties. War means the burying of past discords. I know only one party nowadays— the party of victory."

In the meantime, followers of de Gaulle, radicals, Jews, and Republican Spaniards in Morocco were still being thrown into the jails and deported to the concentration camps in the south. For Patton was alone with his two and a half divisions in a territory of 25,000 square miles. His orders were to cooperate with Nogues. As far as the government of French Morocco was concerned, it was a military dictatorship, since Nogues had received orders from Admiral Darlan empowering the Governor-General to rule the protectorate by decree. Patton is the type of man who would see nothing amiss with a military dictatorship in a region such as Morocco; or perhaps anywhere else.

So Patton's diplomacy remained simple. He paid his respects to Nogues, Michelier, the French admiral who governed Casablanca, and the Sultan of Morocco. There were a number of formal ceremonies, with parades and military bands. The "Marseillaise" was always played first by the American band, followed by the "Star-Spangled Banner." The American musicians had the usual difficulties with the French national anthem, and the French bandsmen gave their customary lugubrious rendering of the American national anthem. But military protocol was always strictly observed, and the Americans wore their "pinks" with full decorations, many of which were new as a result of citations in the recent fighting. All was done with military precision and stateliness, with a total official indifference to the true state of French Morocco.

It was the ordinary American soldier who now ambled down the white streets of Casablanca who glimpsed the real Morocco. This unknown G.I. had begun his wanderings through Africa, regarding all he saw with that simple prejudice with which he was always to judge foreign peoples and foreign ways. He bought souvenirs, drank wine, tried talking to the French women. He ignored the French soldiery. He wandered around the fringes of the Arab compound, called in Casablanca the Medinah, and sometimes he fell into the hands of the pimps and the prostitutes. The sum of his experiences did not move him greatly. He continued to think only of home, and of how much better everything was done in America. Two things, however, did arouse his curiosity and sometimes a stronger emotion: the sottish cruelty of the Arabs to animals, and the cold brutality of the French to the Arabs. Every day he would see an Arab belaboring a donkey over the head with a club; and every night a French gendarme was meting out the same treatment to an "Ay-rab."

To the G.I. there was definitely something wrong somewhere in French Morocco. But Patton was only concerned at this period with two vital military problems. The first was the Spanish Moroccan border; the second was the supply line across North Africa to Tunisia.

Patton's method of dealing with the Spanish was a bold imitation of the Nazi technique. Suddenly he moved the entire 2nd Armored Division, with detachments of the 9th Infantry, up to the Spanish border, and presented his compliments to the Spanish military governor. The Spaniards were maneuvered into stepping across the border and reviewing the American troops. A parade of tanks, with motorized infantry and fighter cover, coupled with some grandiose phrases, resulted in the first "amicable" meeting between Americans and Francoists. Then Patton whirled his 2nd Armored away, leaving the infantry along the frontier.

He had to withdraw his armor, because about this time American tanks fighting in Tunisia had been battered by German Stukas and American P-38s to such an extent that the spearheads of the 1st Armored Division making the drive on Tunis were practically wiped out. Almost the entire equipment of the 2nd Armored was taken away from Patton, and rushed to the battle front 1000 miles to the east. That left an infantry combat team to guard the Spanish Moroccan frontier.

A second combat team of the 9th Infantry was all that was available to guard 500 miles of supply routes between Algiers, the Atlas Mountains, and Casablanca, where thousands of tons of material were already being unloaded and trucked across Africa.

By mid-January, Patton's mission had been accomplished so successfully that Africa was chosen as the scene for the Casablanca Conference. French Morocco had been made safe enough for the two leaders of the Western powers, with their advisers, to step from their planes at the Casablanca airfield and begin the series of discussions which were to take us eventually to Sicily, Italy, and beyond, to the goal of unconditional surrender.

French Morocco was now ours to use for our own military purposes. Spanish Morocco was considered no longer a threat. The supply lines to the east had been secured. And Patton had been assigned his next mission.

On his massive chest were now stitched three more decorations. The United States awarded him an Oak Leaf cluster to his Distinguished Service Medal "for exceptionally meritorious service in a duty of great responsibility. General Patton, as commander of the Western Task Force, was responsible for the planning and execution of the attacks on French Morocco."

"Ability of the highest order," "driving force," "vigor," "dash," "offensive spirit," were the expressions suitably chosen for this citation.

The French promoted him to the rank of Commander in the Legion of Honor.

But the award which most suited his flamboyant personality was the decoration presented by the Sultan of Morocco, who had been so intrigued by the Americans pistols and marksmanship and his way with horses. It was originally a hunter's award and is called the Grand Cross of the Ouissan Alouite. As it was hung round Patton's neck, the citation was solemnly read by the Sultan himself:

". . . et les lions dans leurs tanières tremblent en le voyant approcher."

The language was stilted French; but the significance is subtilely Oriental. "Lions in their dens cower at his approach. . . ."

In a sense, this is the only medal Patton has received for that basic quality which he has glorified into a creed: the quality he calls "guts"—always pronounced with a growl calculated to make lions in their dens tremble.

CHAPTER V
BIRTH OF AN ARMY

I

PATTON took command of all American troops in Tunisia at the beginning of March, 1943. His force consisted of two infantry divisions, the 1st and the 9th; one armored division, the 1st; and a battalion of Rangers. This battle group, known as the American 2nd Corps, was part of the main British First Army, which also included French Foreign Legion and Senegalese troops. The Commander-in-Chief of the First Army was Field Marshall Alexander. The Supreme Commander was General Eisenhower.

Patton's three divisions were the nucleus of the American armies in the western hemisphere. From this little band of professional soldiers grew by mid-1945 seven full-sized American armies: the Seventh which fought in Sicily; the Fifth which fought in Italy; and the First, Third, Seventh, Ninth, and Fifteenth which fought in Europe.

Within two years, therefore, the U. S. European armies expanded from three combat divisions to seventy divisions, from 30,000 fighting men to a million fighting men. Even more rapid than the training of men and the creation of armies was the production of the machines of war. Airplanes, tanks, guns, ships, trucks, jeeps, and a multifarious assortment of gadgets flowed from the industrial reservoir of America until this mechanical torrent inundated occupied

Europe and drowned the armies of Nazi Germany and all its satellites.

Patton's three divisions there in Southern Tunisia had all had experience of battle. They were now professional soldiers, and had ceased to be civilians. They had killed their fellow men, their comrades had been killed, and so they had profoundly changed. In their thinking and their talking, in their daily life and their recollections of home, they were now soldiers, not American boys who a year before had sat in classrooms or worked in offices or perched on stools in corner drug stores, laughing, talking, thinking like American boys. The difference between them, the soldiers who had killed their fellow men in battle and the men who harbored the anticipation of death, and the civilian in battle dress who arrived from America, was profound and fundamental. They were quite changed.

You can always tell the "new boy" at the front. He is still clean. His uniform is tidy. There is polish on his boots, and when he takes his boots off, there are no holes in his socks.

But his manner tells you more than his clothes. He is more "soldierly," and more timid than the veteran. He is tenser, salutes vigorously, and is always wary of officers. He doesn't yet know how to move slowly, and he doesn't yet know his officers as men who lead him into battle.

His face especially is indicative. It is pink and clean and unlined. Some of these new boys appear not to have shaved yet. And their eyes are interesting. They look at you and the harsh world around them with wonderment, and a little anxiously. Theirs are timid eyes.

The replacements are such a contrast to the veterans, they seem like men of a different generation, yet their ages are the same, anywhere from eighteen to thirty-five. But the veteran of twenty-one looks and acts and thinks older than the replacement of thirty-one. The veteran has a deep, quiet aspect. He moves slowly. He doesn't talk much, and is not given to loud laughter. You have to understand that beneath the hard shell of the man is a gentleness, almost a tenderness, reserved for a little circle of friends who have not died beside him.

You wonder sometimes if he will have this same love and gentleness for his wife or mother or friends when he comes home again; or whether his experiences have shut him out from these far-away people. And you hope his wife or some woman he loves will lead him back into a world he has almost forgotten.

The "new boys," or green troops, do not yet have this psychology. They still have the marks of home on them, and the habits of home, and this makes it hard for them.

2

Of Patton's three Tunisian divisions only the 1st Armored had fought Germans. They had been fighting Germans from the beginning of November, 1942, to the end of February, 1943. The 1st Infantry Division, which by tradition, command, officership, and training was destined to greatness, had fought the French at Oran during the initial North African landings in November. They had fought French Marines and sailors and native troops; snipers, 75s, and antiquated Renault tanks, and some coastal artillery. They had fought well and victoriously, and had proven themselves, under a truly professional commander, General Terry Allen, predestined professional soldiers. Their skirmishes around Oran, the killing and the killed, the sound of guns firing in anger, the necessity of knowing and clinging to earth, the terrible excitement of battle, had begun their initiation, and they were no longer sad and bewildered adolescents.

The 9th Infantry Division had stormed ashore at Port Lyautey against shorter but tougher opposition. Their battle experience had been Hollywoodish, with a hot sun, a white beach, colored uniforms, a matter of flame and charging and diabolic uproar. They were to find, as the 1st Infantry found, and the scores of other great American divisions, that war against the Germans was not this heroic Patton formula at all. For them, as for the rest, the war against the Germans was ultimately reduced to gray, without a sun, without a white beach, but with mud and rain, and dead men in blue-green uniforms.

This the 1st Armored Division had already discovered in four months of strange and lonely saga. The 1st Armored had fought the Germans for four months. It had fought Germans, Italians, Stukas, Ju 88s, Messerschmitt 88s, Mark IV tanks; the mountains they call djebels in Africa, and the passes through the mountains; rain and mud, and quagmires of mud and quicksands; cold, hunger, shortage of supplies, confusion in command, and inefficient officers. The 1st Armored had been mauled by the Barenthins, the paratroopers, the 10th Panzer Division. It had been hammered from the air by Ju 87s, which are the Stukas, and by P-38s, which are the Lockheed Lightnings. The latter had caused almost as many casualties and as much damage as the former, when they strafed the American columns on the road to Tunis. The 1st Armored had been driven from Tebourba, fifteen miles outside Tunis, from Djedeida, Medjez-el-bab, Sbeitla, Gafsa, Feriana, and the Kasserine

Pass. It had lost the equipment of almost entire combat commands. It had broken under enemy attacks. It had drowned in mud. It had been chopped up into little units and loaned out to the British and the French. It had changed generals. It had been, in brief, mauled and battered, defeated and mishandled for four months.

For four months, in fact, the 1st Armored had been the only American Army fighting the Germans. As a result, it was—compared to anything else we had—an elite division. It was not as good as the 10th or 15th Panzer Divisions, because its tanks were not as good. American tanks were never as good as German tanks at any stage of the war. When the 1st Armored fought from Grants and Shermans, they were outgunned and outmaneuvered in every tank engagement. But the 1st Armored was now very stout of heart, valorous, proud, tough, and indeed, embittered—embittered as men become who are alone in fighting for their country and seem to have been forgotten.

So at the time Patton took over the command of the American Second Corps, he had only one division of Americans who had fought Germans. They regarded themselves as a band of superior men. America, with its lush life of sunshine and fruit and dance orchestras and comely women and bathrooms and cocktail bars and exuberant inductions into army life and cowboy maneuvers and brass bands and epic military exercises, was remote and unreal to them. Africa and Germans and mud and defeat and death were the realities. They had learned war was these things, not those others. It was not tank charges or horse charges or charges at all. It was not glorious, not red, white, and blue, nor was it fun to die; it was not easy to die, it was not easy to live and endure.

When their new commander, Lieutenant-General George S. Patton, Jr., of "Blood and Guts" and "Green Hornet" fame stood before the officers and men of the 1st Armored Division and harangued them—exhorting and cajoling, blustering and filling the quiet air with profanity—these veterans regarded him with disgust and even loathing. I remember their comments afterwards. They were the comments of angry and insulted men. Patton's exhortations to die, his assurances that death on the battlefield was the finest end any real he-man could desire, his harangues about attacking until the tank was shot out from under them, then going forward on foot, and his grim references to a new disciplinary order, were despised by the officers and grinned at by the men. Their attitude was summed up by a wounded Ranger in an Evacuation Hospital at Gafsa:

"We provide the blood," said the Ranger, "and he provides the guts."

After Patton's victories and powerful personality had fallen with a sharp impact on a flaccid American public, the newspapers began to tell stories of his harangues and exhortations and martinet methods; and these stories were so told to warm the readers far from the battlefields with gentle humor, and they were told to give the impression that the big bluff and blustering general was like a father to his men, and so the men regarded him. They tell, for instance, of the incident at El Guettar. Here, in the heat of the battle, Patton sent a runner to a forward observation post where a young lieutenant and two enlisted men cautiously peered over a rock ledge, directing artillery on the German positions beyond. The lieutenant had reached this post with daring and skill and was doing his duty there. When the runner arrived, says the story, the lieutenant expected a compliment from his commander, and he asked, "What's the message?"

"The General says for you to put your leggings on," said the runner.

I don't think the story is true. It has the marks of a story written on the city desk of a weekly magazine. But though it has been read with a quiet chuckle by many a reader sitting in his safe armchair, if it had happened it would have caused a buzz through the ranks of that little American army in Southern Tunisia like the hum of angry wasps.

Actually, Patton's rule in Tunisia was harsh, but not unreasonable. It affected the soldier in a series of petty annoyances administered by the unfortunate military police. Patton remained a lonely man, and that was how he looked when I first saw him that evening in Feriana.

3

He was standing outside the French railway station at Feriana, smoking his cigar as the sun went down. His large form and face seemed large even in that landscape of vast distances. I was with Frederick Painton, of *Reader's Digest,* the lovable, creased-faced Painton who later died in the Pacific. We went up to the General, having the privilege of the war correspondent and civilian of speaking to generals and G.I.s, when we saw fit. Neither Painton nor I was wearing the helmet which later became regulation throughout the American army and which Patton was then harping about. The Commander of the 2nd Corps gave us that cold glance he reserved for sloppy-looking soldiers, but recognized from our shoulder patches who we were.

And so we stood there in the last sunshine of that African

day, discussing the situation. I was surprised at the quietness and high-pitched quality of Patton's voice. I was surprised at his whole air of quietness and even remoteness, and had the impression he was musing in a time and distance of his own.

Undoubtedly he was musing. Gafsa had fallen according to plan—the Allied plan; but the campaign itself was moving according to Rommel's plan rather than to Patton's. Gafsa had fallen without a shot being fired, and Patton does not care for bloodless victories. He was right. He knew as he stood there pondering over the day's happenings that the Germans had just gone away from the Gafsa plain to positions of their own choosing. His blitz technique and attack tactics were not working at all. He was being held beyond Gafsa, and now he was weighing his chances of cutting behind Rommel's Mareth Line and trapping the German Army in a brilliantly planned and executed maneuver.

What he was thinking about was how different these sawtoothed mountains and immense flower-covered deserts were from the terrain he had roistered over in California. How different were the wadis from the California rivers, how different the roads. Africa was revealing itself in this evening light—as it had done during the white noonday sun—as bigger than his cherished dreams. Africa mocked at his love of war. For three days it had rained, and his tanks lay like stranded behemoths in the soggy mud of dried salt lakes. Africa was bleak, Arab, colonial French, and indifferent. Across its ancient surface, Patton's forces moved about two miles a day. "A man in a track suit could make only half a mile an hour in those hills," said Patton. This was the antithesis of lightning war. It was not even trench war. Out there against the djebels and on the desert it was not like any war at all. Men and machines just disappeared into space. They were as ephemeral as mirages.

A country like this, a war like this, were alien to Patton's whole nature. He thinks only in terms of masses of infantry and armor. He had neither. Yet he had more than Rommel. But Rommel had veterans. He had the 10th Panzer. Patton had the 1st Armored, the 1st and 9th Infantry. His armor could not get away. His infantry were still unseasoned. Standing there at the brick house which they called Feriana Station, Patton smoked his cigar, and thought of still another plan to win a glorious victory which would be recorded in the textbooks as "the Patton break-through to the sea."

How he planned the Benson force and what became of that plan I shall recount later.

4

The strategic situation when Patton took command of the 2nd Corps was a simple textbook one. Rommel and his Germans were being compressed between the mountains and the sea by the First Army, while Montgomery with his Eighth Army thrust like a piston up the coastal plains. The obvious thing for Patton to do, and the thing he tried to do, was to break out from the mountains, get into the coastal plains beyond, and drive to the sea behind the main body of Rommel's army, which was facing Montgomery on the Mareth Line.

If Patton could have done this, he would have won the first American victory of the war. If he could have trapped the majority of Rommel's desert forces, the campaign in North Africa would have finished at least a month earlier.

But the situation was so simple, and the plan so obvious that the Germans had anticipated it three months earlier. At this stage of the war, mid-March, 1943, the German High Command was at the top of its form, and the Allied "strategy of weight" had not been realized in the factories of America.

In a theoretical sense, the Allies had already had two opportunities of making this dash to the sea from Kasserine to Gabes, and thereby trapping the Afrika Corps. The first opportunity had been at the very beginning of the campaign in November, of 1942. If the small Anglo-American forces which had tried to rush Tunis had gone south through Tebessa—Feriana—Gafsa—El Guettar, and so across the great oval plains to Gabes, they would have cut the Tunisian peninsula in half, and isolated Rommel from Tunis and Bizerta. The gamble for rushing Tunis itself was a spectacular gamble, but the odds were against us. For Tunis was nearer to the Italo-German supply resources in Sicily and Italy than they were to Algiers. The Italian merchant fleet managed to make the short sea run from Sicily with heavy reinforcements, while the Luftwaffe held the breach.

The second opportunity of executing this same "steel loop" maneuver had come immediately after the Battle of Kasserine. When Rommel attacked the 1st Armored Division at Kasserine and the British at Thala to the North, he had intended to break through on this southern Tunisian front and get behind the whole length of the First Army's mountain line. It was the same ambitious strategy later employed by von Rundstedt in the Ardennes offensive through Luxemburg and Belgium. Rommel's plan failed because he did not have the weight to exploit his victory, and because Montgomery was snapping at his heels. On February 24,

PATTON'S TUNISIAN CAMPAIGN

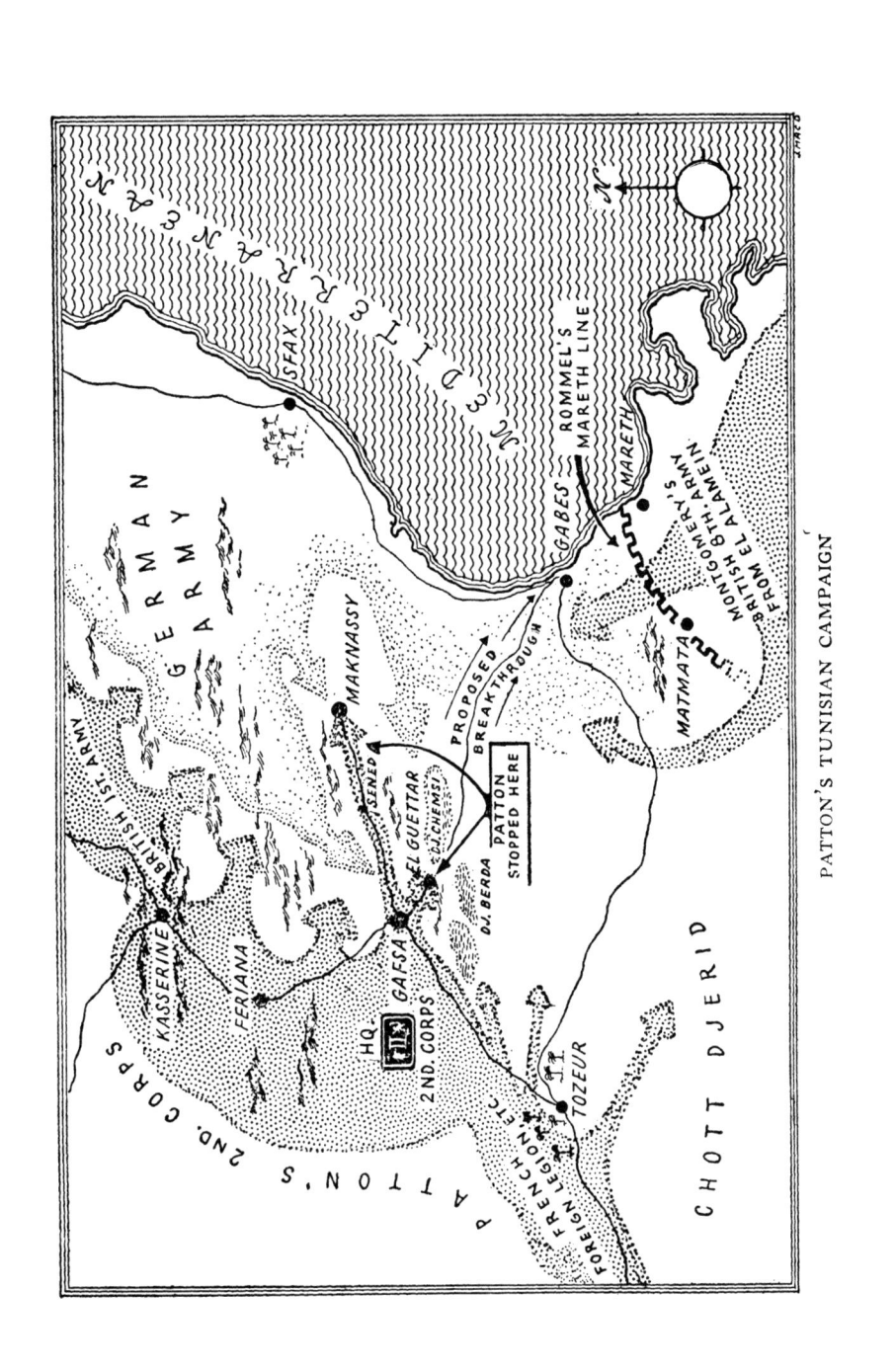

1943, Rommel abandoned his Kasserine battle, having been held too long by Combat Command B of the 1st Armored Division at the Chamri Ridge behind Kasserine Pass, and by the British Guards and Armored Division at Thala. On that day in February, Rommel with his 21st Panzers just faded away across the Gafsa plains, leaving the usual bewildered Italian rear guards to cover his retreat. I returned to the pass of Kasserine the next day, to find it empty and serene, and to hear the birds singing over what had been a brutal battlefield. There was not a sign of men or machines as we peered over the crags which mark the high point of the Pass. The Germans had gone as they always went in Africa, as silently as Bedouins. They left nothing behind, neither wrecked vehicles nor abandoned supplies nor débris of any kind; and we used to say they swept the mountainsides before they went away.

The Germans had obviously gone, but the tired and still dazed Americans could not believe it. They were creeping forward almost on tiptoe, peering over the ridges onto the empty plain in which lay the little square town of Kasserine, with Feriana and Gafsa to the south. In those days, American reconnaissance was haphazard, cautious, and unreliable. Major Martin Phillipsborn, Intelligence officer for CCB of the 1st Armored, often did his own one-man reconnaissance. The professional scout work was done for the Americans by mysterious, aloof, and beautifully efficient British Derby Yeomen, or Phantoms, who took off into the hazy distances on their high-wheeled scout cars, and went whither they wished, a mountain and desert law unto themselves.

Apparently, after Kasserine, there was no proper reconnaissance, and no plan for a swift advance hard on the rear guards of the 21st Panzer, which was racing back to its position in the Mareth Line. Later, in France, it became axiomatic "to go through the same door the enemy leaves by." If the Americans could have rushed the passes at El Guettar and Maknassy, while the Germans were still withdrawing through them, they would have held the gateway to Gabes and the sea.

By the time the 2nd Corps was reorganized, and Patton had arrived to take command, the opportunity had been lost. The Germans had no interest in Feriana or Gafsa. They laid their minefields, and retired to positions of their own choosing in the El Guettar and Maknassy Mountains. From the high ground and peaks, they commanded the passes through these mountains, and the roads which ran through the passes. Patton found himself up against two hostile forces: the Germans and Africa itself.

5

Africa, they say, is the oldest of all the continents. It is old and immense. It has a vast impersonality which makes it fearful and menacing to us. Of the thousands of Anglo-Americans who fought there, only a few liked Africa. The American soldiers hated Africa, and feared it in some indefinable atavistic fashion, because they felt lonely and lost in the djebels and wide oval plains and unexplored salt lakes and forgotten cities of other days.

Geographically, North Africa is a succession of iron folds in the earth which run both vertically and horizontally from the Atlantic Ocean to the Mediterranean. The flat country in between is fertile and cultivated in the north, but gradually changes into a flowering desert in the south. Scattered between are curious salt lakes called chotts, the largest of which is the Chott Djerid, to the south of Gafsa. And here the Sahara Desert proper commences. It is not a land of cities, fields, streams, and woods, but of saw-toothed mountains, deserts, mirages, and ruins. Instead of a neat and orderly civilization it has beauty and mystery. Instead of a static population and industry it has Arabs and goat herds. It is altogether ancient and barbarous. Barbarous are the names, beautiful and mysterious; names like Kasserine, Sbeitla, Youks-les-bains, Thala, Sidi-bouzid, Pont-du-fahs, Medjez-el-bab, Souk-el-arba; names whose harsh music can never be forgotten.

Running east and west are the main arteries of road and rail, built by the French. They are superb examples of civil engineering. But they are only scratches across the face of Africa, and the iron rails and macadamized highways and wayside stations with their brick depots have a lonely and forgotten look, and in places just seem to disappear into the vast impersonality of the landscape.

The strangest thing about Africa was that in the middle of a battle it was hard to believe that there was a war going on. This land engulfed the men and their machines, and whole units literally disappeared in the immensity that surrounded them. Perhaps this was why the Arabs and their goats and camels disregarded the war which was fought all around them. They may not have seen it, even though their camel trains passed superciliously right across the plains where battles were being fought. The war in Southern Tunisia left no marks on the landscape, though thousands of rounds of shells were poured into the mountainsides, though scores of tanks were wrecked, though vehicles were abandoned in the quagmires, though men were killed by the hundreds. Only the minefields seemed to menace you, and that was a menace in the mind, invisible and incalculable, like the loom of Africa itself.

This was strange. We would set off in our jeeps with the windscreens down, because in those days the Luftwaffe was active and hovered like hawks in the clear air, watching for the flash of glass on the roads below. The correspondents drove their own jeeps, usually three men to a vehicle. One drove, the other two watched the skies; and at the appearance of a plane, we stopped the jeep and waited for an identification; if it was the enemy, we proceeded to run as far as we could away from the vehicle. We were all fast runners in those days. Driving along, with the distant rumble of some battle coming nearer, one still became bemused by the majesty and mystery of Africa. The iron battlements of the djebels always had a new form, new colors. Sometimes, from the peaks, you would look down on what appeared to be a picture postcard lake; and this lake would become a field of ultramarine flowers as you descended into the plain. The little Arab-French towns clinging to the mountainsides were prettier than Swiss towns in the high Alps, until you drove into them, and found them a squalor of Arab hutments and cheap white-stuccoed houses.

But it was the lonely and magnificent Roman ruins which gave timelessness to our experiences. There was such a ruin of a Roman city on the way to Kasserine, and eventually those lovely triumphal arches and broken temples of Haidra, Roman city of the second century, became far more wonderful and fascinating than the grim struggle among the crags of the Pass. Further north, at Sbeitla, was the ruin of still another thriving Roman city, with a tremendous amphitheater which the Germans had mined before leaving.

I remember driving up to the amphitheater, walking across a field, and suddenly noting the white tapes with which American engineers had marked the minefield, and thinking how mean and nasty were the Germans to spoil a tourist's pleasure. So, up north in the British sector, the indescribably beautiful ruins of Dougga, Afro-Roman city in the mountains, seized the imagination far more than the bloody struggles at Medjez-el-bab, gateway to Tunis.

The mountains, or djebels, gripped some of us, the ruins others, the flowers still others. To the geographer, the djebels were far more interesting than the war; to the historian, so were the ruins; and to the botanist, so were the desert flowers. Patton was fighting his campaign in the desert spring, in mid-March. Then the desert blossomed, as no spring-fed valley in milder climes ever blossomed. The desert blossomed in a hundred vivid hues and smelled with an intoxicating scent. Color and perfume were so beautiful that they too expunged the reality of war. I recall a trip onto the Maknassy plain and up to Sened Station with Cy Peterman, of the *Philadelphia Inquirer*. Peterman loved flowers, and gradually his attention wandered from the noise of guns and the occasional bursting of shells and the array of tanks drawn up along a ridge to the exquisite garden around us. We got down from our jeep, and Peterman gathered flowers. All that day, I remember, he wandered about from group to group, from command post to command post, clutching a bunch of red and yellow flowers in his hand. So he approached generals and G.I.s, and no one saw anything strange in the spectacle of the portly, red-faced and behelmeted war correspondent with his notebook in one hand and his posy in another.

Peterman's posy was not strange in Africa. In a Command

Post in a phosphate mine, General Patton himself set to work with a pick to pry out two marine fossils to send to his wife, who collects them.

As with the mountains and the ruins and the flowers, so with the oases and their leaning palms and dunes and eternal springs and mirages. Those of us who could, would suddenly turn our jeep south towards the Sahara and the Chott Djerid, and spend a few days at Tozeur or Nefta in a Garden of Allah setting, complete with Meharistes or the French Camel Corps. It was also an opportunity to see the desert gazelles, which are rarer than wars.

To our High Command, the majesty and mystery of Africa were not, of course, important. They had to assess them in terms of war. They were interested not in mountains but in the passes through them; not in deserts, but in roads; not in flowers and ruins, but in supplies. When Patton took command of the 2nd Corps they had worked out their scheme and their plans. Patton's role in these plans was the key one. He knew it as he stood at his headquarters in Feriana smoking his cigar, and within the next few days, he set his plan in motion.

6

The first step in his campaign was the capture of Gafsa. From Gafsa we were to dash to El Guettar and Maknassy across the plain. At El Guettar and Maknassy we were to storm the passes, and stream through them to Gabes and the sea. At this time the bulk of Rommel's Afrika Corps, with reinforcements brought down from von Arnim's Northern Tunisian Army, were fighting it out with Montgomery's Eighth Army along the Mareth Line. Patton's task was to get behind Rommel.

The first step, then, was Gafsa. Patton hoped to attack on March 15, with the 1st Infantry Division as the spearhead. But for three days before March 15 it rained almost unceasingly. It rained, and it was bitterly cold in the mountains and on the plains.

I arrived at the front on March 14, to find the score of front line correspondents who covered the British and American sectors foregathered at the American Advance Press Camp at Tebessa. Some of us were sent to the local Hotel Victoria, which had been built, as far as one could see, into the original Roman walls which encircled this ancient city.

The next three days were spent getting our army into position, which was delayed by the continued raining. Corps headquarters were now at Feriana, midway between Kasserine and Gafsa. Here, on the night of March 16, the correspondents moved into a brick barn; a week previously it had been occupied by German soldiers, who had adorned the walls with excellent crayon sketches, skilful and humorous. There were holes in the roof, and it rained onto our camp beds at night; but we ate at General Patton's mess in the Feriana Hotel, and we ate very well. At breakfast, on the morning of the 17th, Generals Eisenhower, Alexander, and Patton, with their Chiefs of Staff, were present, for the attack went off that day.

We took off for the front lines immediately after breakfast, driving across the desert, round the shoulder of the mountains, past the inevitable Roman ruins, and a salt lake, all of it still mysterious and immemorable; but today, because the sun was shining and a battle was pending, not as impressive as before.

We found the advance infantry of the 1st Infantry Division along a crest of sandy hills, overlooking Gafsa in the plain. Gafsa, from afar, was exquisite. Through field glasses, it was a compact oasis town of white minarets, date palms, and clay walls, and shimmered there in the haze like a mirage.

Here, on the ridge, the late Brigadier-General Theodore Roosevelt, assistant divisional commander under General Terry Allen, had set up his command post. Officers and men were dug into the sand. From these dugouts came the constant peep-peep and sudden harsh voices of the radio. On the American side of the lines there was an air of expectation and strength and all the preparations for battle. From Gafsa, supposedly in German hands, there came nothing but the shimmer of a distant city.

I have stated that in those early days of the North African campaign, our reconnaissance was amateurish and ineffectual. Lying there on the ridge, we did not know who or what was in Gafsa. We took no risks about it, though it was fairly obvious that there was nothing in the town but Arabs and a sprinkling of French civilians. But punctually after dawn a flight of eighteen Mitchell bombers roared in from the west, circled over Gafsa, and dropped their cargo of bombs. It was significant that there was no enemy anti-aircraft fire to impede them. The American bombs fell all over the place. Precision bombing, at that time, was more of a theory than a fact. Synchronized with the aerial bombardment were the batteries of carefully concealed American guns, 105s and 155s, or Long Toms. After this shelling, the infantry moved cautiously forward. It was all according to textbook tactics.

Still nothing stirred in Gafsa, and General Roosevelt,

skeptical and impatient, decided to go and see for himself. He and his aides and retinue jumped aboard their jeeps and set off across the sand like a small flotilla of ships, zigzagging back and forth, bumping through wadis, slipping down dunes, edging closer to the town. There was the occasional cracking of machine guns, and as we approached Gafsa, we saw a long line of men running along a ridge. The jeep convoy stopped, everybody studied the scene through field glasses. Moving on, with every man of us silently anxious about mines—as we were throughout the African campaign—we came to an abandoned road block, topped a rise, rolled down a hill, and into Gafsa.

Simultaneously other small mobile units had moved into the town from the southwest, as we entered from the northeast. In a few moments, Gafsa seemed full of Americans, and the place had been captured without a shot being fired.

The next day, Thursday, March 18, the little oasis of El Guettar, a few miles east of Gafsa, fell, also without resistance. Behind the infantry, the 1st Armored started to roll, and reached Sened to the northeast, and came to Maknassy at the base of the mountains.

Then it started to rain and hail; and rain, hail, mountains —*and* Germans—stopped us.

It was easy now to see what game Rommel was playing. He yielded Gafsa, El Guettar, and Sened without fighting, because from his point of view they were not worth fighting for. Between Patton and the coast was the "dorsal" range, or spine of Tunisia. Rommel had prepared his defenses there. Unless Patton could break them, the American campaign would not be a success. Patton did not break them.

7

Patton tried for three weeks to break Rommel's mountain line. He assaulted it with infantry and guns and tanks and a special task force under Colonel Benson. He tried to break through at Maknassy and El Guettar with his Americans; and further south with a French task force, the Chasseurs D'Afrique. Still further south, the French Foreign Legion lightly scattered around the west side of the vast Chott Djerid were prodding across the mined causeway which French engineers had built over the salt lake in the direction of Kebili. Further south again, on the southern shores of the Chott Djerid, the French Camel Corps was feeling out the wastelands of the Sahara, and coming into occasional contact with the Long Range Desert Patrols of the Eighth Army.

It was obvious enough to Patton, and to every American in those southern Tunisian Mountains, that there was no longer any strategy in the high sense in this Maknassy-El Guettar campaign. After the advances from Kasserine to the "dorsal," the war settled down to a slogging match between guns and mountain-climbing infantrymen. The German observers sat on the mountaintops; their batteries of 88s lay beautifully camouflaged on the far slopes of the hills; they used smokeless powder; and they dug themselves deep into the mountainsides. Thus they controlled the passes through the range at Maknassy and El Guettar, and so north and south along the 300-mile Tunisian front. There was no strategy involved in driving them away from their vantage positions. There were only frontal tactics involved. Patton, the roistering, hard-hitting tank general, was dependent upon the valor and stamina of still-green American infantrymen.

Everybody set to the task of clearing the Germans off the high ground with grimness. The Germans in the mountains were elite troops. They were safe, their approaches covered with mines, the plains below zeroed in with field guns, the skies over them still challenged by their air force. Bombing them in their caves was a waste of time and effort. Bombing our exposed forces was not. The ridge which we held beyond El Guettar became a constant target for dive-bombers, Ju 88s, and Messerschmitts. Our soldiers cursed the lack of air cover in those days. The Luftwaffe, using radar skilfully, waited till the Spitfires had to return to base, then came over in waves and pounded the Americans lying on the hard rock below, and killed them and hit their guns and vehicles.

This happened during the day, and at night the Luftwaffe, by means of a few night bombers, kept the American front alerted and restless, as they went for our roads and supply dumps outside Gafsa. The night was anxious with their flares hovering over roads and towns, and the soldiery expended many rounds of ammunition trying to shoot down these flares. Rumors abounded that pockets of Germans, left in the caves behind Gafsa, were sniping at us. In the morning we sent patrols up the mountainsides to investigate, and found Arab families living their Biblical existence in holes in the ground.

In the meantime, Patton worked tenaciously at driving the Germans from the key points overlooking the El Guettar and Maknassy Passes. Infantrymen of the 1st and 9th Divisions went up into the mountains, working their way along the peaks, driving out the Germans in hand-to-hand fighting. Sometimes they were able to seize some dominating height, but the way was never open for the armor and soft-skinned supply vehicles to roll through. The Rangers went into the mountains, too. I remember a battalion of them dug in on a round hillock on the El Guettar plain, and how when the Germans divebombed us there, they stood up behind rocks and fired ineffectual rifles at them. But they were brave and resolute men, seasoned and professional soldiers, and when the order came to "take off," they formed their long, weary column, and marched into the dusk and the mountains beyond.

Next, Patton tried a break with a specially selected Armored and Infantry force under the command of Colonel C. C. Benson. This Task Force was to rush the El Guettar Gap, and make straight for the sea.

It started with a rush all right. The lead tanks went through the Gap, out onto the plain beyond, and then the German artillery opened up. The column, with tanks blazing, was held and stopped, and before nightfall had to be withdrawn. The infantry, a battalion from the 9th Division, could not be withdrawn. They had fought their way up the bare slopes of Djebel Berda, and here they clung, with orders to hold, while Benson reformed and tried it again. There were many grim counsels of war that night, with the Armored commanders maintaining the infantry should clean out the enemy strong points, and the infantry commanders calling for close tank support. All this time the 9th Infantrymen were clinging to their positions on the Djebel Berda, constantly counterattacked by the Germans and thrust out ahead of our main forces. Benson's tanks tried to break through again; then the plan was abandoned, and the infantrymen were recalled. Getting back was as difficult for them as getting out there, and for several days they became one of the "Lost Battalions" which distinguished this campaign.

To the northeast, the 1st Armored Division's tanks and infantrymen were meeting the same type of resistance in their assaults on the mountain peaks and pass. They tried saturation bombing and massed artillery fire and even last war infantry charges. One of these was lead by General Ward himself, in the brave old style, he ahead of his men and urging them on. The General was wounded. But the Germans held at Maknassy, too.

So it went on for three weeks in an arid mountain wilderness, where the earth's ribs gleamed white in the sunlight. The Nazis took advantage of every rock and boulder to close the three-mile-wide bottleneck through which Patton's armor had to go. Patton was always waiting to get his tanks rolling forward. He was obviously burning to have a tank battle with Rommel.

But the German High Command did not regard war as a means of personal jousts between tanks, and Patton's alleged challenge to Rommel to engage in a personal tank tournament must have given the Germans a dangerously false illusion about the character and mentality of the man who was later to outmaneuver and outfight them right across Europe.

Finally, it was Rommel who hit Patton with tanks. Switching the 10th Panzer Division from the southern front against Montgomery, the German Commander decided on rushing the American 2nd Army Corps, as he had done at Sbeitla and Kasserine. His intention was plainly to panic the Americans, chase them away from the El Guettar and Maknassy Passes, demoralize them, destroy their dumps, and thus relieve the constant pressure on his flanks. Then he expected to deal with the Eighth Army, and restore the situation in Tunisia.

His strategy was good and characteristically German. It was based on the assumption that Americans would never make good soldiers, because they had proved bad soldiers in their first battles. They were, to the Prussian mind, green, timid, and worst of all, civilians. So Rommel threw against these young, serious, and anxious Americans the 10th Panzer Division. His tanks came out from behind the Berda range at El Guettar, and charged straight through the pass and out onto the wide marshy plain, in which lay the oasis of El Guettar. They were making a frontal assault on the American gun positions which lay in an arc across the valley. Each tank had been detailed to rush a certain position; and the theory was that the American gunners would abandon their pieces and run away. After the Mark IVs and Vs had dealt with the guns, they were to turn and charge the infantry on the forward slopes from the rear. And that was to be the end of the American 2nd Corps, and this "ridiculous" Patton.

Thirty-two out of an estimated one hundred tanks of the 10th Panzers came out through the El Guettar bottleneck, and according to plan charged across the plain. From an olive grove—the inevitable olive grove which was supposed to hide our command posts from enemy air and ground observation—I watched the German tanks running like blind beetles back and forth across the plain. A tank battle is fascinating; you can never tell what is going on, because tanks play strange games, sometimes like a mouse coming in and out of a hole, sometimes like beetles, scurrying blindly along, stopping, almost waving their antennae, running again, somehow impersonal until you hear their noise and see their markings, and then they are truly fearful objects.

They were truly fearful objects to the antitank gunners and infantry of the 1st Infantry Division, because they did smash through at first and start towards our rear positions. But the "decadent" Americans did not break and they did not run at all. They started to fire in their own good time, and within minutes eleven German tanks were on fire, and five immobilized. Sixteen out of the thirty-two had received direct hits. The other half of them raced for the foothills, and finally, now spitting like hurt cats, turned and twisted back behind the Pass.

We expected them to try it again. But Rommel had changed his mind about the quality of American troops; and never doubted their prowess after the defeat of the 10th Panzer Division at El Guettar.

After the 10th Panzer had been defeated like this, the Germans were content to wage an entirely defensive war along the entire Tunisian front; and apart from local counterattacks, never again had a chance to launch an offensive against American or British troops. But the quality of their defense in those high African mountain ranges remained good until the Luftwaffe was driven from the skies, and the mass of material, handled by veteran troops, compressed them into a narrow rectangle around Tunis, which was sliced into pieces by our drives to the sea.

But that was in May. And this was only the end of March. For three weeks Patton hammered at Maknassy and El Guettar, probing for a weak spot along these southern defenses. When it was fairly evident that the three American divisions were being held, I went further south to see what the French were doing.

The French had odds and ends of troops operating as loose attachments to the American 2nd Corps and Patton's command. Nobody paid much attention to them, because they had no equipment at this time, except what they had salvaged from the Axis armistice commissions.

North of the Chott Djerid was a French unit called the Chasseurs D'Afrique who were gathered together in the vast loneliness of the desert plain before the Djebel Asker mountain range. I visited them and found their armament consisted of twenty-two light Renault tanks, which had a good silhouette, were fast, but armed with only a 47-caliber gun. They also had a few 75s, AA guns mounted on jeeps, last war rifles and, for the officers, 1875 pistols. From the Americans they had received a couple of six-wheeled trucks, without which they could not have been supplied at all over those desert trails. Chinigo and I passed the two trucks bringing along the supplies. The supplies consisted of barrels of red wine.

They were a lonely, pathetic, almost tragi-comic force, stuck out there in the desert at the base of the Djebel Asker, with their twenty-two tanks, five 75s, ancient muskets, 1875 pistols, and barrels of red wine. We talked to the officers, and it was hard to discover what they were supposed to do. I don't think anyone at higher headquarters cared very much, because if the Americans, with three splendidly equipped divisions, could not break the enemy's mountain line, it was obvious this little band would be held. But the French commander had a vague plan for attacking the Italians who held the pass, and he kept his tanks running back and forth, as much as his supply of fuel would allow. I never knew what happened to the Chasseurs D'Afrique.

They certainly did not break through Djebel Asker. It would have taken five infantry divisions to have done that quickly and effectively.

So I went further south still, around the west side of the great Chott Djerid to a little Arab town called Krise. This was the end of the world as far as the war in Europe was concerned. In fact, the war disappeared and our journey became a Cook's tour through a lovely land of oases, mirages, and shimmering distances. To complete the Hollywood setting was the French Foreign Legion, holding the western end of the causeway which runs across the Chott. The Italians held the town at the eastern end—Kebili. But the causeway had been mined by both sides, and neither side had any adequate weapons or transports, so there was no war, only heat, sand, flies, and the colorful squalor which distinguishes the Legion in its lonely outposts.

Gault MacGowan, of the New York *Sun*, and I paid our respects to the commanding officer of the Foreign Legion at Krise. He was a young, bespectacled lieutenant who probably had his sad tale of love to explain why he was lost on the white borders of a salt lake. We did not ask him. Instead, we asked permission to go out as far as we could across the Chott in the direction of Kebili. No one knew, or cared very much, whether Kebili was still held by the Italians. If it was not, MacGowan thought we might make an advance junction with the Eighth Army. The French lieutenant gave his permission, and we started out across the causeway. What lay around us was far too wonderful for us to take an interest in the war any longer. Africa had reasserted itself. The mirages started to hover over the limitless oval of the Chott. Trees grew upside down in the sky. Roads appeared from nowhere and disappeared into the blue arch of the heavens. Great lakes of shining blue water came and went, now on our right, now on our left.

We kept to the causeway for a mile or so, and then, suspecting mines, left it for the hard-baked salt marsh on either side. Under our wheels, the crust changed from white to brown to black, and within a matter of seconds we were axle-deep in the quagmire. So we walked back, two little figures in a mirage-shimmering emptiness, to Krise, and reported to the lieutenant. He was kind, and sent an American truck back with us to haul out the jeep. The legionnaire driver was a Spaniard, and an articulate man. He talked exceedingly, and drove his truck straight into the quagmire where lay our half-drowned jeep. Then he walked back, to get another.

That was about the extent of the war on this front.

There was still another sector, falling under the general jurisdiction of the Americans. This was on the southeast of Djerid, and was held by the French Meharistes, or Camel Corps. They had their headquarters at Tozeur, and their main outpost at Nefta, a few miles round the lake. Tozeur was pure Garden of Allah, conveniently adapted to tourism. Nefta was indescribably lovely. But Nefta is the garden of the Sahara, an oasis, a green beauty of 10,000 date palms, a hundred waterfalls, and stars tumbled from the jewel box of the night in cascades of emerald and amethyst and opal. From Nefta, the Meharistes disappeared into the white dunes of the Sahara in pursuit of their own magazine-story war. They were officered by three young Frenchmen. Captain Ruat was their commander. He wore sandals to enable his toes to grip his camel's neck, and he wore a white burnoose. These three strange Frenchmen invited MacGowan and me to eat supper with them. We lay on camel's hair blankets under a leaning palm, and ate desert food. The meal that night was soup, kus-kus, a whole barbecued sheep, rice with raisins in it, wine, and a dish of tea. Captain Ruat's men were a "goumier" from a desert tribe. They were black-bearded men, and as we ate they sang desert songs. It was beautiful and strange.

Captain Ruat's war was quite outside Generals Eisenhower's and Alexander's strategy, and as different from Patton's machines as the camel is from the 105 howitzer. And at the moment it was more effective. Captain Ruat's sector happened to be the soft spot in the Axis defense line which held the Allies out of Tunisia. There was no enemy between the Eighth Army and these Meharistes, except for Italian outposts; and it was Captain Ruat's "goumier" which actually made the first contact between the First Army and Le Clerc's Lake Chad Forces.

Captain Ruat thought it was possible to send a fast armored force along the southern shores of the Chott Djerid to harass Rommel's Afrika Corps from the right flank and the rear. This was the northern fringe of the Sahara. The sand was white and firm, and we demonstrated that a jeep could travel over sand faster than their racing dromedaries. Tanks could have crossed this sandy ocean, too. It was surprising that Patton, who longed for wide open country in which to deploy his armor, did not reconnoiter this sector, even though it was almost off the maps of Tunisia and showed only as a wilderness without roads or towns.

But by the end of March, when we visited this forgotten unit of Meharistes, with their two machine guns, muskets, ancient revolvers, and sacks of barley for camel fodder, it was too late to move American forces down to this soft spot in the Axis Tunisian line. Montgomery had begun his Mareth Line battle with a characteristic frontal attack on the Germans' strongest positions along the Wadi Zigzaou. The battle was won for Montgomery by the individual fortitude of his Cockneys and countrymen, and by the dash of the New Zealanders. Gabes was entered on April 7, and Rommel's entire southern front disintegrated.

8

On April 7, on a hot afternoon, Patton's forces, still held at the passes of Maknassy and El Guettar, began to inch forward, as they had tried to do every day for three weeks. This day, tanks nosed their way through the pass, and were not fired on. Our reconnaissance was still unreliable, so the individual tank commanders did their own probing, and they found they were hitting against a vacuum.

Because of our inadequate reconnaissance, we were always suspecting traps, such as Rommel had laid for American armor at Sbeitla and elsewhere. And that was how Patton's army went forward at first. Cautiously, through the El Guettar bottleneck, first the light tanks, then the mediums passed and fanned out, making for the base of the mountains which enclose the immense oval plain beyond. Then, suddenly, as though caution were cowardice, urged on by Patton himself, the entire American force in this sector mounted its vehicles, burst through the pass, and started a massed advance eastward towards the sea. The spectacle that afternoon was a tremendous and futile one. The entire plain which reached thirty miles across from mountains to mountains, was covered that day with American tanks, light and medium, half-tracks, mobile guns, jeeps, trucks surging eastward in line abreast like a Spanish fleet in olden times, with pennants and flags flying.

Jack Barnet, tough Chicago newsreelman, Cuck Corte, another cameraman, and I, aboard our jeep, were somehow tossed forward on the crest of this wave. It was evident now that the Germans had gone. One knew the signs after a time. The Germans had a way of disappearing in the night, like a witch on a broomstick. There was not a sign of them or their equipment. I thought again of that mild joke: they had swept the place with little brush brooms before they went, so as not to leave any litter behind.

Again, as usual, they had abandoned the Italians, who now came streaming out of the mountains, smiling largely, meekly surrendering odds and trifles the loot-loving Americans prized sometimes more than their lives.

Yes, it was a typical Patton spectacle of the Californian Maneuvers variety. Everybody and everything plunged forward as fast as they could go—though no one seemed to know where they were going or why. Our jeepload decided there was a story in it for us, even if there was no victory in it for Patton. We wanted to meet the Eighth Army. Along the Gabes road we saw Colonel Benson sitting in his jeep, smoking his inevitable corncob pipe, and drawing up plans for a tremendous battle which never materialized. For Rommel had disengaged himself from the Americans without losing more than his expendable Italians; and he had made a skilful getaway from Montgomery. He was then racing northward to the mountains of Enfidaville, and Benson was a day's march behind.

So at 2:15 P.M., on Wednesday, April 7, on a vast oval plain, hemmed in by saw-toothed mountains, we of the American 2nd Corps met the British Eighth Army.

Such a meeting had its drama. There was the drama of the setting itself, immense and historical. There was the drama of the men, the behelmeted Americans bundled up in warm clothes suitable to Djebel temperatures, the British in ragged bleached desert uniforms, without helmets. There was drama from blazing tanks, for the Germans had the rear guards concealed in a wadi, and had fallen on a British reconnaissance party.

But apart from the magnificent setting, it was not a stage piece, though the two cameramen "fixed" this omission by posing Yanks and Tommies shaking hands and smiling largely. Actually, our two lightly armored units met suddenly, and there was no time for greetings, because they had to fight before they could greet one another.

What had happened was a German squadron of Mark III tanks had ambushed the British party, when the Americans burst out onto the plain. American light tanks then set upon the Germans, and scored a direct hit on an enemy tank, which lay in the wadi smoking for the rest of the day. Then Patton's men slashed across the line of Nazi tanks, fought a running battle of the naval type, drove off the Germans, and rescued the commander of the British unit, Major Neil Speake, of Northumberland. Thus the situation was restored. Thus the two Allied Armies met. Thus the great historical moment slipped away before the men who made it knew what they had done.

After that came the consciousness of history. The Americans climbed out of their tanks, the British from their reconnaissance cars. They approached each other curiously, the Englishmen diffident and unemotional, the Americans amiable but not overwhelmed. They said "Hello" to each other, but did not shake hands, until the movie men recalled that millions of people in the great smoky cities of America and Britain wanted their money's worth; and tall, wide-toothed Englishman was duly hugged by round, white-toothed American.

Then the men of the two armies and two nations continued with their commonplaces, swapped cigarettes for the sake of tradition, climbed into their vehicles, and so the junction was made.

From the military point of view, it was a junction around a vacuum. From Patton's point of view it was hardly a victory. But from the larger viewpoint, it was most significant to the winning of the war itself. The United States now had the nucleus of a professional army. We had professional fighting men, competent field officers, and experienced generals. We had tried out our equipment.

Thinking it over, Patton concluded that, given some veterans like the 1st Armored, the 1st and 9th Infantry, given the weapons, he could outmaneuver and outfight the Germans.

He also had to be given the chance to prove it. The chance came in July, 1943, when Patton was given command of the first complete American Army to fight in Europe, the Seventh Army which invaded Sicily on the night of Friday, July 9.

CHAPTER VI

"BORN AT SEA, BAPTIZED IN BLOOD . . ."

I

THE Sicilian campaign, which followed our North African victory at a decent interval, was dull, uninspired, and only partially successful.

The purpose of the campaign was twofold: first, to occupy the island as a stepping-stone to Italy and the mainland of Europe; second, to destroy the Axis forces garrisoning the place, with particular attention to the Germans. We succeeded in conquering the whole of Sicily, representing an area of 10,000 square miles in thirty-eight days. We eliminated an entire force of some ten Italian divisions on the island. But we accounted for less than a half of the three German divisions.

These results were satisfactory, but they were not what we had hoped for and they did not represent the best that we could or should have done. Eventually it was admitted, quasi-officially, that we could have subdued in some twenty instead of thirty-eight days; and that we could have trapped the entire German garrison, instead of letting the majority of them trickle back to Italy across the Messina Strait.

Clearly, Sicily was a triumph of force, not of strategy. The force was a combination of engineering, ballistics, and medicine, harnessed to masses of men distinguished by their valor and endurance. It was no victory for the strategists, because no strategy was involved. There was a Plan, of course; but a Plan so prosaic, it would not be found in even the elementary textbooks of war.

The Plan, in its simplest form, called for the hurling of a mass of machines and men, without skill or cunning, at a point nearest to our invasion bases. There was no element of surprise either in the timing or place or manner of our landings. Everything went according to the first lesson in a manual of amphibious operations. The inevitable hazards were experienced. The inevitable mistakes were made. The inevitable success was achieved. All these were inevitable, because the mathematics of the Plan were of the simple computing kind in which the margin of error is negligible.

The use of such a ponderous Plan in the Sicilian campaign was significant. It represented the new Allied policy of smothering the enemy by weight rather than strategy. This policy was indicative of a trend not only in this war, but in the wars to come. Science, engineering, physics, chemistry, medicine, and all industry and technology henceforward were to be adapted to the theory of weight as contrasted to the antiquated strategy of maneuver.

The theory of weight had first been practiced under almost laboratory conditions against the small Mediterranean island of Pantelleria. Scores of thousands of bombs had been dropped on Pantelleria for almost a month between the end of the Tunisian campaign and the beginning of the Sicilian. The use of massed bomber fleets against such a minor target was explained by the Air Commands as "experimental." Even so, it was a heavy-handed experiment, for our military intelligence should have known that a small Italian garrison required no such "softening" to surrender; and, more important, the bombing of Pantelleria revealed, by implication, our intention of moving, step by step, from small to large Mediterranean islands, and so to Italy itself.

Thus the theory of weight was proven by results, and results were what the Allied people and their leaders needed in 1943. Still, many generals—and General Patton was certainly one of them—instinctively viewed this new policy of using a steamroller against a wheelbarrow as incompatible with the true science of war.

While it was almost wholly American science and industry which made possible this strategy of weight—the multitude of amphibious machines were all American inventions—it was British generalship which subscribed most wholeheartedly to the application of it in practice. When the Americans first arrived in the western hemisphere with their curious gadgets, the British General Staff had been surprised and amused at the electric saws, hammers, and riveters. Their old-time generals were instinctively scornful of technological innovations. But their new-line generals, now in the ascendency, were not. Montgomery, for instance, the epitome of the strategist of weight, was enthusiastic for anything which crushed the enemy, whether it flew through the air, swam in the sea, or crawled on land.

Now, at this phase of the war, British generalship was ascendant over American. It had been Montgomery, Commander of the Eighth Army and Alexander, Commander-in-Chief of the Tunisian Armies, and Tedder, commander of the joint Allied Mediterranean air forces, and Cunningham, commander of the Allied navies, who had been the controlling minds in the North African campaigns, and the planning of the Sicilian invasion. All these men were British, and it was right and proper that their ideas should have greater weight with Eisenhower than those of Bradley or Patton.

And so, when the conquest of Sicily was planned, it was the British conception which prevailed at Eisenhower's councils. This British conception was simple and safe. It called for a frontal assault on the southeast corner of the Sicilian triangle, nearest to our bases in Malta and North Africa. This was the plan used on July 10.

The American plan, subscribed to by Eisenhower's chief of staff, General Smith, and the two leading American generals, Bradley and Patton, was more complicated and bolder, a better gamble against longer odds. It proposed two widely separated landings: the Americans on the northwest near Palermo; the British on the southeast at Catania. The two forces were to strike out diagonally across the island and cut Sicily in two in a blitz operation. The fundamental purpose and value of this plan was to prevent the Germans from forming a line at any place or any time. The American plan was based on strategy, speed, and surprise.

It was later stated, by an Army spokesman, that the American plan would have worked, shortening the campaign by perhaps three weeks, reducing casualties, and probably achieving the main object of cutting off the German garrison from their escape route back to Italy.

However, the British Alexander-Montgomery plan, safe and ponderous, was put into effect, with the full and patriotic coöperation of the American commanders. The campaign went through its scheduled phases, and very dull they were. For so pedestrian and orthodox was the general plan that not even a commander as mobile and unpredictable as Patton could materially alter the outcome. We overran all of Sicily except the northeast corner without noticeable opposition from the hordes of disorganized Italians. We captured practically this entire Italian force, abandoned in any case by the Germans as more of a liability than an asset. And we fought the Germans from mountain peak to mountain peak until they decided the moment had come to cut their losses and evacuate.

Any American general other than Patton would have emerged from the Sicilian campaign as a reliable and valuable leader of a new American Army, and would have been judged, principally in military circles, on what he had achieved as a field commander. But with a man of Patton's temperament, it was inevitable he should emerge as the most-discussed general in the Allied armies. For this was his first army command. This was real war. He obviously intended to leave his warlike imprint on the time and occasion. Here was his opportunity to use his men and himself on dangerous missions, to storm up and down the road of war and across battlefields; to imbue the bloody scene with his sanguine personality. General Eisenhower, when placing him in command, had expected this—and worriedly feared it. His parting words to Patton were:

"Now, for Heaven's sake, count ten, George, before you say anything."

But the beloved atmosphere of battle proved too much for Patton. By the time the campaign had ended he had achieved a rare and unenviable reputation among his whole Seventh Army. It was said, not exaggeratedly, that 50,000 G.I.s were waiting to shoot him. Then his conduct became known to the home front. That conduct was epitomized in the ridiculously headlined "slapping" incident. Now Patton found himself in an even more dangerous position than being hated by his soldiers, though that was dangerous enough. Now he found himself being tried and judged by 120,000,000 lay civilians, whose clamors almost grew loud enough to end his career forever.

So what had happened was this: Patton had helped win an important campaign which (1) conquered 10,000 square miles of Axis territory; (2) eliminated some 300,000 Axis troops from the war; (3) placed Italy in such a perilous position she unconditionally surrendered a month later; and (4) gained American soldiers, scientists, and technicians that experience which made feasible a successful assault on the fortress of Europe one year later.

What had concurrently happened was Major-General George S. Patton had struck and abused a private American soldier in the tent of a field hospital.

The world forgot his achievements. It still remembers his mistake. Let us review the former briefly, and tell the story of the latter more fully. For the public was correct in emphasizing the "slap." In the philosophy of history, it was more significant than the success of a prosaic campaign.

2

Everything and everybody, including Patton, started off well in the Sicilian invasion. The planners had mustered men and machines on an unprecedented scale for the operation; 3,266 ships were assembled for the transporting of two armies numbering 160,000 troops. To support the troops air fleets numbering thousands of bombers, fighter-bombers, and fighters patrolled the skies and neutralized the Axis air power. With the men, in the sea convoys, went 1,800 guns, 600 tanks, and 1,400 vehicles. Many newly invented machines designed for amphibious operations were being used for the first time. There were LCIs (landing craft infantry) and LCTs (landing craft tanks) and "ducks," or amphibious

"BORN AT SEA, BAPTIZED IN BLOOD . . ." 111

trucks and amphibious jeeps and floating piers and docks. The Sicilian campaign demonstrated that an amphibious operation was no longer any more hazardous than a land operation.

The two armies served by the tens of thousands of machines were the British Eighth, commanded by General Montgomery; and the American Seventh, commanded by General Patton.

The Seventh Army comprised six full divisions: the 1st, 3rd, 9th, and 45th infantry; the 2nd armored; the 82nd airborne. Patton also had a battalion of Rangers.

The Eighth Army comprised five full divisions, with an armored brigade, airborne infantry, and commandos.

Opposing this Allied force of some eleven divisions, though not all of them were used in the initial assault, were an estimated twelve enemy divisions—ten Italian and two German.

On the nights of July 8 and 9, the Allied ships began sailing from a score of North African ports to their rendezvous. Everything went according to plan. The captains of the large vessels and the skippers of the little ships and the officers on the war boats navigated with traditional skill, both by day and by night, when they sailed without navigation lights. The soldiers in the ships stood or sat about, in conversation or silence, according to their moods, which were the moods of men moving towards a dangerous unknown shore. The chaplains held religious services. The sailors stood their watches. And the generals, in due course, gave their battle addresses, with the customary appeals to the Almighty.

Patton, aboard the American Headquarters warship, was in that exalted mood which always descends on him at such moments, and which, in due course, took the form of rather solemn rhetoric. His first campaign address was read from a gun turret over the ship's loud-speaker system, and was not noteworthy for originality; and, in any case, originality was not required.

"We are indeed honored in having been selected by General Dwight Eisenhower as the American component of this new and greater attack against the Axis," said General Patton. "We are teamed with the justly famous British Eighth Army, which attacks on our right; and we have for the Army group commander that veteran and distinguished soldier, General Sir Harold Alexander."

Amid this polite and diplomatic pronouncement gleamed rare glimpses of the true Patton, such as "attack rapidly, ruthlessly, viciously, without rest. However tired and hungry you may be, the enemy will be more tired, more hungry. Keep punching. God is with us. We shall win."

As was his custom, Patton made reference to the Almighty; but as events turned out, he was not able to commend the Lord for his meteorological aid during the landings, since after a spell of calm, a small gale began to blow from the northwest, with a heavy breaking sea, which made the intricate job of navigation excessively difficult and the bulk of the troops seasick.

It would be interesting to examine the effect of generals' panegyrics on invading soldiers, seasick and otherwise; but in this case, the men of the 1st, 3rd, and 45th divisions who crowded into the rolling LCIs never heard their commander's brave words, but heard only the shrilling of that northwesterly wind and the grinding of the surf on the alien shore and the crackle of guns from the Italian shore batteries.

The battle was joined at 2:45 A.M. on Saturday, July 10. Before that, at Zero Hour minus, airborne troops of the 82nd Division, had been dropped at strategic locations inshore, only to be scattered like chaff over a wide area.

The 1st Division made a good landing at Gela, immediately came to grips with and overpowered the 4th Italian Livorno Division, and started a grim battle, with attack and counterattack, with elements of the Hermann Goering Panzer Grenadiers.

The 3rd Division landed some twenty miles to the west of Gela, against light Italian opposition. The 45th Division, covering the 1st Division's east flank, went ashore at Scoglitti, and quickly moved inland to seize Vittoria and Ragusa.

The 2nd Armored landed in force two days later on July 12. Patton's reserve division, the 9th, was landed two weeks later, after Palermo on the north shore had been captured.

Meantime, General Montgomery's British and Canadian soldiers were undergoing almost exactly similar experiences at Pachino, on the other side of the Cape, fifty miles east of Gela. The British were sped on their way with the literary aid of a Montgomery Order of the Day, addressed simultaneously to his troops, the press, and the Almighty.

The simple plan was thus simply accomplished. The first twenty-four hours of these massive landings were the only anxious ones in the entire campaign; and the anxiety was localized at Gela, where the 1st Infantry had the misfortune to bump into two regiments of the Hermann Goering Division, with Mark IV and VI tanks. Both sides drove back and forth, in and out of Gela. And there was danger on Sunday, July 11, that the German armor would force the American infantry back into the sea.

This was a typical situation for Patton, enabling him to make an heroic and dramatic appearance on the scene by leaping into the surf before his landing craft had grounded, and wading ashore to rally his troops with fiery exhortations and counsel, though it was apparent the troops had need not so much of rallying as of antitank guns.

By July 13, the initial danger of an amphibious operation was over. The British and Americans had made their planned junction at Ragusa. The southeastern tip of Sicily had been seized and secured. Landing parties had made contact with the airborne troops; or vice-versa, since the paratroopers and glider troops, dropped for the most part as much as twenty miles from the designated drop-zone, had spent most of their time wandering about the Sicilian countryside, trying to find their bearings and their seaborne Allies. Airfields had been seized at Gela and Licata. The beachhead for one hundred miles was established. Supplies were coming ashore. Several thousand prisoners, nearly all Italians, had been captured. And, above all, it was now plain that the ten divisions of Italian garrison troops were inferior, cowardly, and potentially disorganized. Sicily seemed ours, except for odds and ends of Germans, notably elements of the Hermann Goering Division and remnants of the 15th Panzer Division.

Our High Command must have already started regretting that they had not used the bolder American plan. The British plan was working admirably, but some indication of its over-cautiousness was revealed by the fact that estimates calculated the initial landings would cost 20,000 casualties. Actually, our casualties from all causes were less than a thousand. Only one large ship, a hospital ship, was sunk by enemy action. Our heaviest loss was one we caused

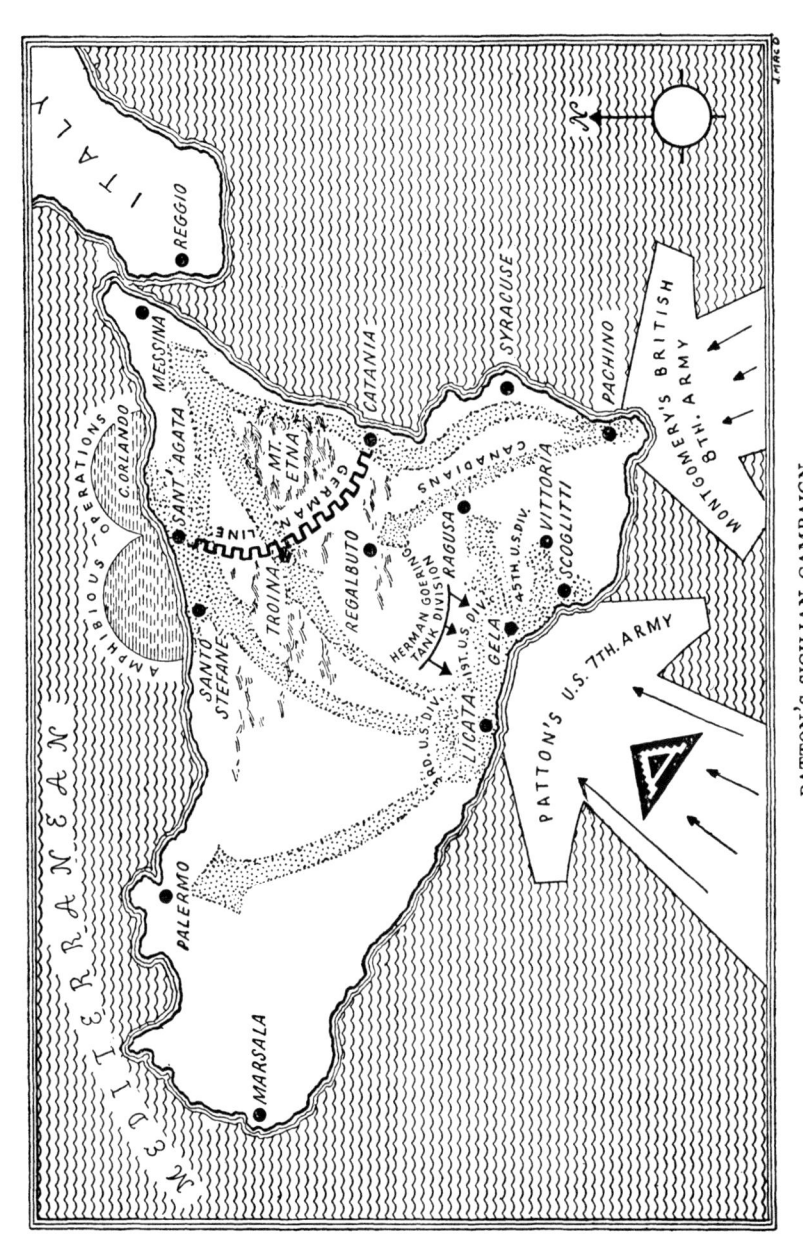

PATTON'S SICILIAN CAMPAIGN

ourselves in a tragic, self-mutilating blow. Forty-three troop-carrying planes were shot down principally by American naval gunners in a short period of hysterical error.

From here on the conquest of Sicily proceeded unspectacularly according to the unspectacular plan. The principal obstacles Patton had to overcome were obstacles of terrain. The advance of the Seventh Army rapidly became a prodigious feat of engineering. The principal hardships Patton's soldiers had to endure were the heavy hardships of heat, thirst, fatigue, and diarrhea. In contrast to Montgomery's Eighth Army men, who were still clad in their miscellaneous and light desert uniforms, the American soldiers were gripped by a severe discipline of dress. They had to wear their thick regulation shirts and pants in the torrid heat of the day. Leggings and helmets were to be worn at all times. Some justification for this régime was apparent when the sun went down and the chill of the craggy mountains descended over the night scene. But the American uniforms were a heritage from the djebels of Africa, and were a hardship to our soldiers on the plains of Sicily. But Patton himself, roaring along in his individual cloud of dust, made it a personal matter to see that his men were clad according to regulations, even if no known Army order called for soldiers to be insufferably hot.

So, "properly dressed" and improperly perspiring, the Seventh Army swept back and forth across the Italian-controlled regions of Sicily in a kind of shadow blitz; while the Germans painstakingly moved into their Etna positions, prepared their defense line, and organized their retreat from Messina. By the 22nd of July, ten days after landing, Patton had cut Sicily in two by reaching Marsala on the north coast. The 45th Division seized 1000 square miles in

"BORN AT SEA, BAPTIZED IN BLOOD . . ."

three weeks. The 2nd Armored dashed to Palermo in a few days, and Patton received the surrender of this important city in grandiose manner. In brief, 50,000 Italian troops surrendered; Italian resistance collapsed entirely; and four-fifths of the island was ours for the firing of a few rounds of artillery.

Against such an enemy, who were even less troublesome and hostile than the colonial French in West Africa, Patton found himself again playing the role of diplomat. It became apparent to him, from the multitude of stories which reached him in intelligence reports, that a large percentage of the Sicilian population had either been in America themselves or had relatives still there; and it was not uncommon for an American soldier to meet his kinsfolk in the scores of dusty, malodorous Sicilian villages through which our columns passed. And so we find one of Patton's few published works appearing in a Sicilian newspaper, the *Liberata* of Palermo. In a letter Patton writes:

"The purpose of the Americans under the leadership of our great President, Franklin D. Roosevelt, is not—I repeat, not—to enslave but to liberate those peoples of the world who have suffered for twenty years under the malign influence of Fascism and Naziism.

"It is with deep regret that we have had to fight the Italian armies in Sicily. . . . Here, in Palermo, we have established excellent relations with His Eminence, the Cardinal, and through him with the church. . . .

"The purpose of the Americans is relentlessly to press on and ruthlessly to destroy Fascism and Naziism, wherever found. . . ."

Commanding Generals do not always write their propaganda. But this document, from internal evidence alone, has the hallmark of Patton's style. He loves such words as "ruthlessly," "relentlessly," and "destroy."

Next, in the first week of August, began the all-out assault on the Germans' Etna line, with the British attacking on the south against Catania, the Canadians in the center at Regalbuto, and the Americans in the north at Troina. It was a battle which cost us heavy casualties, which spoilt the balance of our victory in terms of our own killed and wounded compared with the enemy's, and which should never have had to be fought. It was the result of this ponderous steamroller Plan of pushing the Germans into a corner of Sicily ideal for defense and escape.

Patton set about the reduction of the key Nazi stronghold on top of Mount Troina without fear or faltering, though the divisional generals and officers whose men had to scale the craggy peaks made their plans with many a fear. Battalion after battalion of the 1st Infantry was hurled against Troina before the crag fell to the weight of our air and ground bombardment; and hundreds of infantrymen died on the long slopes of the ridges. General Terry Allen, the beloved commander of the 1st Infantry, later relieved of his command by Patton, wept openly when he saw the fields of dead Americans. Allen's tears did not mix well with Patton's blood and guts. But Allen was loved by the 1st Division; and Patton, I think, will always be hated by them.

Troina was reduced, and the road to Messina was opened by two "end runs," or amphibious landings, the first of which was brilliant because it was a strategic surprise; the second of which was a failure, for the opposite reason.

Patton's first amphibious operation was an example of his boldness which seemed to more conservative military men unduly risky. And most of his advisers and divisional generals advised against the Sant' Agata and San Fratello landings, which were the first of the mid-August amphibious operations along the northern Sicilian coast. But on August 8, Patton sent a light force in landing craft round the vast promontory called Cape Orlando, landed on the beaches near Sant' Agata, and surprised German reinforcements moving west along the seaboard highway to the San Stefano sector. Because of the surprise element, Patton's force ambushed the Germans, routed them, and rapidly moved west themselves, to effect a junction with the main force at San Stefano. It is certain that without this brilliant, unexpected move, the Seventh Army would have been held at the Cape Orlando tunnel, which ran through a mountain and came out on the German side over a wide gorge, across which was the highway bridge, already thoroughly blown by the Germans. Now American engineers were able to respan the gorge, without having the enemy fire on them. This amphibious operation, then, was a brilliant success; and thus Patton rightly characterized it. He said of it:

"People are unduly scared of amphibious operations. No large-scale amphibious operation I can remember offhand ever did fail in the whole of history. Except, that is, the landing of the Athenians at Syracuse in 413 B.C. That was a failure for a lot of reasons. It was not a failure of the Athenian soldiery." *

It would seem that Patton forgot such invasions as the Spanish Armada and Napoleon's attempt in his large generalization, but to remember that date of the Athenian landing offhand is nonetheless a minor triumph of memory.

Gratified with the success of the Sant' Agata landing,

* Quoted by Vincent Sheean in *Satevepost,* June 23, 1945.

Patton determined to try the same strategy again, though this time his advisers argued even more strongly against the attempt, on the additional grounds that the element of surprise was gone. Nonetheless, Patton insisted that it should be done, and so the amphibious landing further east along the coast towards Messina was made, with the invasion troops going ashore at the mouth of Naso River. Patton's advisers were right about the surprise element. This time the Germans were not caught or ambushed, and the landing party was held down on all sides by fierce counterattacks and artillery bombardment. They were rescued in three days by the main forces driving from the West; but apart from harassing the enemy's rear, this second landing party achieved no notable success.

For the Sicilian campaign was almost over. Troina had fallen. Randazzo was captured. The British had broken through to Taormina. And the last of the Germans were scurrying across the Messina Strait. Patton, of course, was eager to be the first into Messina. And he had his way. His troops entered it the night of the 16th of August, to find it a shadowy ruin, in which a few weary Italians stood about waiting to surrender. The last German had gone.

All that remained to be done was for the generals to make their victory speeches, once again addressed to tired and battle-worn soldiers, now resting their hot bodies under the olive trees. Once again, it is doubtful whether the men addressed heard more than echoes of the speeches, as they turned over from their backs to their sides in the long sleep of weary riflemen. But the rest of the world listened respectfully to the speeches; and the American world particularly lauded the address of General Patton, commander of the victorious Seventh Army. It was a characteristic diatribe;

"BORN AT SEA, BAPTIZED IN BLOOD . . ."

nor were the usual corporeal ingredients omitted. There was blood and guts, translated into the civilian language of "glorious achievements," "dash," "tenacity," and "prodigious feats."

This was what he said:

"Born at sea, baptized in blood (bu-lud), and crowned with victory, in the course of thirty-eight days of incessant battle and unceasing labor, you have added a glorious chapter to the history of the war.

"Pitted against the best the Germans and Italians could offer, you have been unfailingly successful. The rapidity of your dash, which culminated in the capture of Palermo, was equaled by the dogged tenacity with which you stormed Troina and captured Messina.

"Your fame shall never die."

Patton also recorded the material successes of his army: the construction of "impossible" roads over impassable country; the laying of over 10,000 miles of wire; the killing or capturing of 113,000 enemy troops; the destruction of 256 tanks, 2324 vehicles, and 1162 large guns.

Patton distributed his praise generously and wisely, omitting no branch of the services. Navies, air forces, infantry, armor, medical services, supply services, all were warmly commended. But perhaps the warmest touch of all, which brought a sudden gleam of humanity to one not accustomed to display this attribute was the little phrase addressed to that unknown corps of men who, during four years of campaigning, spent half their time hanging from poles and trees —the signal and wire men. Of them Patton said with sincere simplicity, "They worked often without food, favor, or affection." It was unfortunate for Patton himself that he could not have used phrases like this more often and phrases like "blood and guts" less frequently.

3

It was plain to all trained observers that General Patton had emerged from the Sicilian campaign as a brilliant, efficient, and extremely energetic field commander. He brought a new genius to American arms. Under his leadership, the hitherto unpredictable American civilian in uniform had changed into a highly efficient fighting man. To the supreme American commanders, and particularly to General Eisenhower, Patton was the answer to the urgent hope that from the small group of Allied professional soldiers a general would be found with the qualities to offset the skill and experience of the German General Staff. The British generals Alexander and Montgomery possessed such qualities, to a certain extent. General Omar Bradley showed them in his handling of the Northern Tunisian campaign. Now came Patton, who added to the skill and experience required a peculiar dynamic quality which none of the other three Allied generals displayed.

Patton, then, was the soldier Eisenhower had been hoping for, the one who combined skill and experience with brilliance and even a genius. The genius lay in Patton's aptitude to accomplish the impossible.

In view of the rising general's ability, Eisenhower was not perturbed overmuch by the continual reports of Patton's personal idiosyncrasies. Eisenhower, as a fellow West Point graduate and student of Patton, knew as much about the man's strange individuality as anybody in the Army. For that matter, Patton's personality was familiar to all those members of the small and exclusive professional army—men who murmured "How" when a toast was drunk. In recent months, Patton's fame had begun to filter through to the public by way of the muddy channels of the newspapers. A man who was called "The Green Hornet," "Flash Gordon," and "Old Blood and Guts" was certainly good for a story, even if he was only conducting a military exercise in the Californian desert.

Now, though Eisenhower had earnestly advised Patton to take it easy and watch his temper, it was evident from some of the reports and rumors that came through to AFHQ in Algiers that "Georgie" Patton was doing neither. Everyone who had been with the Seventh Army in Sicily had seen the Commander roaring about the front, from the beaches of Gela to the gates of Messina. He was, indeed, a front line general, and this was no ground for criticism in Eisenhower's scheme of things. But it also appeared that Patton was doing more than making a personal appearance on the battlefields. He was doing a somewhat immoderate amount of "cussing" and swearing, and it was almost as though his rich profanity could be heard from Adrano to Algiers.

Eisenhower dismissed most of what he heard as gossip. He saw no reason to reprove a highly successful general for using the Anglo-Saxon expression for "backside," or similar strong, harsh monosyllables. Similarly, the complaints centering on Patton's adamant discipline in the matter of uniforms, helmets, and leggings Eisenhower wisely disregarded as none of his affair. He already knew his subordinate's ideas about discipline. Patton had expressed them himself, forcefully and unmistakably:

"Goddamit, man, a soldier should salute an officer even in the latrine."

But there were incidents more disturbing. One involved the relieving of General Terry Allen from the command of his 1st Division. Patton had requested this on reasonable grounds. But Patton pressed for the change of command in the middle of a battle—at Troina; and Eisenhower was informed that all the officers and men of that famous division were "sore as hell about it."

Here, too, Eisenhower refused to interfere.

Then came strange stories of Patton's threats, which some said included reaching for his pistol, against a foot-worn infantryman who was lying in a field without his leggings, socks, or boots on. Also, the not unlikely story of the mule cart which was blocking a convoy, with Patton personally shooting the mule and helping to shove the entire equipage into the ravine beside the road.

As the reports came in, Eisenhower must have grinned wryly when he read the statement of a visiting prelate that the clergyman found the man everybody now called "Old Blood and Guts" with a Bible on his desk.

But all grins and chuckles and expressions of resignation and anxieties that Patton would not go too far were suddenly ended for General Eisenhower when the American Surgeon-General Frederick Blesse came to see the Commander-in-Chief one evening in August with a secret report which revealed that the new and long-awaited genius of the American Army had committed an act which exposed him to the disgrace of a court-martial for a military offense almost as grave as treason.

General Patton had struck an American soldier. He had struck that soldier in a hospital. He had struck a sick man.

CHAPTER VII
THE SLAP HEARD ROUND THE WORLD

I

ON August 3, General Patton abused, struck across the face with his gloves, and threw bodily out of a hospital tent a sick American soldier.

On August 10, the commanding general of the U. S. Seventh Army again abused and again cuffed another sick soldier in the same Evacuation Hospital in Sicily.

The two incidents were quite separate and independent; but they became confused in newspaper accounts and in the public clamor which followed the revelation of Patton's misdeeds three months later, in November, 1943.

The first incident, that of August 3, was described in a military report, submitted to the American Surgeon-General Blesse by Lieutenant-Colonel H. Long, commanding officer of the 15th Evacuation Hospital, in the C Company of the 1st Medical battalion of which the assault occurred.

As soon as the Surgeon-General received Colonel Long's report, he took it directly to General Eisenhower.

The next day, the Commander-in-Chief received a visit from a war correspondent, Demaree Bess, of *The Saturday Evening Post,* who described a second case of an assault on a soldier by General Patton; this assault being the one committed on August 10.

General Eisenhower was deeply disturbed by these reports. For him, a personal friend of Patton and an admirer of his military genius, the grave probability that the commander of the only American Army in Europe was subject to court-martial, was the worst news he had had in the whole Mediterranean campaign.

Eisenhower immediately despatched the Surgeon-General himself to Italy to make a full investigation. He also sent a scathing letter of protest to General Patton, demanding an immediate explanation. And he asked those war correspondents who had the story to give him time to examine the matter further and make his decisions before the unhappy business was publicized.

General Eisenhower spent three days and nights of something very like anguish in thinking about the Patton affair, in wondering what to do for the best interests of his country, and in discussing with his closest advisers how to punish General Patton.

Three courses of action were possible: Patton could be court-martialed; he could be relieved of his command and sent home; or he could be reprimanded and ordered to make the best possible retribution.

Some of those involved in the affair asked Eisenhower to court-martial Patton; or at least to relieve him immediately of his command.

To them Eisenhower's reply was simple and rather grim. "You are asking me to get rid of my only good general."

It was this fact which made Eisenhower's decision almost unbearably difficult; and which, literally, kept him awake for three nights. In the small hours of the morning, he would wander into Commander (now Captain) Butcher's room—Commander Butcher was his aide—to sit with his head down, thinking aloud, over and over, the problem of how to save his best commander and how to punish a man guilty of a crime almost as grave as treason in the list of military offenses.

Gradually, he decided that he did not have enough rank to court-martial a major-general, without reducing Patton to his then permanent rank of Colonel.

An alternative was to relieve Patton of his command and send him home for court-martial by a properly constituted court. This meant removing Patton from Sicily in the middle of the last fierce battles of the campaign. It also meant losing the services of a brilliant field commander for the rest of the war.

Finally, Eisenhower hammered out the solution. He decided he had to keep Patton. The man's military record weighed heavier than his personal indiscretions. At the same time, he was to be punished as severely as possible, and no one will gainsay that the final retribution for Patton was heavy indeed.

The commander of the Seventh Army was required to apologize fully and unconditionally to the soldiers he had struck. He was required to apologize to the doctors, nurses, and orderlies who had witnessed the scenes. And he was required to apologize to the officers of every division in the Seventh Army, with the request that his regrets be conveyed to every man in that army.

In addition, censorship restrictions were removed on the writing of the incident, so that eventually the whole world was to know that an American officer and gentleman had been unable to control his temper and his fists in the presence of a sick man.

It was still not all. Congress took up the matter. Senators stated flatly that Patton should have been court-martialed for the offense. Others recommended that his promotion to the permanent rank of major-general be delayed. Letters of protest flooded the newspapers. Abusive letters and jeers were directed at Mrs. Patton and the three children.

It cannot be said that Patton went unpunished; and in all the emotion which his own emotion had unleashed, the premonition that he was actually or potentially hated by every soldier, good or bad, in the American Army, weighed heaviest.

What had he actually done?

On August 3, states Colonel Long's report, he had visited an aid station of the 15th Evacuation Hospital and conversed with the wounded men there. Then he came to the cot of Private Charles K. Kuhl, rifleman of the 26th Infantry of the 1st Division. The General asked the private why he was hospitalized, and the soldier replied,

"I guess I can't take it, sir."

Then, continues the report, the General began to abuse the patient, striking him across the face with his gloves and trying to throw him out of the tent. After General Patton left, Private Kuhl was helped back to his cot.

Next day the lad had a temperature of 102 degrees, and his diagnosis, which originally read "Psycho-neurosis anxiety—moderate," was changed to "Chronic dysentery and malaria."

Further facts about Private Kuhl are given. He was twenty-six years old and had been in the army eight months. He had fought as an infantryman in Africa and Sicily. During the Sicilian campaign he had been admitted to hospital three times as an "exhaustion" case. He had had chronic diarrhea for a month. The third time he had applied for hospitalization he had diagnosed his own case as "not being able to take it up front." It was not until after his case had been brought to General Patton's enraged attention that the private's condition was correctly diagnosed as chronic dysentery and malaria.

On August 10, a similar incident occurred in the same 15th Evacuation Hospital, and this incident is the one contained in the report of Demaree Bess and Merrill Mueller. It was made by these two correspondents at the hospital in a series of interviews with eyewitnesses and the patient himself twenty-four hours after the episode itself. Mueller's account of the matter was given quasi-official status when he was invited by General Smith, General Eisenhower's chief-of-staff, to present his facts to the rest of his colleagues at Headquarters in Algiers.

On this occasion, said Mueller, General Patton, accompanied by a colonel and a nurse, went from bed to bed, as was his custom, making friendly and complimentary remarks to each wounded man in turn. Then he came to a soldier sitting up in bed with a helmet liner on his head; and to the General's inquiries the soldier stated:

"It's my nerves. I can't stand the shelling."

Thereupon General Patton launched into a tirade, all of it profane and abusive, with such expletives as "yellow-bellied son of a bitch" frequent and typical. The soldier placed his head between his knees and wept.

The tirade continued, with a definite order for the soldier to get out of that bed and return to duty. It ended with a blow across the man's helmeted head.

Then the General continued on his way through the hospital tent and the silent rows of wounded men. And nobody's breathing was audible. All that was audible was Patton's continually reiterated mutterings about "cowardly bastards" and "yellow-bellies."

Before General Patton left the tent, concludes Mueller, he returned to the soldier's bedside and hit the boy again, this time knocking the helmet liner out of the tent.

Mueller does not give the name of this soldier. He was twenty-one years old, also an infantryman, and diagnosed as "a very bad nervous case." His hospitalization, it is said, had been ordered after he had initially refused to leave the front. After Patton's blow he asked to return to duty. The doctors refused to let him go at first, but after a week he did return. And thus passes an unknown soldier, out of history as he came into it.

2

While the two episodes are separate and distinct, they are also complementary, and spring from the same set of circumstances and the same motivations. Nothing could illustrate more vividly the passion of Patton's nature than two such scenes, staged in the strange green light of a hospital tent somewhere in Sicily, with its rows of mutilated men and its noise of their thick breathing and its smell of their wounds. Nothing could more terribly symbolize the clash between Patton's love of war and a soldier's hatred of it than the spectacle of a general striking a private. Nothing could more sharply etch the schism in Patton's own soul than the tears he wept for the physically wounded and the blows he heaped upon the mentally distressed.

The General's conduct is understandable, and to some critics, therefore, justifiable. These argue their case on premises which Patton himself has laid down. Patton's premises are simple enough.

He says, rightly, that all men have battle nerves and

THE SLAP HEARD ROUND THE WORLD 131

suffer from battle fatigue. Patton has never denied the existence of fear. He loudly recognizes the sensations of fatigue, hunger, and cold. His whole argument is that the good soldier conquers these feelings and these failings by training, discipline, and his own special attribute called "guts." I believe every soldier, including Private Kuhl and that other unknown soldier, would, however grudgingly, agree with him.

But it is also true that no soldier, however trained, disciplined, and, if Patton likes, "gutted," can conquer chronic malaria and dysentery. Private Kuhl could not; but he did not know why, and the doctors in their hasty examination of the case did not actually know either.

Patton was not to blame for not recognizing what even the doctor had not recognized—that Private Kuhl was no more afraid of battle than the average weary rifleman, but that he had more colic and malarial germs than the average. Many of those who condemned Patton did so on the grounds that he struck an ailing man. He did not. He struck a man who said, pitifully and prosaically, "I guess I can't take it." Let us be honest and admit this was a stupid reply.

So when Patton struck the soldier, he was not striking Private Kuhl as a man, but as the sudden embodiment of an idea, a concept, and an emotion which suddenly and blindingly enraged him. The simple explanation—and the one Patton undoubtedly gives himself—is that he was infuriated by the contrast between the gravely wounded men who represented the good soldiers who could, and would, take it, and the unscathed psycho-neurotic case who typified the bad soldier who couldn't, and wouldn't, take it. His blow against Private Kuhl, according to this explanation, is supposed to symbolize his scorn of all cowards and weaklings.

I suggest the origin of the blow will be found deeper in Patton's nature than that.

In the hospital that afternoon Patton was undergoing an emotional crisis which culminated in a more violent spiritual clash than his outward violence indicated. For what Patton was thinking, with subconscious anguish, as he went from cot to cot, gazing down on one wounded man after another, was that his self-created god of war was a hideous and brutal idol whose gospel of hate preached mutilation, suffering, and death. The poet who wrote "what painted glass can lovelier shadows cast than those of starlit skies," the husband and father, the lover of strong, living things, suddenly reasserted themselves in a paroxysm of rage against the swashbuckler and the booted soldier and the archpriest of martial violence.

If the unwarlike Patton had triumphed over the other Patton compounded of blood and guts, a general might have sat down beside a private, as a father sits down beside a sick son. Instead, "Blood and Guts" raised his hand, and he let loose a spate of abuse, and the moment he did so, he purged himself of his other self—the unwarlike self he had spent a lifetime in repressing. Once again he was justifying the harsh ideal he has set for himself; and once again he was paying homage to the ugly idol he has created.

In this essential warlike part of his nature and thinking, Patton was justified in pommeling a soldier, as he was justified in enforcing his harsh discipline on young trainees in the California desert; or in his brutal yelling at frightened men on the Fedhala beaches to get the hell out of their safe holes and attack; or in his frontal assaults on Troina; or in his pronouncements about greasing his tank treads with Germans' living guts; or in his poem, "God of Battle," printed in the *Woman's Home Companion.* Women and Home and Companion.

The same public which had smiled or gasped at or secretly applauded these and other manifestations of Patton's warlike rage had no particular cause or justification to be righteously indignant at this latest example of his fury.

If Patton's blow was symptomatic of his own inner sickness, then it is symptomatic not only of his sickness, but of the sickness of all people who compromise between ideals of love and the expediency of hate.

CHAPTER VIII
THE GETHSEMANE OF THE HEDGEROWS

I

FOR the Second Front, Patton was given an Army as shiningly splendid to his warlike nature as an electric railway, complete with locomotive, cars, rails, signals, and sidings, to an eight-year-old boy. The Third Army was the Patton Model Army. It raced, roared, and sparkled. It was the 1944 version of a Crusader's army, with tanks instead of charging horses, radio antennae for flying pennants, helmets for visors. And Berlin was its far Jerusalem.

In military terms, the Third Army was a Blitz Army, or a complete army on wheels. Its function was to roll right across Europe; and if Patton could have had his way, to go on rolling right round the earth's curve, until it was lost in myth, like the Flying Dutchman. A whole army, motorized and steel-skinned, mechanized like no other army in the world; such was the Third Army, which landed on the beaches of Normandy in July, 1944.

George S. Patton was the natural choice of the Allied High Command to lead this spectacular army, for the Third Army was the Allies' Blitz Army, and Patton was our only Blitz general.

But the actual invasion was never envisaged as a blitz operation. The planners wanted nothing spectacular and unpredictable about it. They didn't want Light Brigade charges or generals with pearl-handled pistols and an over-

THE GETHSEMANE OF THE HEDGEROWS 135

developed desire for glory getting mixed up with the mechanics of beach parties. The invasion, in brief, was a job of ballistics, not heroics.

It was also a job for a general who husbanded his forces, who preferred to consolidate what he had won instead of pressing on with half a division while the other half was still pinned down on the beaches. In short, the only objective of the first phase of the invasion was to get ashore and stay there, because if we had ever been driven off, the war might have gone on for the rest of our lives.

So Eisenhower skilfully chose General Omar Bradley to command the American invasion forces; and General Sir Bernard Montgomery to command the British.

General Bradley was perhaps the best and the soundest of the Allied field commanders in the formal sense. He belongs, in his training and thinking, to the safe school in American military tradition, and his strategy always had the cleanness and precision of a chronometer. He shows his modest and almost academic character in his appearance. Tall, with a creased, bespectacled face and the parchment-like skin of a mule-skinner, he enunciates his views with a nasal timbreless voice, which somehow conveys tremendous confidence to those who hear it. He looks altogether undistinguished, yet distinctly American. When I first met him, as Patton's second in command in Southern Tunisia, I thought he appeared more like a professor from a midwestern Methodist College than a professional soldier and brilliant strategist. Later, in North Africa, he proved his genius in the campaign which smashed through to the sea at Bizerte parallel with the British First and Eighth Armies on the right which drove into Tunis. This was a victory Patton had not been able to accomplish at Gafsa. Patton had never taken Maknassy or El Guettar. Bradley took Bald and Green Hills, considered impregnable natural fortresses. And he took Mateur and Bizerte.

We correspondents did not see much of Bradley in those days, and though he was always available and held regular press conferences during the European campaign, he was never concerned with publicity for himself, and his personality, like his appearance, was not adapted to newspaper accounts of war. During the final phases of the European War, and particularly during the Ardennes offensive, he became involved, against his whole wishes, with politics; and he appeared in a different light. Bradley was responsible for the Allied reverses in the Ardennes and he admitted it, and explained in his careful and honest way what had happened. But before he could do so, Field Marshal Montgomery had also done some explaining, not so careful and not so honest. And it was then that Bradley, for the first time, became concerned with military politics, and spoke to us like a military politician. I was present at his conference in Luxemburg, on January 9, 1945, when he announced that Montgomery's command of the American Twenty-first Army Group was temporary only. I know Bradley was angry and bitter over what had happened, especially over Montgomery's tactless claims and extravagant statements about stopping von Rundstedt, but he faced the occasion in his usual dry, honest, Missourian way, and all of us, including the British correspondents serving with American armies, sympathized with him.

Bradley's genius was different from Patton's in all ways. Bradley was solid and American. Patton was American but not solid. Bradley won his victories—and they were as conclusive as Patton's—with his mind; Patton won his by his

THE GETHSEMANE OF THE HEDGEROWS 137

personality. Bradley loved his soldiers for what they were—American civilians in uniform. He cherished and husbanded them. Patton loved his soldiers for what they came to be—fighting men in battle units. I don't think he cherished or husbanded them. Conversely, American soldiers loved Bradley. Bradley had an immense following in the American army, and the disturbing, even dangerous aspect of the Bradley-Montgomery dispute over the Ardennes was Montgomery's implied disrespect for Bradley, the favorite general of the American troops. For in Bradley's First and Ninth Armies were many veterans of the North African and Sicilian campaigns, and these men believed in Bradley, not Montgomery. I never met an American soldier who loved Patton in this way. I have told how, when Patton took command of the 2nd Corps in Tunisia, our soldiers hated him. They hated him bitterly after Sicily, and it was this hate which nearly ended his career as a general, because what General Eisenhower and the War Department were really concerned with, was the morale of our troops under a leader the fighting men hated.

Bradley had his genius, and this again was different from Patton's. Bradley's genius was strategic, Patton's more tactical. Bradley, as Commander-in-Chief of the American army groups in the field, was responsible for drawing the large arrows on the map which later became the Patton, Hodges, and Simpson drives.

General Bradley, then, was the natural and proper choice for the commander of the American invasion forces. We remember that this was the biggest and most responsible job ever given to an American soldier. And we remember that it was accomplished successfully.

From General Eisenhower's point of view, thinking of

the British generals, Montgomery was the natural and proper commander to lead the British into Europe. In June, 1944, Montgomery was the most successful of the Allied soldiers, not only in terms of accomplishments, but in the important sense of personality. In modern war, a general's personality is as important as his genius, because newspapers condition the way wars are run and their ultimate results. Newspapers, in turn, require colorful personalities to make readers read about war and like the way the war is being run; hence the success of generals like Montgomery and Patton and MacArthur, whose military genius is actually obscured in the vividness of their newspaper personalities.

Field Marshal Montgomery was such a vivid personality to the English newspapers; and they began, methodically, after the end of the Desert and Tunisian campaigns to groom him into the victorious Second Front general. Montgomery coöperated patriotically and eagerly, and really was what the newspapers intended him to be, which was a religious, crusading man who ardently believed in God and victory. To those of us who knew Montgomery at close quarters over four years of war, this ardor became wearisome; and we had a sense of irritation over the difficulty of discovering whether Monty was actually a good general or merely a good military politician. I did my best to formulate at least a personal opinion, and I concluded that he was a safe if not brilliant general, with a degree of military cunning which sometimes is as good as brilliance. At any rate he was a field commander and a soldier, and from him radiated the light of professional soldiering, so that his subordinate commanders, and under them the field officers,

THE GETHSEMANE OF THE HEDGEROWS 139

and, in turn, the fighting men or British Tommies, were professional and safe.

These two Allied commanders, then—Generals Bradley and Montgomery—were the wise choice of General Eisenhower and our war counselors to undertake the invasion of Europe. Their genius, experience, and personalities were requisite; neither was reckless nor unpredictable.

But the Allied High Command calculated that, in addition to the necessary weight for a successful landfall on the beaches of France, our war potential was now so tremendous that the time had come when we could afford spare armies and unformalistic generals like Patton. Thus the Third U. S. Army was conceived almost as an extravaganza of modern war; and thus it was given to our most extravagant general to command. Patton was the type to do unpredictable and logically unmilitary things. He was likely to do things which were confusing to us. How much more confusing would they be to the enemy!

In the beginning of the invasion of Europe there was simply no room for another army in the rectangle of coastland we held in Normandy. It was, therefore, a month before Patton's army embarked and landed, without having to fire a shot or wet their feet on Utah Beach, July 6, 1944.

We of the Third Army crossed the channel in the largest convoy I had seen since D Day. The lines of Liberty ships were so long and spread so far out over the sea that we could not see our escorting warships. We reached France in the evening, and were appropriately welcomed to Normandy beaches by a summer storm. We lay off Utah Beach until morning, when the LCTs came out to ferry men and cargo to the sandy beach. I was struck by the casual stage the war had already reached after only a month. The front lines were some twenty miles from the beaches where we were landing, but there were no signs of battle. The LCT serving our Liberty ship *Dan Beard* was called the *Stork Club* and was skippered by Ensign Billingsley of the New York night club. Billingsley and his odd craft typified the atmosphere on Utah Beach on that morning of July 7. The ensign—tanned, easy, and casual—bumped the *Stork Club* into the *Dan Beard,* and the crew of neither ship seemed fired with zeal to make the LCT fast, and thereby to proceed with the job of landing the Third Army and getting on with the war. Well, it was a fine summer morning, and these men were all veterans of the D Day and subsequent landings, and the certain mark of the veteran is his easy and casual way in the face of great events. So, as the passengers waited anxiously to set foot in France, the *Stork Club* bumped against the *Dan Beard,* ropes trailed in the water, and the latrine from the big Liberty ship poured over the side into the small LCT. The Third Army's arrival in Europe was no more romantic than this.

One could see immediately on landing how crowded was the Norman countryside with the tremendous forces the Allies had already put onto the continent. The stretches of landing beaches were packed with vehicles, which rolled in sand and dust clouds onto the roads, and were parked in hundreds of fields. The feeling was that we were really winning. You could travel without fear of German planes or long-range guns. It was very different from North Africa, Sicily, and Italy.

2

Patton established his headquarters in a country of apple orchards around the Norman villages of Nehou and Saint

THE GETHSEMANE OF THE HEDGEROWS 141

Sauveur le Vicomte. The headquarters spread over a wide area, and part of it was the G 6, or Psychological and Press Department. Here thirty correspondents had their own camp in their own apple orchard and there foregathered some old hands at war reporting and some on their first big assignment: Ernest Hemingway, Ira Wolfert, Jack Belden, Joe Driscoll of the *New York Herald Tribune,* Tom Treanor, who died in France, Tom Wolfe, Duke Shoop (or Dook the Shoop as we called him), Richard Stokes, and Norman Clark, and John Prince of the English Press were among those present. We set up house in three large tents, under the "command" of a lieutenant-colonel, who was not, most of us felt, either a sympathetic or efficient public relations officer. But public relations officers were a curious offshoot of this war, and their job of controlling large groups of war correspondents who were civilians and individualists, antipathetic to regimentation in conduct or dress, was not an easy one. I met very few public relations officers who were universally liked and respected, and I consider the American army handled this branch of the war clumsily and ineffectually. The British, with more experience and wisdom, handled it extremely well.

General Patton, acutely conscious, since Sicily, of the power of the press, soon visited this unmilitary establishment which was set down in the midst of his professionally military headquarters. He came into our apple orchard the day after we settled in, and was greeted by the permeating stink of many boxes of Camembert cheese which provident journalists had stored away under their camp beds. He was also greeted by men in helmets, men without helmets or any headgear at all, and some in caps of varying hues and shapes. His orders were for all military personnel to wear their helmets on pain of court-martial, but many of us managed to follow the Third Army from Normandy to Czechoslovakia in service caps. The military policemen used to stop us in the beginning, but hearing we were correspondents, they assumed we were beyond disciplining, which was roughly the case.

Patton shamed us in his appearance. He was resplendent. His helmet was lacquered and shone with paint and three stars. His tunic, cut on the cadet model, carried three rows of ribbons on his left breast. His beloved pistols were strapped at his waist, and he carried a riding crop. He was upright, soldierly, and amiable, and gave me—as he managed to give most civilians—the impression that I was an intruder in a warlike world.

To me, Patton's appearance and manner were always astonishing. There is nothing of the swashbuckler about him on the surface. He is a quiet man, even with well-controlled signs of nervousness. His voice is high and thin. He speaks for long periods without manifesting in outbursts the extreme emotionalism of his nature. He can, if he wishes, speak without profanity, which he does not use as most soldiers use it to distinguish them from civilians. His use of language is, in fact, rather Elizabethan. It is lusty, and he likes words. I noted that he pronounced French names correctly, which only one out of ten thousand American soldiers did. I noted, too, that he is a man who by his fine stature and strong personality elicits sycophancy from other men. Our group around Patton that afternoon under the apple trees flattered and indulged him, partly from awe, partly from a desire to exploit him.

The approach was successful, and Patton did give us a detailed account of his forthcoming battle plans. He said

THE GETHSEMANE OF THE HEDGEROWS 143

we would first make a hole in the German lines, probably in the western or Lessay sector, and through this hole he would hurl his armor, fanning it out in two great spearheads, one of which was to go west to Brest and cut off the Brittany peninsula; the other to go east and encircle the German Seventh Army. He said he would be ready to go within two weeks.

He had bet the war would be won by November 11.

While waiting for Patton to make his break-through, we wandered about the front, through Bradley's First Army and Montgomery's Second Army sectors. I was able to orient myself again to the martial life, renewing my acquaintance with divisions I had known in the Mediterranean, and above all, readjusting my senses to the sights and sounds of war.

I could see from my wanderings along the front that the Germans were much weaker here in France than they had been in Italy. We never saw a Nazi plane, and we were seldom shelled by Nazi guns. The absence of German air force and artillery was significant. It enabled us to dispose our forces without interference. It prevented the Germans from anticipating our moves, and though their agents reported the whereabouts of Patton, they could not discover the size or mission of his army. The fact was, Patton actually had no army at this time. The army was formed at the last minute from newly arrived divisions and from First Army units, which were transferred from Bradley's to Patton's command.

The Germans, though greatly outnumbered and outweighed, were fighting with extraordinary skill and cunning. We had a decisive superiority in men and armaments, but they had the advantages of terrain, camouflage, and subterfuge. We were fighting then in the hedgerow country. Normandy is divided into thousands of little fields, separated by high-banked hedges and flanked by trees. The Germans dug into the rear of these banked hedges which formed natural tank barriers. Our infantry had to pry them out, hedge by hedge. Our losses were heavy. All over the countryside they had built woodland fortresses such as the Japanese used in the jungles of Asia. Camouflaged ladders led up to tree platforms from which snipers could fire, using flashless powder. I examined some of these places. They were made with characteristic Teutonic skill, and the ladders, made out of the same wood as the trees they leaned against, were beautiful examples of German carpentry.

This art of camouflage, which the Germans developed to perfection and which the Americans seemed to make no attempts to develop at all, almost counteracted our tremendous air superiority. Our fighters and bombers were after the German convoys all day, and seldom could find any. Yet the enemy was constantly moving supplies to the front. For a long time our intelligence was puzzled by the complete absence of enemy vehicles on the roads. The answer was that the Germans were cutting long sections out of the hedgerows, and filling them in with their convoy trains, which were netted and painted to resemble the original hedges. The convoy drivers stayed in their vehicles until night, when the train side-slipped onto the road and rolled frontwards again.

Bradley and Montgomery kept battering away frontally at the German lines, and our progress was so slow it looked as though we would be months breaking out of a country which the infantryman now called the "Gethsemane of the Hedgerows." Our strategy at this time started to resemble

THE GETHSEMANE OF THE HEDGEROWS 145

the strategy of the last war. We were using weight in a straightforward, pounding way. Mass bombing was tried again and again. On July 24, the major part of the Allied air forces was supposed to blast a hole through the German lines in the St. Lo sector. During the morning we watched a long procession of medium and heavy bombers flying east, but learned at the 19th Corps of the First Army that the attack had had to be postponed on account of the overcast.

The next day the air attack did go in, with 2,215 Fortresses, Liberators, Marauders, and other airplanes, dropping an estimated 4,000 tons of bombs along a narrow sector of the front facing the 7th Corps. Two hundred tons of these bombs, or five per cent of the total, fell on our own forward troops, killing and wounding many of them, including a general, Major-General L. S. McNair, Chief of Air Corps Ground Forces.

Everybody, Americans as well as Germans, was shaken by this earth-rending bombardment. I talked to Germans who survived it, and were taken prisoner in the subsequent American infantry attack. They said the 4,000 tons of bombs had stunned them, but had not killed many, as they knew it was coming. They had watched the abortive air armada the day before, and divined we would try it again as soon as the weather favored. So they had dug their holes in the ground, and survived the storm; but the American infantry was on them before they had time to get out of their holes and reform.

By July 26, Bradley had broken the German's Normandy line. Using the 1st, 5th, and 9th Infantry divisions, veterans of Africa and Sicily, he was shoving the whole German Seventh Army back. The signs of a break-through were now increasing. Our tanks had begun to break loose. We began to see the litter of wrecked or abandoned German equipment; burning tanks, swollen corpses, bloated cattle, lay all over the countryside, stinking in the hot sun. Bradley started by-passing German strong points, like Marigny, which was held for a few hours by fanatical Nazi rear guards. There was still no German rout, but they were breaking.

By July 28, Patton was ready to go. He had the hole in the German lines which he wanted. It was in the desired place, on the west side of the Normandy peninsula, with the sea on his right flank.

3

On the 28th, I went to the "hole" where Patton had said he would pass through. It was at the little town of Lessay, on the Ay River. The river had been a natural defensive position in the Germans' east-west defense line across the Cotentin peninsula, which rises into the Atlantic in the shape of a cat's head, with Cherbourg at the top. The Nazis had abandoned Lessay without a fight, when Bradley broke their line in the center and outflanked it. Now it was a ghost town. I remember walking in with a company of American combat engineers, each of us walking in the footsteps of the man ahead. We knew the town would be heavily mined and booby-trapped. On such occasions, every man is silent. He watches the ground, and the silent shoes of the man ahead. You wonder then in whose footsteps the first man is walking. Our entry into Lessay was silent and uneventful, though we were expecting snipers. The combat engineers who were these first men in, have to expect something of everything in their job. They may have to lift mines under artillery fire, repair bridges under machine gun fire, or tape

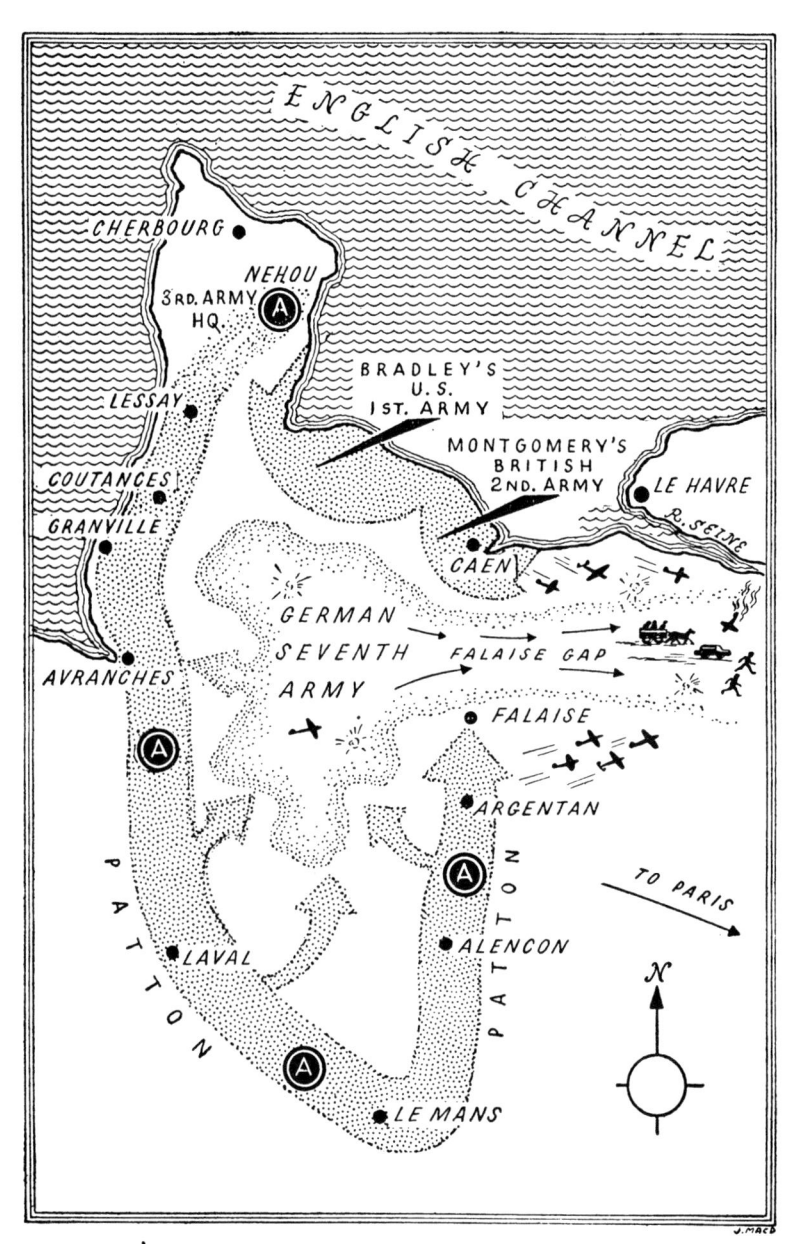

PATTON'S ENCIRCLEMENT OF GERMAN 7TH ARMY IN NORMANDY

out safe roads while being sniped at. But all we met in Lessay was death and the stink of German corpses. The town had been hammered into piles of rubble by our artillery. It was empty, and no faces showed behind the fluttering shreds of curtains. No one was sitting in the local cinema, which had the roof blown off, though the rows of wooden seats remained. The place was typified in a fully clad German infantryman lying on his back by the roadside. He was very dead. His face had swollen and blackened until it resembled a gas mask. And from his pack, which contained the "souvenirs" so beloved by Americans, ran a fine wire. The German corpse, like everything else in Lessay, was booby-trapped.

CHAPTER IX

THE COVERED WAGON WAR

I

SUDDENLY the war became fun. It became exciting, carnivalesque, tremendous. It became victorious and even safe. We awoke on the morning of Sunday, the 30th of July, with the feeling that the war was won—in spirit, if not in fact.

Patton and the Third Army were away.

Those were indeed tremendous and even delirious days. You would walk into Corps Headquarters to find the G 2s (Intelligence Officers) wiping out entire dispositions on their celluloid-covered war maps. All the little red squares and circles representing German positions on the Cotentin peninsula and all the little blue ones representing Allied dispositions were being rubbed off with big sponges, and bald-headed sergeants, with pockets full of draftsmen's pencils were re-disposing the entire war fronts.

At the 8th Corps, which held the western sector of the Normandy front, the G 2 colonel said: "We've lost contact with the enemy."

Patton gave us his last press conference in his apple orchard headquarters. He was the same as ever, resplendent in khaki and medals, with his smooth womanish face, small mouth, colorless eyes, and quiet manner. This day, however, his white bull terrier, Willy Patton, Jr., tended to steal the limelight from his master. During the conference, the white-eyed hound stood in front of the respectful war correspondents, chose a lap, and climbed on.

Patton announced that he was ready to go. The 4th Armored Division was already moving down the Lessay-Coutances road.

My jeep party, consisting of Norman Clark of the London *News Chronicle* and Cornelius Ryan of the London *Daily Telegraph,* decided to move on with it. We packed our belongings in the trailer attached to our jeep, and said good-by to the press camp in the apple orchard for the last time. We had no destination, because the war was suddenly moving so fast, nobody could say exactly where our advanced units were. Everything in the Third Army was now roaring south through the Lessay gap, and down the coast highway through Coutances and Avranches. Avranches marked the shoulder of the Brittany peninsula, and it was the gateway to the interior of all of France.

We could see, as we rode along in the clear, white sunlight of that morning, July 30, that the "Gethsemane of the Hedgerows" was over. No more banked hedges, ditches, and flanking poplars. South of Lessay the country rolled and heaved in a sweeping landscape. The roads were wide and fast to travel over. Down these roads, on this July morning, was rolling the 4th Armored Division, as though there was nothing now to stop it between the Normandy beaches and the German frontier. This was the feeling we had that morning, and the feeling proved to be almost the fact of the matter.

The 4th Armored, now in action for the first time, was largely responsible for this impression of urgency. It had been trained with the power and speed of a panther. It took to tank warfare as a trained swimmer to a pool of blue water. Its tank crews and armored infantrymen were uncannily fearless and skilful. It began its battle career in this way, and eventually raced across France and across Germany and into Czechoslovakia as cleanly and swiftly as a bullet. It was an altogether incredible battle unit, and Patton invariably used it to spearhead all his major drives.

It was the 4th Armored we followed that morning; and we found, as we were always to find whenever this division "took off," that our rear echelons had lost contact with them. The lead tanks had "just gone." Gradually, as we went south of Coutances, we found the countryside becoming emptier of troops and we had that disagreeable feeling of being between our own advanced elements and our own rear. In this war, No Man's Land lay not between our forward units and the enemy, but *behind* our most advanced tanks. In this zone, pockets of the enemy had been by-passed. The infantry came along later and cleaned them out of woods, trenches, and houses. Along the lonely stretches of road friendly vehicles raced as fast as they could, anxiously scanning the fields and woods on either side.

This was how we were riding, when we came across a little group of jeeps at a crossroads south of Coutances called Trelly. One of the jeeps bore the two-star insignia of a major-general. This was General Wood, commander of the 4th Armored. He was a hard-faced, leather-booted cavalryman, and was concerned at the moment with keeping his tanks rolling. I asked him where he wanted them to go. He said, "It doesn't matter, so long as they keep rolling." He did not yet know whether, once through the Avranches bottleneck, he would swing west and cut across the Brittany peninsula or whether he would turn east behind the German Seventh Army. I said, "What happens,

General, if the Germans cut you off by driving through to the coast behind you?" The General said:

"Let 'em. That's what we want 'em to do."

This, then, was now the spirit of the war. This was not the mechanics, the ballistics of invasion. It was not aerial or artillery bombardments, saturation bombing, frontal assaults, hedgerow war, war of attrition. It was not the Bradley or Montgomery strategy. It was pure Patton. A whole armored division was being hurled through a narrow bottleneck, and ordered to keep rolling as far and as fast as it could. It was brilliant, dangerous, and unpredictable. It was the piratical technique applied to modern war.

What had already happened to the 4th Armored was what had to happen. Some of their lead tanks had been ambushed and knocked out. Others had gone so far ahead, they had lost contact with the main force. Others were behind the Germans, without either side knowing how or where. Tanks had begun that cutting and slicing technique which was Patton's favorite and most brilliant tactic. In the darkness and the confusion, they had bumped head-on into powerful German units, and battles of annihilation had been fought all night.

General Wood himself directed us to a place down a side road from the Trelly crossroads where the Third Army's first big battle had been fought. "Go take a look at that road," he said. "You'll see something unusual." Then he climbed aboard his jeep, and his little column roared away. I thought they were more like Indian fighters on little white horses than modern soldiers in jeeps.

The spectacle General Wood was referring to was one of the most awesome I had seen in four years of war. It was a column of seventy German vehicles which had been ambushed by a single American medium tank, and the whole seventy, tanks, field guns, half-tracks, ambulances, trucks, private cars, the General's caravan—in fact, the entire headquarters column of an SS Panzer division—had been methodically knocked out.

We wandered down the country road along which this dead column lay black between high hedges. Its head was a Mark IV tank, knocked out with the second shot from the American Sherman which lay, also dead, under a tree, a hundred yards further down the road. Next came an enormous mobile cannon. Then came half-tracks, more tanks, three captured American tanks, trucks, private cars, the German General's caravan. All over these vehicles, on the road, in the ditches, in the fields, lay the SS men. Their corpses were truncated, bisected, mangled, and sometimes unmarked, so that I saw many of them sitting at the wheels of private cars, as though still in the act of driving. In the backs of other cars sat wounded men, with their arms in slings, sitting upright and relaxed, like sleepers.

Some sad-eyed G.I.s were wandering along the road, and they took us to see the officer who had fought this battle. He was a big, quiet captain, and his eyes were bloodshot with fatigue, and he was not elated or impressed by his victory. His name was W. C. Johnson, and he was once a football coach at Lafayette University, Indiana. The captain had commanded the regiment of the armored infantrymen out of the 4th Armored which had completed the ambush of this SS column, and had fought the SS men all through the night. The SS had fought to the last man. They could not go forward, because the Sherman had knocked out their lead tank. They could not turn round, because the road was too narrow. They could not go over the fields because the hedges were too high. They could not go back because the Americans had closed the Trelly crossroads.

Captain Johnson, with his infantrymen, had arrived on the scene at eleven o'clock the previous night. The battle had ended at six o'clock that morning. Hundreds of SS men had died, and scores of Americans had died, too. The adjacent field was full of dead men. Some of them, American and German, lay head to head, because towards morning, said Johnson, the fighting had become hand-to-hand.

The SS headquarters men had brought all their loot with them. Fur coats, women's silk underwear, musical instruments, giant cheeses, boxes of cigars, bottles of wine, mounds of wool, shoes, shirts, hats, uniforms, lay scattered all over the road. There was enough loot in that column to have stocked a department store.

I believe this was the first time in this war any Allied unit ambushed a German column of this size and importance. It was also the first time Allied armies had broken through and got behind the Germans. What we were now seeing was quite different from what we saw in Africa, Sicily, and Italy. What we were seeing was the beginning of a German rout, which became within the next few weeks the biggest rout of armies in the history of the world.

The signs were all around us. German vehicles and equipment lay littered over the countryside. Their tanks were smoldering beside the roads. Their guns stood abandoned in the fields. In the ditches rested the Nazi dead in gray-blue field uniforms. It became evident, as we went further in the wake of the 4th Armored Division, that a major disaster was beginning to overtake the Reichswehr.

The most significant aspects of this impending defeat were the hundreds of high-wheeled, narrow farm carts which lay wrecked beside the Coutances-Avranches highway. Beside the carts dead horses stuck rigid legs into the air. From the carts overflowed the personal belongings of the German infantrymen. The great number of these carts became more and more impressive. As we rode by in our jeep, I tried to understand what this could mean, and what it resembled. I had never seen carts used in war before—except by the Senegalese and Colonial French troops in Southern Tunisia. It was at first hard to reconcile these carts with war, and hard to believe that the German Army, of all armies, was using them.

Then I remembered where I had seen similar carts before. I had seen them in pictures of Napoleon's retreat from Moscow. So, if the evidence of these carts was valid, the German Army was retreating as Napoleon retreated out of Russia. They were requisitioning horse-drawn vehicles to carry their possessions, and themselves walking on foot.

This was only the beginning, for through the little hole which began at Lessay and ran like a bottleneck down the west side of the Cherbourg Peninsula, through Coutances, Granville, and Avranches, Patton poured the greatest flood of armor and men which Europe had seen since the German blitz of 1940. Within a week the entire Third Army, as it was then constituted, had rolled down this one highway, and fanned out to the west across the Brittany peninsula and to the east behind the whole length of the German Seventh Army. The speed and weight of Patton's attack actually broke the three German armies in western Europe. In the strictly military sense, the Wehrmacht was decisively beaten by a single American armored division, the 4th, which spearheaded the offensive, and turned the whole Nazi Normandy line. The German High Command knew from that moment that the war was lost. Cliques within the High Command had by their attempted assassination of Hitler, tried to save something of their army, conquests, and national resources by seeking terms in July. They knew they could fight on for a year; but they also knew Germany was potentially defeated when the Allied armies began elbowing their way out of the Normandy peninsula and began running like a flood over the plains of central France.

Soon it became apparent, even to the non-professional observer, that the Wehrmacht had suddenly collapsed. That was the meaning of the wrecked farm carts. As Patton's armor poured through the Avranches gap, sliced across the German lines to the south, overran their outposts, crushed their headquarters under tank tracks, and attacked their field positions from the rear, the Germans, as a last resort, stole every vehicle from the countryside, from horse-traps to wheelbarrows, and ran away. They threw their belongings into these decrepit wooden carts, and started—sometimes south, sometimes west or east—without direction or guidance and finally without discipline.

Next, the air forces caught them. The weather had come in fine. There were no clouds. The days were long. From five o'clock in the morning till after ten at night, our fighters strafed and bombed the long, straight, tree-lined roads of France. The result was an incredible spectacle of upturned farm carts, hurriedly camouflaged, dust-brown, and besporting pitiful withered tree branches; and beside the carts, the distended carcasses of dead horses, and broken-down wheelbarrows, knocked-out tanks, burning half-tracks, and bullet-riddled private cars.

2

What had happened was this: When the Third Army started moving through the Avranches hole—and continued to pass through despite the German armored counteroffensive designed to drive back to the sea on the west and cut off all American forces south of Avranches—all German forces in Brittany were in danger of being cut off from the rest of France. So the German High Command ordered a double movement of German troops in this area. Some were to retreat westward to the Atlantic ports of Brest, L'Orient, and St. Nazaire; the remainder were supposed to retreat eastward towards Paris.

The German General staff calculated that Patton was after the Brittany peninsula and the great submarine bases of Brest, L'Orient, and St. Nazaire. They believed Eisenhower would need adequate ports and docks before he attempted to drive east. They were partly right. We needed ports other than Cherbourg, which had been our only sea supply route for two months, with everything else still coming into France over the beaches. What the German High Command did not anticipate was that Patton would split his army into two, and put his main strength into his eastward drive. In other words, Patton was not after ports or submarine bases. He was after trapping the entire German Seventh Army. At the beginning of August he started the biggest encircling movement of the Western European war. He started it on August 1, and completed it by reaching Falaise on August 11, without the Germans knowing where he was or what he was doing.

The power and speed of Patton's multiple drives—one

west to Brest, another southwest to L'Orient, another south to St. Nazaire, and the fourth, an all-out blitz straight behind the German Seventh Army—accounted for the incredible confusion we were now seeing on the roads of France.

We saw the results of this chaos in the form of the wrecked Nazi transport, the knocked-out equipment, the truckloads of German prisoners who had been rounded up, and the hundreds of them who were still wandering about the countryside waiting to give themselves up. The French Maqui saw the real chaos, and helped increase it in a hundred ways.

They told me at Vitré what the scene had looked like to them. It appeared a German infantry division had been ordered to evacuate Rennes on August 1, and make its way east through Vitré and Laval to the Paris region. A French colonel, chief of the FFI of the area and agent for the Allies, sat himself in a hotel window in Vitré, sipped his ersatz coffee, and watched the following spectacle provided by the mighty German Army: First, he said, came ten tanks and about a score of cannon, mostly 88s. Next came a fleet of Rennes buses, painted white and marked with red crosses. Some of these buses carried medical personnel and material, others were loaded with infantrymen, supplies, and oil drums. Behind came an assortment of military and private cars, carrying high-ranking officers. Then came the ragtag and bobtail on foot. The French colonel, who, like the rest of us during those tremendous days, was inclined to mix emotion with facts, swore the entire German division was drunk. They came along, he said, in shreds of shoes, their uniforms unbuttoned, their caps on the backs of their heads, tired but cheerful and, indeed, singing lustily. From their coat pockets projected the necks of cognac bottles. Intermingled with these groups of tramping and singing soldiers were horse-drawn guns, farm wagons, wheelbarrows, and bicycles. There was no sign of any discipline, and the officers who went by were alone or in groups of two or three. The astonishing thing to the colonel was the complete indifference this motley army displayed to their surroundings and the French people who stood gawking by the roadside. These Germans were not at all arrogant or even distant. They sat down on park benches in Vitré beside the local citizens, took out their bottle of wine and their rations, took off their shoes, enjoyed an al fresco lunch, brushed the crumbs off their clothes, put on their shoes, and walked away. This went on for two days. By the end of those two days Patton's armor had captured Laval where the German division was supposed to re-assemble.

The fact was, Patton's forces—armored and infantry—during those eleven days, went on the biggest rampage in the history of this war. In the tight military sense, the Third Army was out of control. Three armored divisions—the 6th driving to Brest, the 4th to St. Nazaire, the 2nd French to Laval and beyond—were never in direct contact with Patton's headquarters after the first few days. The wiremen tried to keep telephone lines out, but the effective length of a field telephone wire is only sixty miles; and the advance elements of the armored divisions had gone another twenty miles by the time the wires were laid. But Patton, tearing around his vast front, moving his headquarters every day, was elated and more confident than ever. He had instructed his commanders to keep on driving, irrespective of resistance, irrespective of where they arrived. His army flowed all over the Brittany peninsula. The 6th Armored went 150 miles to Brest in four days, and lost contact with the main forces for over a week. The 4th Armored went nearly 200 miles to L'Orient in five days, and stayed by themselves down there without infantry or siege guns. The 83rd Division laid siege to St. Malo. Rennes was captured. Another powerful force—the main force—swung south from Avranches, raced through Laval, Le Mans, and up to Falaise through Argentan, a distance of 170 miles in twelve days. Literally, the Third Army no longer had cohesion, except for Patton, who drove madly along the wide, white roads, concerning himself with the direction and flow of his supplies, turning non-military vehicles off the road, roaring at soldiers who violated disciplinary orders, questioning anybody who did not look and talk like an American soldier.

But this mad and piratical use of a modern army paid tremendous dividends. It was obviously smashing the entire German armies and defenses in the west. It was smashing them collectively and individually. The 4th Armored in the neighborhood of Rennes overran remnants of eight German divisions, capturing German command posts intact, taking so many prisoners they did not know what to do with them. Whole units of Germans suddenly threw down their arms and rushed out to meet our lone tank squadrons, before the French killed them in the woods. A single German corporal was put in charge of 500 prisoners, and told to march to the rear—five days' march away. German officers were put on their honor to lead their men back to the prison cages. A 6th Armored Division combat team knocked out the remnants of an entire German division for two soldiers killed in the engagement. Our armor arrived at a German headquarters in Vitré while German commanders were at dinner, and received a cool surrender from the German officers who suggested the Americans join them for the meal. The Americans declined the invitation on the grounds that they knew of another German headquarters twenty miles further on, and they wanted to reach it that night. They reached it.

The French 2nd Armored Division, commanded by General Le Clerc, advanced seventy miles in twenty-four hours, right behind the German Seventh Army which was still facing Bradley's and Montgomery's armies on the Normandy beaches. By this time nobody quite knew what was happening or where our forces were. Patton himself did not know. He had given his last orders. They were simple: "Go where you can, as fast as you can." It may not have seemed practical back in the offices of the Supreme Command in London, but out here in the rolling countryside of France, it was actually working, as it had worked in the California desert on maneuvers. Patton had proved his theory: that modern armies can defeat the enemy without fighting him, if they move while the enemy tries to stay in position. He was, in effect, defeating the German armies in the west simply by hurling his armor into the blue.

This, then, was the war against Germany in August, 1944. Patton had broken through and the entire German front was collapsing on the western sector covering Brittany. For a few days nobody knew what had happened or what would happen next. Those of us who were not in the fighting vanguard were carried along on a tide of emotion and champagne. We had lost contact with headquarters and the press camp. But everybody had lost contact with everybody else. This was how Patton wanted it. His armor was still driving and slashing across the German rear. The German defeat was becoming a rout, and the rout a collapse. General Patton had effected the greatest movement of armor and infantry in history.

CHAPTER X

THE FALAISE GAP

WHAT Patton had done was this: He had sent an entire army along a single highway and through a gap about twelve miles wide. The road was the Lessay-Coutances-Avranches highway, and the gap, or bottleneck, through which he passed his divisions was at Avranches.

He had then divided his army into two forces. One of these forces, the Westbound or Brittany force, he had scattered piecemeal, and dispatched on special independent missions. The main, or Eastbound force, he had first sent south, as though threatening Paris, and then swung east and north, behind the entire length of the German Seventh Army, commanded by von Kluge.

The Germans had been outwitted, outmaneuvered. Their High Command had miscalculated on every important decision since the initial French landings. First, they had decided to seal off our invasion forces in the Cotentin or Cherbourg peninsula, by building a defense line across from Caen and westward through St. Lo to Lessay, and the sea. This defensive strategy lost them the initiative; and after the first week, when they failed to counterattack our forces clinging to the coast-line, they were outnumbered and outweighed, and had no hope of driving us back into the sea.

Next, they decided that we would try and break out of the narrow coastal rectangle to the east, in the direction of

Le Havre and the French Channel ports. So they massed their armor opposite Montgomery's forces. We broke through on the extreme west.

They next miscalculated the direction and intention of Patton's drive. They thought he was bound only west to the Biscay submarine bases in Brest, L'Orient, and St. Nazaire.

Once they realized that Patton's westbound forces represented only a heavy feint, and that his main force was driving south and east, they misjudged his objective and assumed he was Paris-bound. They, therefore, decided they had time to swing back von Kluge's Army on the Caen hinge, and thus cover a Caen-Paris line, protecting the Channel ports, the V-1 launching sites, and the Low Countries.

Finally, caught in a dilemma, they risked everything on a massive armored counterattack calculated to cut the Avranches bottleneck and divorce Patton's Third Army from the American First and the British Second Armies.

During the week of August 4-11, they threw everything they had in armor and air against the Avranches corridor. To do so, they switched panzer divisions from in front of Montgomery, infantry and artillery units from in front of Bradley, and attacked fanatically the sides of the corridor.

This is what we expected and wanted them to do. The sides of the Avranches corridor were steel-lined, with guns and dug-in infantry holding the high ground to the East of the Coutances-Avranches highway. Bradley was able to meet the German counterattack from the north. Montgomery was able to move down from Caen to Falaise. And the weather being fine, the RAF turned loose the rocket-firing typhoons on the German tanks.

Meanwhile, there was nothing in front of Patton. He

made his encirclement without opposition, and within ten days, the trap was closed around the German Seventh Army.

The brilliance of the Allied Plan and the mistakes of the enemy counterplan lost Germany the Battle of Normandy, of France and the Low Countries, and the war.

What was happening during those first days of August was happening so fast that neither the Germans nor the majority of Allied military commentators knew what events portended. If you look at the newspapers of the time, you will see that they were headlining distances from Paris, and such towns as Orleans. The British Broadcasting Corporation, which we used to listen to at night, gave an entirely false picture of Patton's drive, and many American listeners were angry about it. I assume now that the BBC, together with other Allied news sources was deliberately given certain half truths and allowed to draw false deductions in order to confuse the Germans even more. For the Germans were incredibly confused. By the time Patton had raced along their rear and cut off the Seventh Army from France, they had lost control of the situation, because they had lost proper communications with the central command. When that happens, armies disintegrate.

By August 12, the German Seventh Army was about to disintegrate. It had been encircled and trapped by Patton's armor and infantry in the most daring operation of the war. By August 12, the French 2nd Armored Division, commanded by General Le Clerc, with the American 90th Infantry pacing the tanks and consolidating behind them, had reached Argentan. The Canadians of Montgomery's Second Army, with a Polish Armored Division, had moved down from Caen, and were outside Falaise. The entire German Seventh Army, therefore, had only one road running through

Falaise and one narrow corridor through which to escape. That escape gap was interdicted by the Canadian guns to the north, and the American guns to the south.

By this time, my jeep party of correspondents had finished with St. Malo and the Brittany battles, and we were chasing along behind the 15th Corps, commanded by Major-General Wade Haislip. In an apple orchard near Argentan we met General Haislip and the Commander-in-Chief, General Patton, and heard the full story of the Third Army's victory. Patton stalked up to our little group of correspondents gathered outside General Haislip's caravan, and greeted us with his customary sunless smile. His first words were praise for General Haislip whose 15th Corps had spearheaded the Argentan run. Haislip was a Patton soldier. He, too, believed in almost reckless speed, in by-passing enemy strong points, in keeping tanks always moving, in keeping his headquarters within cannon range of the front, in living in the open, and stopping for the night in some grove. General Haislip had obeyed orders and reached his objective in less than scheduled time. Now Patton had ordered him to stop at Argentan. Patton, in turn, had been ordered to stop. The French 2nd Armored—which was almost recklessly excited by the success of its drive and burned to keep going, on to Falaise, until they closed the gap between them and the Canadians to the north—had been ordered to stop. The gap was being left open.

We asked Patton why. He implied it was not his idea or wish; but, as best he could, he justified the Allied High Command's policy. He said: "Some of the greatest pursuits in history have been planned to leave an escape hole, through which the enemy forces funnel, only to be annihilated as they flow through."

He said the gap was closed with artillery and aerial bombardment. I gathered that we were afraid to edge our ground forces closer, after what had happened at St. Lo, where five per cent of our bombs fell within our own lines. This was a good argument for leaving plenty of room for the bombers, if they were capable of closing the gap from the air.

But I didn't understand then, nor do I understand now, why the Argentan-Falaise escape gap was not closed by a junction of Patton's and Montgomery's forces. I thought at the time it was a conservative policy—even more than that, a stupid one, because no army is trapped until the ring of steel is looped right round it. And this is particularly true of the German armies. Patton was sure he could hold von Kluge from the south, where he might have attempted to burst out. All along the Avranches-Fourgeres-Laval-Le Mans-Argentan road, Patton had disposed tanks, guns, and infantry to steel-line the huge enveloping bag within which lay von Kluge's estimated 150,000 troops. To the north were Bradley and Montgomery. To the west the sea. I could not understand the purpose of the Argentan-Falaise escape gap, which the Germans did use with skill to extricate their elite panzer and infantry troops.

But this was a High Command decision. Patton had achieved his objective, and completed his drive. And now we could see for ourselves what he had done.

CHAPTER XI

EISENHOWER MAKES HIS DECISION

I

LEAVING the destruction of the German Seventh Army to Bradley and Montgomery, Patton started in mid-August, 1944, his drive east to the German borders.

This, the second drive of the Third Army, was a classic in the history of warfare. It was to take Patton's lead tanks from Le Mans to Metz, right across France, nearly 500 miles in just over two weeks. In fact, when reconnaissance elements of the Third Army approached Germany against light German opposition at the beginning of September, the war was almost won. German armies in France had been so heavily defeated, their order of battle was so confused, their High Command was so out of control of the situation that victory was nearer to the Allies at the beginning of September, 1944 than ever again until the total and inevitable collapse of the Hitler-Himmler régime itself.

What Patton had done was to drive like a long spear clear across central France, splitting the country into two. His route was Le Mans-Chartres-Fontainebleau-Meaux-Château-Thierry-Soissons-Verdun-Metz-Luxemburg. Along this magnificent French highway, which the Germans had kept in a good state of repair as their principal supply route to the West, Patton's tanks, infantry, and supply trains hurtled night and day for two weeks in the greatest blitz in warfare. Patton drove east with such speed, there was no organized opposition even in the defensible regions of the First World War battlefields at Château-Thierry, the Marne, Verdun, Metz. Reconnaissance found the Maginot Line abandoned and overgrown with jungle growth. Later, prods at the Siegfried Line indicated this, Germany's main defense belt, was undermanned and easily penetrated.

Under these circumstances, Patton was determined to keep advancing, through the Maginot Line, through the Siegfried Line, across the Rhine, and into Germany. I believe, from what he had said at his conferences back in the Normandy apple orchards, that he would have taken the vanguard of his Army to Berlin, if he had been allowed to do so. For a moment the opportunity was given him to win the greatest victory in the history of wars; for it would have been the victory of one General and one army, comparable with the victories of the ancient soldiers, like Alexander, Hannibal, and Caesar. Patton's nature was such that he would willingly have taken the risk involved: and the risk was having an entire army nearly a thousand miles away from its bases, which were still back on the Channel beaches.

But on September 3, the entire Third Army, which now reached from the docks of Cherbourg on the English Channel to the walls of Metz, came to a stop. All along the main west-east highway from Avranches through Le Mans and east across the 500 miles of France, the tanks, guns, trucks, and jeeps just ceased moving, and coasted to a halt at the sides of the roads. The lead tanks were called back from east of Metz. They lumbered into bivouac areas, their tanks were filled with oil, and they were told they could get no more. The trucks carrying the infantry were drawn up in small towns; the infantrymen were de-trucked, and started walking. Drivers of vehicles began begging gas from passing vehicles. Third Army correspondents in a camp at Villeneuve, west of Verdun, were told there was no more gas for their jeeps, so we could not ride even as far as the 7th Corps to see what was happening. It was unnecessary to go there, because nothing was happening. The drive into Germany had ended; the moment for victory was past.

Patton started a furious telegraphic conference with Eisenhower, demanding, begging, cajoling gasoline. His men, he said, would willingly go without food, and even ammunition, if they could have oil to keep rolling. Patton was right in assessing the situation. Food was obtainable in France in harvest time. Ammunition was hardly necessary, as little or none was being expended. The farther and faster his tanks went into Germany, the less need of ammunition there would be.

Patton has a genius for living off himself, when there is no alternative. For instance, when the First and Ninth Armies were being built up in November and December, the Third Army was getting no replacements, though its casualties in the endless succession of river crossings and frontal attacks on the Siegfried Line were still the greatest of any American European army. But Patton could get no replacements, so he took them from within his own army, turning quartermaster troops, clerks, and headquarters troops, into combat infantrymen, and streamlining every rear echelon to keep the front line units up to strength. Now, with his army out of gas supplies, he tried by a great feat of organization to resolve the crisis. He organized the Red Ball Express route which ran right across France, using six-wheeled trucks, forming a convoy hundreds of miles long. These trucks carried nothing but gasoline. They rolled night and day the 500 miles from the gas dumps to the front lines. That was a 1000-mile round trip, during which the truck itself burned a hundred gallons of gas to deliver 500 gallons. Patton ran this fleet of gas trucks with the speed, efficiency, and peculiarly American recklessness of frontier days. I well remember passing these supply trains on the Verdun-Paris highway in September, 1944, and being struck with the almost nightmarish quality of the task they were trying to perform. In the cab of each truck sat the driver, usually a Negro, with a mate beside him. They drove like maniacs, hitting the bumps at full speed, rounding curves on the wrong side of the road, roaring through towns; and always the air was filled with the screeching of their brakes and gears. I believe these truck drivers usually ate on the road, and slept in their cabs. They were an epic fraternity, and the story of the Red Ball Express ranks with the story of the covered wagons. It was typically American.

But not the Red Ball Express, nor the appeals to Eisenhower, nor the greatness of the moment itself sufficed. Patton did not get his oil. He had to fall back from the approaches to Germany. He had to relinquish Metz, the taking of which just one month later cost thousands of American lives. He had to abandon his tank drives, and get his infantry up to consolidate his most defensible forward positions from Nancy to Luxemburg. He had to forget his dream of being Conqueror of Berlin, for the time and for all time.

The reasons why Patton outran and ran out of his supplies are obvious. They were chiefly military reasons, and partly political. Militarily, what had happened was that Bradley's First Army and Montgomery's Second British had broken loose from their Normandy bridgeheads, and

EISENHOWER MAKES HIS DECISION

were streaming across France and the Low Countries with a speed comparable with Patton's. Bradley was away soon after Patton, and went 350 miles in thirty days, from the Cherbourg Peninsula to the Belgian-Luxemburg border. Montgomery, driving the sizable remnants of the German Seventh Army across the Seine, drove 300 miles in twenty-five days, from Caen to Brussels. Each army needed millions of gallons of gasoline, and thousands of tons of supplies.

Eisenhower's problem was to divide his available resources equitably among his three field commanders. He had three choices: He could give top priority to Patton, and allow the Third Army to plunge on deep into Germany.

He could give equal priority to the two American armies, finding sufficient supplies for Patton to continue his blitz, while ordering Bradley to drive northeast, and thus pinch out Montgomery.

Or he could apportion each of the three armies an equal part of the available supplies, and make a three-army frontal drive across Western Europe.

He chose the last.

Militarily, the choice was safe. It was safe, because it meant the German armies in France and the Low Countries would be routed and defeated, and the territory would be liberated. More important, it meant that a chain of Channel ports from Brest round to Antwerp should be available for the feeding of the Allied armies in the coming winter. Those armies could not be fed during the winter across the Normandy beaches. The ports indicated were Brest, St. Malo, Cherbourg, Le Havre, Boulogne, Calais, Dunkirk, and Antwerp.

Politically, the choice was wise. The politics of it involved two main factors: The first was the almost unbearable strain the German V-1's, or flying bombs, were putting on the citizens of London; the second factor was the matter of British prestige.

2

About the flying bombs. These had begun to fall on London in mid-June, of 1944. The Londoners had first regarded their coming as a strange and mysterious phenomenon of war. I was in London the night they first arrived, and on subsequent nights until I left for France in early July. I watched, in myself and in my neighbors, our curiosity grow into dread and our dread into a great terror. The statistics eventually published tell no facts worth knowing about the flying bombs, except perhaps the indication of the number of people made homeless. The true facts involved rather the danger of a nervous breakdown on a national scale, the strain on the war workers, the dislocation of human resources, the undermining of the national health from days and nights of danger and hardship. First, therefore, on the list of Britain's requirements was the destruction of the flying bomb launching sites in the Pas de Calais. Churchill himself had emphasized this to Roosevelt and Eisenhower. The British Second Army was within striking distance of the Calais sites. It was imperative that Montgomery clean out this area. Priority, therefore, went to the British Second Army for its drive along the Channel Coast into the Low Countries.

And there was a second consideration: that of British prestige. At the time Eisenhower simply had to make his decision, the war seemed almost won. It looked as though it was going to be won by an American army. The British point of view was that they had fought Germany since 1939, much of the time alone, and they did not want to be still on the beaches of Normandy when American armies were sweeping into the Reich.

Eisenhower's greatness lay in his ability to rise above nationalistic considerations. His belief in Anglo-American solidarity had been his guiding principle since he was Commander-in-Chief in North Africa. To Eisenhower, the British claims were legitimate and right. If he had disregarded them on a gamble for a quick American victory, and had lost; if Patton had become bogged down in the center of Germany and Bradley in the center of France, and the Germans had gone on shooting flying bombs into the center of London, Anglo-American ties might have been strained to a snapping point.

Eisenhower saw the war not simply as a struggle between armies in which soldiers died, but as a struggle between peoples in which civilians died. In England, civilians were dying from blasts and falling masonry faster than soldiers were dying from bullets and shrapnel. From my own experience, I knew it was safer at the front in those days than it was in London.

The Commander-in-Chief, therefore, gave top priority to the British Second Army, with the second priority going to Bradley, the third to Patton. I believed at the time that this prolonged the war; that the gamble of giving everything to Patton might have brought us a sudden, spectacular victory. It would certainly have enabled the Third Army to get through the Siegfried Line with a minimum of difficulty; and this might have resulted in the Germans organizing their last defenses behind the Rhine.

But this is speculation, and the full facts from the military and political archives are not yet available. In the meantime, great things were happening in those days, and one of those great events was the fall of Paris, which was an offshoot of the Third Army's tremendous victories.

CHAPTER XII
THE TANKS STOP

PARIS fell melodramatically, and in a matter of hours had nothing more to do with the war. Patton was almost at Verdun, Bradley at Namur, and Montgomery at Brussels, before the citizens of Paris had finished shouting "Vive!"

All the turbulence of Paris, the premature liberations, the final fall, and the celebrations, were incidental and immaterial to the Third Army, which was still plunging eastward, winning more spectacular victories every day. Paris meant for Patton the loss of the French and Armored Division. Whether he regretted the loss, I never heard. I suspect that he did, because, though there were a lot of hard feelings towards the French, among both tank and infantrymen of the Third Army, with the usual implications of French incompetence and intransigence, the 2nd Armored remained nonetheless a hard hitting, valorous, though somewhat reckless outfit—and Patton wanted just those qualities in his armor. Patton liked the French in general, and Le Clerc, commander of their 2nd Armored Division in particular. I record the high praise and commendation bestowed on this French division by Major-General Wade Haislip, commanding the 15th Corps which spearheaded the Third Army's Argentan offensive. The French 2nd Armored led that run through Le Mans to Argentan, and General Haislip, in the presence of General Patton, commended them highly, and at the same time denied that they were mistreating their prisoners.

Paris fell on Friday, August 25. On Sunday, I left for the Third Army front, leaving Paris without much regret, being tired of a diet of K ration and champagne; also being tired of the continuous popping of rifles by mysterious blackguards called "milices," who inhabited the rooftops of the city and sniped at the rest of the world in the streets below.

In the lovely, sweeping countryside east of Paris, we found Patton still pursuing an enemy so beaten and disorganized that he was no longer putting up even a pretense of orderly resistance. Strange things were happening all along the front. I got the impression, in those late August days, that the German High Command back in Berlin had lost all control of their armies west of the Reich, had written them all off as lost, and were preparing themselves for the sudden collapse of all German resistance on the Western Front.

In the surge of the three complete Allied armies across France and into the Low Countries, Patton's Third Army still plunged forward with its entire right flank exposed to large German forces scattered throughout southwestern and southern France. Five hundred miles to the south, the Seventh Army from Italy had landed without serious opposition on the Côte d'Azur and were moving slowly northward. Tens of thousands of German troops lying between the Third and Seventh armies were moving in all directions, shepherded about by our fighters and fighter bombers.

By the end of August, the retreat of the German armies in eastern France had become another rout. By August 31, the Nazis were running before Patton as they had never run before any other army in history. What was more significant than their speed, was their confusion. Our intelligence picked up their radio messages from headquarters to various elements, instructing the by-passed units to assemble at certain cities for regrouping. Third Army units had already reached such cities, and were beyond them, even as the German High Command radioed its orders. When the stragglers arrived at their assembly points they were ambushed or surrounded.

Every day, Patton's plunging tanks overran enemy headquarters staffs and rear supply dumps. The 4th Armored Division, heading for the Meuse River near Sedan, rolled in upon a German garrison which was taking sun baths, while the officers strolled around in dress uniforms.

In a few days, Patton had crossed the Seine, Loire, Marne, and Aisne Rivers on a wide front. In this territory, which was the scene of the bloodiest battles of the previous World War—a region crossed by rivers and covered with forests—Patton was able to sweep aside hastily erected German defenses, and reduce Château-Thierry, Belleau Woods, Soissons, and Reims for the loss of a handful of men, whose fathers had died in their tens of thousands a generation before.

As we drove eastward, trying to contact the Third Army's forward elements, which were now rumored beyond Verdun—and even in Germany itself—we passed the World War I cemeteries, with their neat white crosses and grandiose winged monuments.

Eventually, we made contact with the 7th Corps, commanded by Major-General Joe Collins, of Cherbourg fame. Sitting in a schoolhouse which General Collins had taken over for his headquarters, we were told that the American advance was controlled now by one factor only: gasoline supplies.

"We are moving as fast as our gasoline can keep up with us," said General Collins. "Crossing the German border and driving deep into Germany is now largely a matter of transportation."

He did not tell us, and we did not know, that even then the last gallons of gasoline were being poured into the engines of our tanks, and that in a few days the whole Third Army was to run dry at once.

General Collins advised us to go to a little town called Braine to see two German trains his troops had ambushed. The ambushed trains were typical, he said, of what had been happening to the Germans in the last week. So we went to Braine, and pieced together the story of the ambushed trains.

In the little station at Braine stood one train of forty cars. Further along the line was a second train, of thirty cars. Both were still smoking.

The station master at Braine told us what had happened. The two trains, he said, were loaded with hundreds of the German Paris garrison, who had left the capital the night before the city fell. They brought with them their women, children, and loot. Also, the freight cars were loaded with Tiger tanks and anti-aircraft guns.

The trains had rolled out of the Gare du Nord at ten-thirty on Thursday night. By seven-thirty Monday evening they had been ambushed by American tanks and artillery, 120 miles east of Paris. The German trains had got as far as Braine. They were making for Reims, not knowing this city, too, was in our hands.

THE TANKS STOP

The ambushing of the trains was pure Hollywood—and pure Patton. As the first locomotive came round the hillside at Braine, a squadron of General Collins' tanks came over the crest of the hill and opened fire, knocking out the engine just as its bogie wheels were on the level crossing. The Lieutenant Colonel in command of the American tank squadron said he had never seen anything like the astonishment and stupefaction on the faces of the Germans when his tanks suddenly swung over the hill and opened fire, knocking out the locomotive with the first shot and shooting up the entire length of the train over open sights.

Behind the engine were long freight cars, carrying three Tiger tanks, which were manned in the German manner and these Tigers fought back, knocking out two American tanks. Then the Americans closed in under the guns of these monsters to within fifty yards of the train, rapidly silencing the three Tigers and a fourth German tank further back along the train. Next, with their machine guns, they drilled the carriages, from which the German troops were firing with rifles and pistols. In half an hour it was all over and the entire personnel aboard the train surrendered.

Further down the line, the second Nazi train was being ambushed by American field guns, placed in position by the gunners who had been forewarned by the station master's sixteen-year-old son, Hubert. Six tank destroyers moved into position, and demolished the second train—which was also carrying tanks—without loss.

The German engineer of the second train tried to keep up steam until his boiler exploded.

The result of the ambush was five Tiger tanks destroyed and two Mark IVs, with 500 prisoners, fifty killed, and a hundred wounded.

The ambush of the German trains was typical of this stage of the war. It was the essence of the thing. When it happened, you began to see the end of all organized resistance. The end did not come then, or later, even when our columns had crossed into Germany itself, because Nazi Germany was not finished politically. After the attempt to end the war by surrendering, engineered in the near assassination of Hitler, in July, the Nazis had eliminated all possibilities of a normal military surrender; and it soon was to become plain that the defeat of Germany meant only one thing: the destruction of the nation.

I recount the history of the ambushed trains, because it was so characteristic of the war at this stage. Once again I was to hear of German trains being ambushed—and this is always high drama. The second instance occurred just west of the Elbe River, near Hanover. Here a little group of Americans were standing one day, well behind our advance lines, when they heard the whistle of a locomotive. They could hardly believe their ears—or eyes—when a German freight train, loaded with tanks and boxcars, rolled past them. They radioed ahead, and this train was neatly knocked out by our forward tanks.

It was now plain that we were advancing faster than the Germans could retreat. The enemy had not even defended the Aisne River crossings from the high ground overlooking them. They had not defended Château-Thierry, Soissons, Belleau Woods, nor the great fortress of Verdun. There was nobody in Metz, when our patrols probed it.

German strategy and tactics were simply explainable at this stage of the war. They were outmaneuvered and beaten, and though they kept on fighting in swirling lines and isolated pockets, they were no longer fighting as an organized army.

Even their small battle units, hastily regrouped all over eastern France, were curious formations. Four hundred prisoners captured by one American division, included representatives of fifty-four different German units—panzer grenadiers, infantrymen, signalers, engineers, cooks, and clerks—from German divisions in every part of Europe.

By the end of August, ten weeks after he had landed in Normandy, Patton had captured 150,519 prisoners—an average of 2,000 a day. Estimated killed and wounded brought the grand total up to some half a million.

We had knocked out hundreds of tanks and guns. We had overrun more than a hundred air fields in the last four weeks of the Third Army's advance.

Yes, at the end of August, the Germans were staggering about the ring of Western Europe, and Patton seemed to be gathering his strength for the knock-out blow.

There was no knock-out blow. There was no blow at all. Suddenly the battlefields grew silent. The tanks stopped. The guns ceased to fire. There was only the soft tread of the infantrymen's rubber boots along the roads leading to the front.

First Patton's Army, then Bradley's, ran out of gasoline. Everyone knew we had stopped, for everyone heard the strange silence. We did not realize at first that the war was not yet ended. The Germans, in fact, felt this first.

We were all to realize it when the first rains fell.

CHAPTER XIII

GERMANY DECLARES A NEW WAR

I

THE change in the course of the war from impetuous speed to sober immobility, from headlong attack to static defense, from riding all day and through the night along the wide roads eastwards to sitting under trees in orchards and groves, was so sudden, unexpected, and incomprehensible that a kind of daze descended over the Third Army; and all of us suddenly felt very tired, and wanted just to lie where we were and sleep.

It could have been a period of very great peril for Patton's entire army. If, on that September 4th, the Germans could have mustered just three full-strength and fully equipped Panzer Divisions, they could have slashed back through our immobile armored vanguards, back to the soft core of our rear echelons, overran our command posts and headquarters, and perhaps have driven back to the gates of Paris.

It was the ideal time for a counterattack. Normally, the Germans always counterattacked at such a moment. That is, they waited until our objective had been reached or almost reached, when we were most exhausted and before we had consolidated. Then, in the classic style, they hit us with fresh troops, drove us back, and frittered away our strength.

That is what they would have done at this historic moment, and that is what their High Command had planned, on paper. But Patton had outmaneuvered them in this, the

GERMANY DECLARES A NEW WAR 183

high strategy, as he had outmaneuvered them in field tactics.

Patton had gone so far and so fast that the Germans had nothing left with which to counterattack.

According to the formal rules of warfare, Patton should have halted his army when Paris had been enveloped and the Meuse River reached. With the river as a holding line, he should have consolidated his gains. Instead, he gambled on a last run, though by then he must have known his supplies, particularly gasoline, could no longer keep up with the rate of his advance. But the gamble was that he would crumble the last German organized resistance in France—the last resistance, in fact, west of the Reich. And this is what he had done.

So when he did have to halt, there was no danger from a counterattack. There were no Germans between him and the Rhine.

The events of the last month had been so spectacular, Patton's victories had been so decisive, that we at the front—and even those in the rear at Supreme Headquarters—still thought we had an indisputable victory within our reach. The mood of the Third Army was still a holiday one. Everyone, gleefully or soberly, according to his temperament, predicted the war would be over in a matter of weeks. None of us dreamed we would be fighting the greatest battle of the war at Christmas time.

The armor proceeded to move into bivouac areas for a rest and refitting. The infantry made themselves comfortable in the fields. Headquarters' staffs moved into châteaux and comfortable farmhouses. Crates of Reims champagne, and the alcoholic loot of the Wehrmacht warehouses were broken open. The correspondents headed for Paris and London.

This was all legitimate enough in view of the circumstances. Patton had taken Verdun. He had entered Metz, and there was no strong resistance even in Europe's mightiest fortress. We assumed the gasoline would come, and soon we should be riding again, this time along the roads of Germany.

What we did not anticipate in our optimistic calculations was a spiritual resurgence within Germany itself.

For within a few days, the German High Command realized that the Allied advances across France and into the Low Countries had halted for lack of supplies. They estimated it would take us at least two weeks to refuel our columns, so they had at least two weeks of grace.

They also had (1) the Siegfried Line; (2) the Rhine River; (3) the Volkssturm; and (4) their secret weapons.

The first three were sufficient military material for reorganizing their defenses of the Heimat. The fourth was sufficient propaganda incentive to rally the home front.

All of Germany suddenly regained hope. They began their new war.

They began it cautiously and expertly. The entire Reichswehr was reorganized. The land forces were strengthened. The Volkssturm was called up. Civilian services were combed for more men. Industry was reorganized to exploit the secret weapons.

On Friday, September 8, the first rockets fell on the city of London. Soon after, the jet planes made their appearance in the skies over Germany. Later still, the new submarines started their work in the seas.

Within a month, all talk of a 1944 victory over Germany had ended. We began to fight the war all over again.

More slowly, more wearily, the American and British

people settled down to a phase of grinding battle and underwent their own resurgence, without which armies in the field are powerless.

2

By mid-September, when Patton was ready to advance again, the Germans had organized their Saar defenses. Recognizing the importance of the fortress of Metz, they manned the twelve forts with officer cadets from a Wehrmacht training school. It took many weeks, with the fiasco of Fort Driant, to get them out.

Now began Patton's greatest campaign—the Saar campaign. It was not a spectacular campaign from the news headline standpoint. It was a dreary campaign for the Third Army troops who fought it. It was costly and heroic and extremely intricate. It entailed crossing a dozen rivers, some, like the Moselle, nearly a mile wide when in flood, some narrow like rapids, with mountains on the far shore. As the rains came in that gray, mysterious Lorraine country, the ground turned to mud. The tanks stuck in the mud, so the infantry began to fight the war.

Patton now proved in this coming campaign that he was a great infantry commander as well as a great tank general. Under his inspiration, the Third Army developed some of the finest infantry divisions in the world. The 5th, 35th, and 90th, were such divisions.

The object of Patton's new campaign was a frontal assault on the Saar industrial area and the Siegfried Line. It was the hardest assignment an American army could have in the winter.

Patton's first task was to capture the city of Nancy, reduce the fortress of Metz, cross the lower Moselle, and advance frontally onto the Saar. His campaign was part of the Allied strategy of crushing German industry, instead of crushing its armies. The Saar was Patton's mission. The Ruhr was Hodges' of the First Army and Simpson's of the Ninth. Silesia, the third great German industrial zone, was an objective of the Russians. Czechoslovakia was assigned to our heavy bombers.

The change in the Allied high strategy was noteworthy. Our war leaders had had to decide almost overnight that German armies were now almost out of our reach. The German High Command had recovered. It had reformed the defenses of the Reich. The supply of manpower was still greater than we could now neutralize. A defensive war, such as they were determined to wage, is light on casualties. Neither our tanks nor guns nor planes could reach soldiers sheltering under concrete forts.

Above all, we feared German scientific and industrial power. The V-2 had materialized. The jet planes were materializing. We were afraid of both weapons. The V-2 had come a little too late in the war to determine the outcome. The Germans had now too many targets; and their main target, our armies in the field, was comparatively immune from this form of attack.

The jet plane was a different menace. It was, militarily, the finest war weapon the Germans had devised. Our air chiefs later admitted that the German jets had them worried almost to the point of distraction. If German factories had been able to produce jets in larger numbers, we might still have lost the war. They would certainly have cleared our bomber fleets and our fighters from the skies.

In addition to the jet fighters, we knew they were working on jet bombers. These would have been an almost ungovernable menace to our ports, supply lines, and armies.

What else they might produce, we did not wholly know. We believed they were working on new explosives and the atomic bomb. German propaganda boasts that they would blow the world to pieces were not to be sneered at.

Nor were their new field weapons—their cannons, automatic rifles, bazookas or panzerfausts (better than ours), and tanks (better than ours).

In the Nazis' design for world conquest, no part of the industrial Reich played a more important part than the Saar, and its adjoining region. Notably in Luxemburg and Lorraine, German military engineers and scientists had planned their new industry, because they could put it all underground. The iron mountains of this strange zone of Europe are honeycombed with workings and tunnels. Herein, the Nazis had built their underground V factories, and planned mass production by means of slave labor.

Patton's first mission, urged upon him by the Allied High Command, was to rush this outer Saar belt which reaches into Lorraine and Luxemburg, and to seize the Nazis' underground installations. This he did, and the results were astonishing.

But first he insured his tactical position by capturing Nancy and prodding at Metz. Nancy, with the last German headquarters in France, fell on September 15. The great road and rail junction where King Stanislaus of Poland once held his court, was taken by a maneuver which was to become a classic of the Patton strategy. The secret of it lay in attacking where the terrain was least favorable; where the local German commander, because of the wooded heights, least expected the major blow to fall. So Patton plunged his tanks and infantry through the Haye Forest to the north of Nancy, then crossed the Moselle before swinging round to take the city from behind. Another force, which the Germans supposed was the main force, came round from the south; and thus Nancy was encircled.

When Patton finally took the fortress of Metz, captured for the first time in a thousand years, he employed this same daring and dangerous tactic, of crossing the wide Moselle River, then in flood, and outflanking the strong point.

Even after Patton had taken Nancy, and crossed the Lower Moselle, the Germans held onto their river line, with Metz as the anchor. They were determined to defend the Saar, and everything here was advantageous for defense. The rivers ran north and south. Behind the Moselle, and running roughly parallel to it, was the Saar River. And behind the Saar River was the Siegfried Line, which had been constructed in this zone in two belts of forts. In between lay the abandoned Maginot Line, some of whose vast forts we were now able to visit. The parts of the Maginot forts which lay above ground looked like stranded whales along the line of the Lorraine hills.

The Germans were now fighting more skilfully and tenaciously than they had ever fought before. The resurgence of their national spirit was apparent. Their soldiers were fighting in defense of the Homeland. Naziism was stronger than ever among them. The battle of the Moselle River became bitter and bloody, and for the first time, Patton's Third Army was making only slow progress at a high cost.

It was the rivers which resulted in the high casualties. Across the wide Moselle, above and below Nancy, above and below Metz, the engineers had built first their light pontoon bridges, then more massive bridges of steel and wood. Nearly all of these bridges were under direct enemy observation, and were constantly shelled, though a thousand smoke-pots sent a gray fog into the sky above them.

As German resistance grew stronger, the terrain more disadvantageous, and the weather less favorable, Patton's aggressive and confident tactics increased. He started about now his classic "steamroller" campaign, which was based on continuous daily attacks and short rushes, across Lorraine to the Saar River and the Siegfried Line.

To attack constantly, with a new limited drive every day, in this terrain and with this weather, was an unprecedented undertaking. The circumstances were these. The autumn rains had set in—and Lorraine is one of the rainiest regions of France. The terrain was rolling and wooded, and crossed with rivers and canals, now in flood. The Moselle was nearly half a mile wide, and growing wider and wilder. Beyond the Moselle were the Meurthe River and the Marne-Rhine Canal. Further to the east was the Saar River, and then the Siegfried Line. One hundred and fifty miles beyond the Saar River was the Rhine.

These were the natural obstacles Patton was attempting to reduce.

More significant was the condition of his army. I have said that the Third Army was designed as a mobile or Blitz army. The emphasis had been on armor. But this terrain was now unsuited for armor. Patton's tank commanders reported that their machines were bogged down in the ooze.

Patton's reply was characteristic. He ordered his subordinates to get their tanks out and keep rolling. Otherwise, he would find commanders who could and would.

It was at this time that he advanced his theory that neither weather nor terrain should stop tanks. He maintained there was a solution. He was determined to fight a winter campaign with a summer army.

There was still another difficulty, even graver than these others. The Allies now had five active armies in the field on the Western Front. In the far north were the Canadians; below them the British. Below them again the First U. S. Army. Next came Patton's Third. And at the bottom of the line, Patch's Seventh.

The Allied Supreme Command was determined to keep all these five armies at full fighting strength, even while forming three new ones. Priority was to go to the new U. S. Ninth Army, whose mission was to be the attack on the Ruhr. A French Army, the Second, was being built up for a drive, with the Seventh U. S. Army, against the lower Rhine and towards Bavaria, which our Intelligence estimated would become a Nazi Redoubt area. And still another army, the shadowy Fifteenth, was envisaged on paper.

The maintenance and creation of these eight armies, comprising some five million armed men, was, for the moment, actually beyond our industrial capacity. Eisenhower again had to make grave decisions as to priority in men and supplies. Every army commander was making heavy demands. For his part, Patton needed, above all, infantry replacements, tanks and tank parts, and heavy ammunition. He never got them in the quantities he wanted, until the war against Germany was nearly ended.

Eisenhower decided that top priority would have to go to our northern armies, for two reasons. First, the classic road into Germany was in the north, across the central German plains to Berlin. Secondly, the heart of German industry—the Ruhr—was opposite the American First and the Ninth Armies. Looking at the terrain—the mountains,

GERMANY DECLARES A NEW WAR 191

rivers, and fortified zones which faced Patton—our High Command decided that his was a fruitless and perhaps impossible assignment. Later, he was given the famous order, to conduct an "active defense"—which was a polite way of telling an aggressive general to stay where he was and make a nuisance of himself.

There was some talk up and down the front at the time that Patton was being discreetly discouraged for political reasons. This was nonsense. General Eisenhower, and our whole High Command, was, in the larger sense, above politics. There were politics between individuals; and some subordinate officers on the joint Anglo-American staff disturbed unity by their personal prejudices and conduct. But no major decision was ever made on petty political or nationalistic grounds. Everything was determined by the urgency of our peril and the desire to defeat Nazi Germany expeditiously and professionally. I can think of no decision or policy or plan which sacrificed this purpose to politics.

And General Patton showed himself above the pettiness of political bickering—even if some of his staff officers did not. He accepted the decisions of the High Command and his Commander-in-Chief Eisenhower as proper and inevitable. He had access to most of the facts, of course, though I was often surprised how little army commanders knew or had been told about our overall strategy, in its political as well as its military ramifications.

Thus, General Simpson of the Ninth Army knew that his army had to stop at the Elbe River in May, 1945; but he did not know why.

Patton's reaction to the necessary starving of his army and the subsequent order to conduct an "active defense" was more stimulating than discouraging to his character. In the days to come he did not change his plan of continuously attacking and advancing at all. He did not change his strategy. He changed his methods.

He told us at a staff conference in Luxemburg, in January, 1945, about the order given him and his army to place a role of "active defense," and the idea amused him and us.

"I don't know what the term means," he said dryly. "Maybe one of you can tell me."

He knew, however, what it did *not* mean—in his thinking. It did not mean establishing a line or being on the defensive. Defense is atheism in Patton's military creed. He has said more times than his listeners can remember that defense is synonymous with defeat.

"Nobody ever successfully defended anything," he says with an air of finality, and off he goes into history, ancient and modern, with references to the Great Wall of China, Troy, Syracuse, and the Maginot Line.

"An army is defeated when it digs in."

His shrewd generalization is prophetic and certainly sums up the German defeat. For that defeat dates from the moment they started building the Atlantic Wall.

3

In September, 1944, even after it became apparent that the Third Army was not at the top of the priority list for men and supplies, Patton nonetheless started his tremendous offensive towards the Saar. Every day, usually in the mornings, when the September mists provided ideal cover, the infantry "went over the top"; and by the day's end, had advanced another two miles, and cleared another half a dozen of the poor, manure-stacked Lorraine villages.

GERMANY DECLARES A NEW WAR 193

During the next three months, Patton's Third Army men were to fight a hundred local engagements, fighting them day after day without cessation, always creeping forward over the low hills, and grinding down the German opposition.

At this time, Hitler called on the two strongest men in the Reich to help shoulder the new war which was now waged on the propaganda level for Germany's survival. Himmler moved into the military picture, as the power behind the Army. Von Rundstedt was recalled, after his eclipse following the Normandy defeats and the suspicion which clouded his name as a representative of the Junker clique which had attempted to kill the Führer. Both Himmler and von Rundstedt personally attended to Patton. Himmler found the men von Rundstedt demanded. Von Rundstedt disposed of them along the Moselle Front.

By October, of 1944, when the first messengers of winter were winging over Europe in tiny, frozen snowflakes, it was obvious that the Germans were almost holding the Allies on the Western Front. The British and Canadians in the far north were facing an immense flood in Holland, and eventually fought their skirmishes from boats, like medieval gondolamen. The First U. S. Army was engaged in a costly, bloody, and unremunerative jungle battle in the Hurtgen Forest. The Seventh Army in the extreme south was held up in the Vosges Mountains.

It was like this for three months. During that period, Patton's was the only army which made any decisive advances at all.

During the week of September 15, Patton destroyed the entire German 16th Infantry Division, 112th Panzer Brigade, many regiments, battalions, or brigades from other units, scores of tanks, hundreds of guns and trucks and enemy rolling stock.

The 112th Panzer brigade was annihilated in a classic battle. Patton sent his infantry against the German tanks, and with artillery and bazookas, drove them back into and through the Forest de Haye, east of Nancy. Meantime, he sent flying armored columns ahead to ambush the Germans as they came out of the forest. By sundown on the day of the battle, this Panzer unit was officially described as annihilated. Of 2,000 men, 500 were killed, 900 captured, and the rest missing.

It was only another local engagement, another day's normal fighting. But Patton was doing it every day—and did it every day for three months, until von Rundstedt's Ardennes offensive, endangering our whole northern front, forced him to call off the Saar offensive at the end of December, just when Patton was about to burst through.

CHAPTER XIV

THE BATTLE OF THE TUNNELS

ABOUT the end of September, it became obvious to Patton that he would have to reduce Metz.

Metz is the mightiest Fortress in Europe. It is one of the fortresses whose foundations were laid in Caesar's time. Metz is symbolic of the dark turmoil of Europe itself. It is more than a fortress. It is a memorial of the fact that in modern wars, fortresses are no longer symbols of strength. Every fortress in the world, when attacked with determination, has fallen. But Metz had never fallen to attack since the time the Huns, in 451, fell upon its soft garrison and sacked the town. It always survived sieges and wars themselves, to change hands endlessly in the dickerings of peace parleys. And so became German, French, German, French, through the centuries. During the Religious Wars of the Sixteenth Century, it stood out against the attacks of Charles the Fifth. It resisted two more sieges in the Napoleonic wars.

It passed to the Germans in the Franco-Prussian War. It never fell to the French in the War of 1914-1918. It passed back to them after the Armistice.

And back it went to the Germans in 1940.

A double ring of giant forts surrounds Metz, and by the time Patton decided to lay siege to the place, the Germans had completed the modernization of the defenses as near to an impregnable fortress as they could make it.

Now the cannon of Fort Driant, one of the twelve bastions which defend the town, were not ancient pieces projecting through stone walls, but modern rifles which could be raised and lowered from steel turrets, sinking down to the safety of concrete chambers. The garrison were immune from shelling and aerial bombardment. And these guns, manned by this safe garrison, controlled the crossings of the Moselle, and its confluence with the Seille River. They also controlled the network of roads which run north to Luxemburg, west to the Saar, and south to Nancy. Metz, indeed, was the crossroads of this region of Europe, and that was why it was a fortress, and why Patton had to reduce it.

The General told us at a conference why he had decided to lay direct siege to Metz, instead of by-passing it. His reason was simple enough—though at the time it seemed strange from a commander whose creed was never to delay for strong points, but to swirl round and beyond them.

Metz, General Patton estimated, would hold down three full American divisions, just to sit outside the fortress and contain it. Further, it would lengthen his route into Germany by over a hundred miles. Without the Metz road net, Patton's forces would have to swing either south through Nancy, or north through Luxemburg before turning east to the Reich frontiers.

On October 1, Patton began his first attack on the medieval fortress. For some reason which was never satisfactorily explained this first assault on Metz was a conventional frontal assault, most nearly resembling the medieval type of siege of any fighting I saw on the battlefields of Europe. Later, when this assault was called off, a failure and a defeat for Patton, it was intimated by spokesmen of his General staff that the Fort Driant attack had been only an experiment.

It had nothing of the appearance of an experiment. As far as I could see in my daily visits to the 5th Infantry Division's command post just outside Driant, we were attempting to assault a medieval fortress in a medieval manner. For almost two weeks a small band of infantrymen attempted to scale the walls of the fortress, dig tunnels beneath it, overpower the defenders in close quarter fighting, and penetrate to the citadel—as warriors had done from the time of the siege of Troy. At first the unfortunate American soldiers who were sent against the walls and into the tunnels of Driant made some progress, which was measured in feet. Eventually, two points in the perimetral defense were supposedly controlled by us—the northwest and southwest corners. To reach these objectives our men had scaled the concrete walls, blasted their way into tunnels, and actually crossed a moat. But the nut of Driant lay deep underground, where the German commander and staff of the garrison controlled, through instruments, the firepower of the bastion. From here, deep underground, the defenders of Driant continued to fire the heavy guns of the fort and the enfilading machine gun fire which made it possible to approach the place only at night.

I went every day for almost a week to the command post of the so-called Warnock Force, which was attached to the 11th Regiment of the 5th Infantry Division, which was making the attack on Driant. The 5th was now one of Patton's elite divisions. There was no question of timidity or holding back, though every man who made that night journey into the tunnels of the fort expected not to return.

So we used to spend the day, sitting in a hillside dugout,

almost overlooking Driant, consulting the detailed maps of the place, and listening to the reports of the grim, red-eyed officers who had just come out of the tunnels. The battle had now settled down to a weird subterranean guerilla warfare, with strange workings through which men crawled not knowing where they were going and suddenly coming to a halt in front of steel doors. They took gas masks with them to survive the fumes. They took acetylene torches and electric drills into the tunnels, and started to bore through the steel doors. Then one brave man would climb through, and they would go a little further to find the tunnel blocked by another door or a pile of rubble. It was a game of ferret and rabbits—and Germans and Americans were both hunters and hunted.

Those who came out of Driant now said it was impossible even to move for hours at a time. They said the Germans were ambushing them in the tunnels, appearing and disappearing as though through trap doors. The infantrymen would run across a level space of ground, only to be machine gunned from the rear, as a miniature turret rose out of the earth and fired into them. Both sides blew in tunnel walls, entombing one another.

This went on for almost two weeks, and soon it became plain that we were sacrificing brave men like rats in tunnels. Patton and his commanding officers had tried everything from artillery barrages to tank rushes to pouring hot oil through the embrasures of the gun turrets. It was daily becoming more medieval and more fruitless. Finally, it was admitted that even though we held 120 yards of the Driant tunnels, we did not know where we were or where to go.

At the end of eight days, we had gained 120 yards of tunnels, lost sixty yards through counterattacks, and captured sixty prisoners. Our own losses were small, because only a few men at a time could get into the fortress enclosure and tunnels. Most of our casualties were caused through subterranean gases and fumes.

After ten days, Patton decided to abandon the assault. I cannot agree that he was wise to have attempted it, and the reason—"for experimental purposes"—was a poor one. He was certainly wise to halt it, on two grounds: first, the simple military ground that he was frittering away material, and time; secondly, the "political" ground, that Fort Driant was fast becoming in the eyes of the uninformed newspaper world another Stalingrad. The eerie "Battle of the Tunnels" had caught the public imagination, and with the usual lack of perspective, people had begun to attach great importance to the success or failure of the Driant siege.

I remember we were summoned by General Gay, Patton's chief of staff and informed that "our troops are withdrawing from Driant." We were also instructed not to send the story to our newspapers. The following official statement was issued as an apology for the Driant failure: "Our casualties were numerically light. Much valuable information on the construction of the forts in the Metz area was gained by our engineers. If it had been thought wise, the fort might have been taken by frontal assault. However, it would not have been worth the necessary casualties involved, inasmuch as Driant was under direct fire from neighboring fortifications. There was never more than one battalion at a time involved in the action against the fort. In action we lost six tanks, less than fifty killed and 300 wounded."

CHAPTER XV

ASSAULT ON THE SAAR

I

ALL during the period that the 5th Infantry was attacking Fort Driant, Patton's army was driving forward across Lorraine in a series of daily battles which no one but a general supremely confident of his men's stamina would have launched. Patton had always expected his tanks and infantry to do superhuman things. This was embodied in his old battle-cry: Attack, attack, and when you can't go forward any longer, attack again. He had expected this of American soldiers in Tunisia, but our troops down there had not yet acquired this ruthless philosophy of the professional soldier. They had begun to acquire it in Sicily, where they did overcome the unendurable heat and the insurmountable terrain.

But hitherto, Patton had always had his tanks. His army, in its drive across France, could attack all he wanted, because it was not a tired army; and most of the time it was not fighting at all, but riding trucks along the highways, cleaning out pockets of enemy resistance and snipers in towns, woods, and fields.

Now it was winter. Now the tanks could move only on the roads, and only on some roads. Now Patton's army was depleted. A comparatively small force of some six experienced divisions had the whole task of driving forward, day after day. These divisions were always attacking—the 5th and 90th Infantry, the 4th and 6th Armored. They always had a new river to cross, a new strong point in some town to reduce. And ahead of them lay other rivers, becoming wider and deeper, until the Rhine itself.

In those October-November days, when a great sense of weariness and apathy fell over the Third Army, so that men became more grim-faced, more silent, more bundled up in old clothes every week, Patton retained his love of war and his faith in the gospel of attack. His headquarters were in Nancy. He was not seen much at this time, for he was planning the fall of Metz. The assault of Driant had been brushed aside as an engineering experiment which did not work. Patton was now about to use strategy.

The plan of attack looked terrifying on the maps, and even more terrifying on the actual terrain itself. Conventionally, it was a wide flanking movement, with the customary two arms of the pincers swinging round the fortress city and closing in behind. But what Patton was now about to undertake was certainly not conventional. Indeed, it looked scarcely possible. For what he was calling on his battle-weary troops to do was to fight an amphibious action across a river some three-quarters of a mile wide in places.

The river which had to be crossed above Metz was the Moselle. The autumnal rains and drizzle had flooded the banks, so that the little islands around which the flood swirled were all under water. On the eastern side of the Moselle, the ground rose to dominating heights, and these heights were held by the enemy. The German defense of the Moselle had been completed by the time Patton decided to attack. It was a characteristically thorough and efficient defense. On the high ground were the observation posts. Beyond lay their big guns. On the forward slopes were many batteries of 88s, interconnected by trenches and barbed wire. Along the river bank itself were their machine gun nests and infantry outposts.

Patton selected his veteran 90th Infantry division to make this water jump. The 90th had been fighting all the way across France. Elements of it had landed on D Day, when the division had been attached to Bradley's First Army. It had been the infantry division which had ridden with the spearhead armor in the encirclement of von Kluge's Seventh Army. It had marched and trucked its way across France, and wherever Patton needed experienced infantry, the 90th was likely to appear. Its casualties had been heavy. Its replacements numbered thousands. It had had several commanding generals. I remember a young-old rifleman of the 90th, relaxing over a glass of beer in a café saying that the company commanders came and went so fast that the guys didn't even have time to learn their names. These lieutenants and captains came from the replacement centers. They went into little graves all over Europe.

The southern arm of Patton's pincers on Metz was fashioned from the 5th Infantry, whose combat experience, length of service, and unit valor were comparable with the 90th.

The 95th division was to be used in a frontal feint.

The attack went off according to plan, but how inadequately that trite military cliché describes the gray morning when the first assault troops slipped their rubber boats into the swirling river and started their watery journey. Patton's artillery was giving them full support, of course. But once out on the tide, there was nothing to do but keep paddling until they reached the far shore. Meantime, other assault infantrymen were scrambling across the wreckage

ASSAULT ON THE SAAR

of a bridge, swinging through the water, sometimes falling into it and being swept away by the current. Behind the infantrymen came the engineers, and they started their pontoon bridges under observed enemy shellfire.

These river crossing attacks, of which Patton made over thirty in his European campaign, were to me always the most unbelievable, grim, and even impossible feats of arms. A river crossing has an almost painfully dramatic aspect, for in no other type of offensive do the ordinary soldiers seem so touched with tragedy and marked for death. River crossings always begin the same way. The night before, the men move down to the bank in preparation for the assault. They march down the dust roads or lanes or through a wood, one behind the other, and all their faces are quite expressionless, as they step each in the other's footsteps. The riflemen carry their rifles and spare ammunition. Bazooka men march along with their queer iron pipes. Aid men, with their four red crosses on each side of the helmets, intersperse the column. This man carries a walkie-talkie. That man is borne down by a heavy machine gun or mortar. The narrow-faced captain who commands the company is moving back and forth along the line. The round-faced lieutenant keeps his position. Jeeps loaded with supplies follow the column. So they all go down to the river, and on the bank quietly sink down, to lie on their backs and gaze at the night sky. When I went with them I used to half wonder of what they were thinking. But I say it was painful to see them and wonder about them. And the only thing to do was to share their silence and their fear.

I remember following such a river assault party down to the Saar River, south of Trier. The double column of men was just the same: the same weapons, the same uniform, the same expressions or lack of expressions. We assembled in a village, where the infantrymen sat against the walls of the German houses. As we drove by one house, there was a rifle shot, and then the cry of "Medics! Medics!" A soldier had just shot himself in the foot. Nobody took much notice. The divisional general was there at the head of the column, waiting for zero hour. There was supposed to be an artillery barrage, which never came. He was deciding whether or not to cross without it. His regimental colonel was discussing it. The captains and lieutenants stood by, awaiting orders. The infantrymen sat or stood where they had halted. I noticed one boy with the iron pipe of a bazooka over his shoulder. His chin was wobbling up and down. I tried to smile at him as best as I could, and said, "Hallo." All he said, for some strange reason, was, "How long you been away from the States?" It showed what he was thinking about. Not he, or the others, from the general to the riflemen, were thinking about the man who had shot himself through the foot. Their supreme indifference was strange and significant.

That was what the river crossings were like, except this crossing of the Moselle by the 90th was, on the map and on the spot, seemingly impossible. And that was why Patton chose it for his major attack on Metz. He was not supposed to cross here, on the maps or on this terrain.

Perhaps that was why the 90th got across, and received from Patton his highest commendation. They got across, according to that plan you heard so much about. That means some of the rubber boats arrived safely on the east bank of the river. Some riflemen got away and up the slopes of the hills. Some engineers lived to span the river with a pontoon bridge. And some tanks and supplies were landed on the far shore.

The 90th's immortal feat in crossing the Moselle in mid-November, and the successful attacks of the 5th and 95th Divisions completed the encirclement of Metz within a week; and we fought our way into the town itself on November 19. This did not mean that the twelve forts which ring it had fallen. Most of these, including the main bastion Driant, never fell to direct assault. But one by one they surrendered. I record that they surrendered, because we were not allowed to say so at the time, for some specious and surely foolish reason that the families of the fortress commanders would have been persecuted and perhaps killed by the Gestapo or SS, if the fact of surrender had been known. We were told by Patton's chief of staff that this would have a discouraging effect on other German commanders wishing to surrender on this front or other fronts. Obviously, the German High Command knew that the forts surrendered. And I could not see how it was our responsibility if the Germans were killing the wives and families of their own soldiers. I do not think we had any control over the passions of the Nazis at any period of the war.

So I record that all the main Metz forts—Driant, Jeanne d'Arc, Marival, Verdun, and Queuleu—surrendered and were not captured. Most of them surrendered to our parleying officers—often a junior officer of Jewish descent.

The capture of Metz and the surrender of all its forts was, I think, the greatest victory won by American soldiers over German soldiers. Patton's plan had been brilliant. But in a sense, it had been illegitimate, because it could rightly have been criticized as impossible from the soldiers' point of view. A general must make his plans always with two human factors in mind, because these human factors determine the success or failure of the plan; the norm of his troops' courage is the first human factor. Thus, experienced troops have more courage than green troops, and fanatical troops more courage than experienced troops. The endurance of the average soldier is the second consideration. Fatigue, hunger, and wet feet are digits in the mathematics of high strategy.

In expecting civilian soldiers to make this crossing of the Moselle, Patton showed his love of war, with its resultant attitude that the good soldier is superhuman in his capability for daring and enduring. It was only because, under this stern and inhuman régime that a division like the 90th had become a unit of incredibly good soldiers that the plan had succeeded. A month later, Patton was to use this same 90th Division in another "impossible" offensive into the Siegfried Line at Dillingen. I will tell of the Dillingen episode in its place. It also illustrates what Patton could do with young men who had once been clerks, laborers, and students in the peace-loving communities of America.

Metz was a great strategic victory, and even a rather merry one. All manner of important and curious German characters were taken in the town; of whom the most important and the most curious was SS General Anton Dunckern.

Since General Patton informed SS General Dunckern to his face that he was "the lowest form of animal life I have met," the Nazi deserves a comment.

2

Anton Dunckern was captured slipping across a bridge from the old Île of the city, where he had been trapped with his headquarters staff. There was a rumor that he had been caught hiding behind a huge barrel of beer in the town brewery, and this was the story the more exuberant reporters cabled out to the world. He was caught on the bridge with his aide and a lone German soldier by a 5th Division patrol which was riding through the streets of the liberated town. The tired, dirty G.I.s had no idea of the importance of their captive, but turned the SS general over to the military police, and so he found his way to Division headquarters.

Dunckern was put on display in a not strictly military manner, but such a vile man could expect no other. I never saw a Nazi thug typify so strongly the peculiar foulness of his caste and creed. Dunckern was a Hollywood Nazi. To begin with, he was round and piglike, with most of his weight round his belly and his buttocks. He was lashed in with a thick leather belt. Above his huge girth was a bull-like neck, rising into a pink, smooth face, in which popped forth two froglike eyes. Dunckern's aide was a Colonel Constantine Meyer, who, now that the pair were in the hands of the Americans, demanded to be kept as far from the SS General as possible.

Dunckern began by being truculent. He demanded to see General Leroy Irvin, commander of the 5th Division. He was told the American general was busy fighting a war, and had no time to converse with a policeman, which was apparently the SS General's function. Then Dunckern demanded special food, specially served. He was informed he could eat what the American officers ate, when they ate it. He wanted hot water and soap.

Dunckern, who, investigation showed, was actually Gestapo chief for the entire Moselle area, was responsible to no one but Himmler. He was not strictly a soldier. The defense of Metz had been in Colonel Meyer's hands. Another Gestapo chieftain taken at Metz was a Major Schmidt, whose title was "Executioner for Metz." Schmidt was responsible to Dunckern. Schmidt and 250 Gestapo men were captured in the Metz barracks.

Patton asked to see Dunckern and Meyer. We correspondents were not present at the interview, but the General told us about it later. The two generals, American and German, were a strange contrast. Patton, as always on these occasions, had bedecked himself in his most splendid uniform; and across his round chest ran five rows of decorations and orders. Patton can stand very straight and tall and impassive. Before and below him stood the SS Gestapo General, frog-eyed, round-mouthed, pink-skinned, barrel-waisted, thick-legged.

Coldly, Patton asked the German why he had not stayed with his men, to fight and die with them, as he had announced he would. Dunckern protested that he had the right, as a soldier, to surrender honorably. Patton replied Dunckern was not a soldier, but a Gestapo agent; and his surrender, hiding in a brewery and running across a bridge, without trying to fight his way through, was not honorable. Patton closed the interview by informing Dunckern that he was a coward and "the lowest form of animal life I have met."

Patton's scorn and hatred of this Nazi-Gestapo type are

significant of his attitude. Conversely, his courtesy towards the stiff, Prussianized Colonel Meyer, who was a soldier and not a Nazi official, was indicative. Meyer, with good reason, protested that Dunckern had spied on his activities as commander of the Metz garrison; that he, Meyer, detested the man, and asked only that he should not be imprisoned with the SS General or made to ride in the same vehicle with him.

Patton commended Meyer as a soldier of the old school, and granted him his wishes.

It raises the question whether Patton hated Germans. There is no argument concerning his often stated intention to kill as many of them as he could—an intention he translated into grim action. But in his own conduct, thinking, and words he had always seemed to express a similar philosophy to that which the Prussian Colonel Meyer no doubt held: the philosophy of the soldier caste, which emphasized the virtues of duty, discipline, valor, and death on the field of battle. Patton and Meyer were soldiers with the same creed. The fact of nationality alone made them enemies. But they were enemies by necessity, not inclination. That is simply the fact of the matter. But it does not make Patton a Nazi, as is shown by his reaction to Dunckern, who was the epitome of Naziism.

As Patton hated Nazis and their Dunckerns, so they hated him. They took the trouble to drop leaflets on a German prison camp at the medieval walled city of Toul, behind the Third Army front, in which they urged the prisoners to escape, on one side, and warned them they were in the hands of America's leading gangster and Public Enemy Number One, on the other. This was General Patton, who was accused among other things, of mistreating his prisoners.

The "mistreated" prisoners meekly turned over the leaflets to their American guards.

3

With Metz reduced, Patton began his massive assault on the Saar basin. He used his entire army of six infantry and three armored divisions in a steamroller attack, which pressed back the Germans a few miles each day, along a front extending from Luxemburg in the north to the foothills of the Vosges Mountains in the south.

This Saar offensive was one of the greatest sustained campaigns in modern history. It was made during the worst European weather on record. Every day on this dreary Lorraine front it rained. It was a teeming rain, which gradually gave the fields, forests and hillsides an underwater look, so that after two weeks of it, only the raised roads, railways, dikes and high ground stood out above the gray lakes which the rain had made. Trees and bushes projected, and in the covered fields, you could see the stiff legs of dead cattle pointing heavenward. The cows and horses which had escaped the constant artillery barrages could find no fodder and stood forlornly beside the abandoned farms.

Just to drive along the roads under these conditions was a grim experience. We all froze and shivered, and wiped the mud from our faces. For the infantrymen it was the acme of war's misery; and toiling through the mud, fording streams, digging their little slit trenches at sundown, they began to hate war with as much fervor as Patton loved it.

For Patton, still located in a big house in Nancy, this

ASSAULT ON THE SAAR

relentless, massive drive to the Saar, was a beautiful example of war. It was beautiful on the maps. We used to study the campaign in the War Room at headquarters on a vast map which showed the position of every company in the Third Army and every enemy unit. This War Room was the nerve center of Patton's army, and it was kept by a flock of staff officers and soldiers in a typical Patton style. Into this room, and onto the maps, flowed every detail of information from the front, relayed back from company command posts, through the Battalion, through the Regiment, through the Division, through the Corps, and so into Army. Correspondents who had been that morning with a company were somewhat surprised to see the kind of report which the Intelligence officers were chalking onto the master map, because there was often a wide variance in the facts. Two enemy tanks with a company of infantry had a way of becoming ten tanks with a battalion of infantry.

Every day at five o'clock in the evening, there was a briefing by the staff officers. Punctually at five, the sergeant-at-arms at the door of the War Room would shout "Hup!" and the Commander of the Army would march in, followed by the quiet chief-of-staff, General Gay. Patton would look coldly round the room, say "Sit down, gentlemen," and the briefing would begin.

Usually Patton had come in from the field. During those wet, cold days, he was bundled up, like any G.I. The cold and rain gave him a tired, aged appearance, and if he decided to add anything to the briefing, it was in a quiet, high-pitched voice. When he spoke he would leave his mouth rounded between sentences, and seemed to go off into a daydream.

What we saw on the vast map was this: Three columns

of combined armor and infantry were driving steadily on Saarbrücken, key city of the Saar basin and vital road, rail, and industrial center.

One column was coming up from the southwest, paced by tanks of General Wood's 4th Armored Division and supported by the 35th Infantry. Wood's tanks were now, after a long delay, fitted with "Ducks' Feet," which enabled their treads to find some traction in the muddy fields. Mile by mile, they had rolled across fifty miles of Lorraine to the small town of Saint Jean Rohrbach, fifteen miles from Saarbrücken and eight miles from the German border.

A second column, making the central drive, was lead by the 6th Armored Division, supported by the 80th Infantry. In this type of fighting, the infantry usually preceeded the tanks—or more likely the tanks got stuck in the mud, where they had to await special trucks with winches to drag them out. This often took several days. But the advance went on; and the 6th and 80th fought to within eighteen miles of Saarbrücken and nine of the German border.

Further north, the 90th Infantry and the 10th Armored were driving to the satellite towns north of Saarbrücken—Saarlautern, Dillingen, and Merzig.

As the Americans advanced, they passed through the main and switch fortifications of the Maginot Line. This monstrous French fiasco was now derelict, and the Germans rightly made no attempt to use it. I spent a day inside one of those big forts, Brehain, near Aumetz, wandering along its two miles of tunnels, looking at its workshops and underground factories, climbing into its turrets, and learning that 650 men, with thirty-six officers had been confined in this damp tomb for eight months.

The function of these 686 officers and men was to tend

two 135 cannon; four 75s, and various small machine guns. The officers carried pistols. The men had no weapons at all. These 686 men, entombed underground, to tend six smallish cannon, was about the most futile example of war I had yet seen. In the open field—where the guns could be moved around, as guns must be to be effective—some forty men could have handled these pieces, offensively or defensively, as the situation demanded.

The French had spent many millions of dollars in building this single fort, which was hidden deep in a dark forest; with their money had gone their hopes. And however stupid the concept of the Maginot Line may have been, the hopes which built it were legitimate enough. The French had built a wall round their prosperous, peaceful country, as the Romans had built a wall across the north of England to keep out the barbarous Picts and Scots; and the Chinese had built a wall to keep out the Mongols. The Maginot Wall proved, indeed, Patton's theory: that walls never stopped anybody. This was literally true of the Maginot Line. The weird French engineer who showed me over Brehain told me that the 686 men emerged from it after the armistice without ever having fired a shot from their six cannon.

"They were very discontented," he said. "It is not a nice place in which to spend eight months, especially as they let the soldiers out for only an hour or two once a week. When they finally came out for good, their skins were not white, but blue."

The Maginot Forts, I used to think, as we drove past them, standing like neolithic mounds on the rolling hillsides, are now as remote in history as the pyramids. They have the same ineffable and mysterious quietness, so that if you were not told what had been their purpose and function, you would associate them with some strange Druidic rites.

The Germans did not trouble to use the Maginot Line even as a stopgap. First the line was built to face east, though the fortress guns had a 360-degree traverse. Secondly, the Germans had already stripped the serviceable cannons from the Maginot, and had used them to increment their Atlantic Wall. So Patton's troops passed through the Maginot Forts without much difficulty. There was one strange incident. One day Sergeant William H. Whiteside, of the 80th Division wandered into a fort called Bambesch, unarmed except for a candle, by whose light he was investigating the tunnels in search of loot, for which the American soldier would have passed through the Gates of Hades. In the story we wrote of Sergeant Whiteside, the illegal pursuit of loot became a legitimate search for a mattress, on which to lay his weary limbs. Whiteside picked up a Nazi bayonet in his meanderings. He was accompanied by Lieutenant Donald Hall of his artillery battalion, and the two of them descended fourteen flights of the stone stairways, leaving their rifles and walkie-talkie equipment propped against the steel door at ground level.

Down in the bowels of the earth, the two men lost each other; and from what I saw of that deep concrete tomb called Fort Brehain, this would have been a nightmare to a man not in search of subterranean treasure. Whiteside, with candle and souvenir bayonet, wandered about happily, until he heard a voice in the darkness say, "Hallo, Hans."

Whiteside rapidly changed from souvenir hunter to soldier. He put out his candle and stood against the wall, as a figure came along the tunnel, still calling peremptorily for "Hans!"

When the German passed, Whiteside jumped behind

him, and stuck his bayonet against the man's back.

Whiteside did not speak German, but he had learned a few phrases from one of those pocket guidebooks the Army issued to soldiers, in Ireland, England, North Africa, France, and Germany. By means of Anglo-German gibberish, Whiteside discovered he had his bayonet in the back of a German lieutenant. He concluded that there were other "Krauts" in the fort, and told the German lieutenant it would be advisable to round them up. "Quick! Boom, boom," said Sergeant Whiteside.

So they proceeded downstairs and upstairs, and along the corridors, and into the little cell-like barrack rooms; and at each stop, the lieutenant shouted, "Raus!"

From barracks, storehouses, and engine rooms, came the Germans, singly, by two's and three's, and in little groups of six, until the line marching ahead of the lieutenant, who marched ahead of the sergeant, contained sixty-three men.

The column, in good military formation, then marched up the fourteen flights of stairs to the entrance. Lieutenant Hall was waiting here, and that was what he saw march out of the underground bastion: sixty-three German soldiers, one officer, and Sergeant Whiteside.

This little incident is strange and true and significant. It is significant of the kind of soldier the ordinary American civilian had turned into in Patton's Third Army. In appearance, he was a large, slow-moving, slow-speaking young man in a rather dirty uniform, his head covered by an extinguisher-like bowl, his steel helmet. Over his back hung his rifle, which did not look as though it had been used much. This soldier was always looking for souvenirs, poking around houses, turning over piles of abandoned German equipment, sitting in cafés, drinking beer with a bovine look, and avoiding all officers and what he called brass in general.

Back of the front line, in the rest areas, this immortal unknown soldier, called the G.I., was a simple, inarticulate man whose reactions always seemed to me essentially child-like. I remember telling a group of them who had just been relieved from outpost duty that I could cable a short letter home for all of them who lived in Chicago. They did not really believe me—that the letter would arrive in Chicago that afternoon, or that I would trouble to send it, for them individually and for nothing. Because I was a correspondent, and a bit like an officer, they thought they were really being told to do something. So they did it—they went each to a corner of the garden where we were standing, squatted on one leg in the way they had, and began laboriously to write their little notes. I was able to persuade them eventually that neither my paper nor I were philanthropists or Red Cross workers; but this was a newspaper stunt, and their letters would appear in print, as well as being delivered to the addressees—and so it was a good thing for all of us, if they liked to do it.

Then their basic personality reasserted itself a little, and the smart ones began their humorous patter and the eager ones consulted me for more details, and the slow ones licked their pencils with their tongues. I looked at them all, sitting with their little pieces of paper, their expressions grave and concentrated, and their innocence and youth were such as to pain the heart a little. So did their letters, written in large, round script, sending their love to their wives and children in poignantly trite phrases like "I love you, darling."

These men, who in their battle setting always seemed touched with battle's strange beauty, were the result of Patton's love of war. That love had, by keeping these infantrymen constantly in danger, metamorphosed them from adolescent civilians into "old" soldiers. It had made them into expert killers, which was a source of constant gratification to Patton, who considered that his theories of training, discipline, and self-abnegation had been vindicated. But the vindication was at the expense of the bodies, minds, and souls of these big, simple men, who fought every day more like automata, growing every day more mentally and physically tired, until some of them seemed like the shells of men.

It explains why Sergeant Whiteside, with a candle and a souvenir bayonet, wandered into a Maginot Fort and emerged with sixty-four German prisoners. Whiteside was just another big, old Patton soldier, and to him, darkness, tunnels, and subterranean whisperings were threads in the pattern of his life.

What Patton had done to Americans was epitomized in the saga of Dillingen, which was to come later, and about which I shall tell.

CHAPTER XVI

PATTON'S GOOSE—AND THE SIEGFRIED LINE

I

THESE incidents related in the foregoing chapter concern individuals in the Saar offensive. In them I have tried to tell something of what the conditions of terrain and weather and just ordinary events were like. All these things, when translated into the blue and red rings and lines and arrows on Patton's maps, began to add up to a massive offensive which was again swinging the war on the Western Front in favor of the Allies.

This could not be said of the offensives on the other fronts. The British, Canadians, and Poles in the extreme north, the Ninth and First U. S. Armies below them, and the Seventh and First French Army to the south of Patton, were all attacking at this time, with as much weight and perhaps with as much skill, but without the progress which distinguished Patton's campaign.

For by the end of November, Patton had reached the Saar and the German frontier on a fifty-mile front, having advanced his whole Army over sixty miles in thirty days, clearing 2,000 square miles of territory, capturing hundreds of towns and villages, and accounting for 100,000 Germans, killed, captured, or wounded.

Strategically, he had reached his objective. He was on the Saar. Now, without pausing, he prepared to smash through the Siegfried Line, and storm into Germany itself.

PATTON'S GOOSE—AND THE SIEGFRIED LINE 219

Merzig, Saarlautern, Dillingen, Volklingen, Saarbrücken, and Sarreguemines—all the great industrial towns of the Saar—were now within range of Patton's heavy guns. A massed artillery bombardment, preparatory to continued infantry assaults, began.

Patton told us at his staff conferences that he was going to assault the Siegfried Line. Earlier he had said, "We'll go through the Siegfried Line like crap through a goose." But from the aerial reconnaissance photos and ground reports which were coming in, some of us began to say that Patton's goose looked as though it might be more constipated than he had anticipated.

The task of assaulting a line like the Siegfried was the biggest Patton or any other general so far had faced in this war. Actually, it needed far more men than Patton had available in his Third Army. That army had been seriously depleted by the grinding, relentless offensive up to the Saar. Patton was not getting replacements in the numbers he needed. About now, he started feeding his army from its own body. He streamlined staff and service personnel, and many officers and men who had sat in the safety of houses now found themselves in foxholes at the front.

Where Patton said he would attack the Siegfried was also where it happened to be strongest. It ran along the Saar River in a thick belt, which even on the maps looked like the thickest defenses I had ever seen. These defenses consisted roughly of machine gun concrete emplacements as outposts. Behind were the dragon's teeth or tank traps. Between outposts and tank traps ran barbed wire to catch the infantry. Beyond lay the subterranean forts, all interconnected by trenches and telephone. Further back lay the main forts. And in the rear waited the big guns.

This formed the main belt. There was a secondary belt, or switch, in the hills beyond. For not only had Patton to attack fixed defenses—he had to attack up hill.

The German counter-strategy seemed to be to let Patton come. They intended to grind up his tanks and infantry between the teeth of the Siegfried fortifications. They also kept small reserve forces of armor to counterattack any penetrations.

In spite of the awful difficulties and obstacles, Patton confidently announced he would assault the Siegfried Line— and assault it frontally.

The attack began on November 29, when one of the newer divisions which had come to Patton's Army, the 95th Infantry, edged its way to the top of an 1100-foot hill, from where forward observers could look down on Saarlautern, three miles away. All along the front, Patton pushed forward his veteran and war-weary divisions closer to the Line. The 5th and 80th moved up. The 90th moved into position for its assault on Dillingen. The Germans suddenly reacted violently to Patton's pressure. The reason became apparent later. For at this very period, November-December, 1944, von Rundstedt was planning, in his headquarters at Trier on the Moselle, the last German offensive of the war—the Ardennes offensive. Therefore, Patton's continuous and relentless drive into the Saar was upsetting von Rundstedt's calculations. Von Rundstedt intended to strike further north, across the Luxemburg frontier; but his chances of succeeding were threatened, if Patton broke through the Siegfried Line to the south. For then the Third Army would be on von Rundstedt's flank, and, in some places, behind his Panzer army.

And so reserve forces, now gathering in the forests along

the Luxemburg-German border, were quickly moved south to try and stop Patton's penetrations. They were moved hurriedly, and they were moved in insufficient strength. That was where von Rundstedt blundered fatally. Urged on by Nazi quasi-military hopes of a decisive blow against the weak center of the Allied Western line, von Rundstedt did not spare enough troops to effectively hold Patton.

Instead, he tried a series of sharp counterattacks over a period of three or four days, which had no effect on Patton's drive, frittered away the reserves of the Ardennes Panzer army, and eventually caused von Rundstedt to strike in the Ardennes almost two weeks earlier than he had intended.

Nobody in the Allied ranks, from General Eisenhower down to the company rifleman, knew at this time of von Rundstedt's counter-plans, which were to materialize a few weeks later in the desperate and dangerous Ardennes breakthrough. All we knew on the Third Army front was that for three days the Germans put in a series of savage counterattacks, coming out of the white mists which swirled in wraiths over the gloomy landscape as many as twelve times in a day. Patton remarked at the time that these counterattacks were curious. He understood their intention, but did not understand why they were so inadequately mounted. The Germans came behind occasional tanks, which made hit and run raids on the Americans, then disappeared into the misty hinterland which was Germany. In other words, von Rundstedt was making a feint of resistance—and Patton was never stopped by feints.

We counted almost fifty sizable counterattacks along the Third Army front on the last day of November and the first day of December. All were grim and determined, but none was strong enough to do more than shock our troops, who withstood the shock and pressed on again.

Then the counterattacks ceased as suddenly as they had begun. Von Rundstedt had withdrawn his reserves to re-assemble them in the forests across the Luxemburg border. He gambled on the Siegfried Line holding Patton.

The Line did not hold him. First, the 4th Armored Division crossed the Saar River south of Sarreguemines. In the extreme north, the 10th Armored drove to the same river and stood within sight of the industrial town of Merzig, marking the northern limit of the Saar zone. In between, the 90th Division crossed the river and fought its way into Dillingen. South again, the 95th finally broke into Saarlautern.

Patton was now into the Saar, and into the Siegfried Line itself. To the correspondents, riding sixty and seventy miles to the front from Nancy, and back in the same day, it didn't seem to mean much, because the rain was still streaming down, the whole earth had turned into mud, the tanks lay all over the waterlogged fields with tracks torn off, and the infantry was desperately weary. But the General was unusually cheerful and confident. Everything was going according to plan.

The 10th Armored was waiting outside Merzig. The 90th Infantry was waiting to go into Dillingen. The 95th was in Saarlautern. Five more divisions, two armored and three infantry, were closing in on the Saarbrücken-Sarreguemines-Forbach triangle. In brief, Patton was attacking with eight divisions on a forty-mile front, and the German resistance showed signs of collapsing under his hammerlike blows. This was what was meant by "according to plan."

Things began to move fast now. By December 7, the entire Saar region west of the Rhine, was threatened by the

PATTON'S GOOSE—AND THE SIEGFRIED LINE 223

Third Army. Patton was on the High Command objective. He now had six beachheads on the east bank of the Saar River. The major cities of the Saar itself had been captured or fired by long-range artillery and aerial bombardment. Patton's gunners had poured 3360 rounds from 155-millimeter guns, eight-inch guns and 240 howitzers into Saarbrücken alone during the last seven days. Further back, Zweibrücken, Neunkirchen, and Kaiserslautern were blazing from bombing. Germany's third largest industrial zone was about to be reduced.

It seemed that about now Patton began to do more impossible things; and nothing was more indicative of his warlike mentality and the effect of that mentality on the American army than his assault on the Siegfried Line. The Line here was directly across the Saar River, and we were to discover that the great industrial cities on the banks of the river—Merzig, Fremersdorf, Dillingen, Roden, Saarlautern, Fraulautern, Saarbrücken, and Sarreguemines—were actually and literally fortress towns built into the wall, as watchtowers and inhabited places were built into the Roman walls.

2

The most remarkable example of an entire town designed and built as a fortress was Dillingen, which the 90th Division attacked and entered on December 7. For a general even to undertake such a mission as the attack on Dillingen seemed, on the face of it, futile and suicidal, for this is what the tired, battle-drunk 90th had to do:

It had to cross a river, now in flood and loose from its channel—the river, with the contingent mudflats, being over a mile wide. It had to cross this river in boats directly against Siegfried forts and defenses which extended from the east bank of the river to the summit of the hills ten miles further back. When it landed, the advance elements of the Division were required to enter the town of Dillingen, clean it out, move further inland, reduce opposition from the pillboxes and forts built into the overlooking hillsides, and clear the high ground beyond, which the enemy was using for observation over the entire area and the action being fought there.

Nor was Patton's assault on Dillingen the only frontal attack on Siegfried towns. Further down the river, the 95th Infantry was required to make a similar attack on Roden and Fraulautern; and further south still, the 35th was engaged in like manner on the lesser fortress of Sarreguemines.

The reason Patton's assaults across the Saar looked suicidal was the apparent impossibility of building and maintaining bridges across a river which was dominated by fortified heights. The most desperate adventure of war is to place men, whether airborne or waterborne, in a position where they are cut off from their rear and their supplies.

Patton now began placing his forces in this position. It is true the 95th and 35th Divisions not only had bridgeheads across the Saar, but bridges. But these supply lines were too slender and too impermanent to support the attacking forces. And at Dillingen it proved impossible to build a bridge at all. Every time the engineers got their pontoons a little way out into the tide, the Germans, by direct observation, sunk them by artillery fire.

Even when it became obvious that a bridge could not be built across the Saar at Dillingen, Patton ordered General Van Fleet, commanding the 90th, to press the attack. And this is what was done, resulting in perhaps the most astonish-

PATTON'S GOOSE—AND THE SIEGFRIED LINE 225

ing and incredible feat achieved by any infantry division in the war. For here at Dillingen, across a wide river and into the heart of the Siegfried defenses, was ferried almost the entire division, which was supplied and maneuvered on the far banks for sixteen days, without a single bridge to support their attack.

The story of the 90th's saga in Dillingen cannot be told in detail here,* but it is an example of what had happened to the individual American soldier under a field commander whose creed of war is that nothing is impossible. These once-green American boys from the towns and villages of America were now able to live for three days on a single K ration per man, drinking water taken from shell craters, carrying their comrades with trench feet back to their posts, and fighting with rifles and bazookas against concrete fortifications, for the sixteen days they were ordered to stay there. Food and ammunition were sent across the river at night, with a long line of men handling the boxes down to the river banks. Ferries then made the crossing under shell and machine gun fire. Medical supplies were flown in by Piper Cub observation planes. A few tanks were ferried across, and rolled up the far banks on cordwood roads.

The doughboys began to live a fantastic life in the strange city, in which a garage, motion picture house, toolhouse, or even a pigpen would turn out to be a blockhouse or pillbox. They reduced a slaughter-house, and had steaks for breakfast. They overran a brewery, and had steaks and beer for breakfast. They captured fire trucks, and rode around the conquered part of the city in German firemen's uniforms. They broke into a department store, and went "shopping."

* For a full account see the feature in the *Toronto Star Weekly*, February 4, 1945.

This went on for sixteen days. And the corpses began to pile high in the streets and the basements of the houses, many of which had brick walls around concrete bastions. The German casualties were high. Ours were small. The old-young riflemen of the 90th reckoned on killing six Germans a day, each with his M-1.

Sixteen days. At the end of that time, something had happened on the First Army front which made all of Patton's calculations of the last two weeks, and all the strange achievements of his Army, invalid. Von Rundstedt attacked in the Ardennes. Suddenly, dramatically, Patton was told to halt his Saar offensive. The Third Army was needed at a danger spot nearly one hundred miles away—at right angles to the direction he was now facing.

How Patton moved his entire army almost overnight is the next story to be told; and part of that story was the withdrawal of the 90th Division from Dillingen. They had gone across the river without bridges. They had lived across it for sixteen days without bridges. Now they were told to come back—the entire division of them—without bridges.

Grumbling and a little bitter, they came back. Some 8,000 men, with all their equipment, tanks, and a hundred vehicles, were ferried across the Saar, without suffering a single casualty.

So you can see that Patton, by this time, was doing incredible things with incredible soldiers. What he was to do next, in the moment of the Allies' greatest danger since the defeat at Kasserine, was the final proof of his doctrine that the most successful plan strategically is always the most impossible tactically.

CHAPTER XVII

"I'LL TAKE VON RUNDSTEDT AND SHOVE HIM . . ."

I

BEFORE we examine Patton's role in the Ardennes, let us glance at what he had achieved in the Saar, because what he had achieved was the result of a month and a half of intensive campaigning, under the worst possible conditions of weather and terrain, and at the sacrifice of many brave men. What he had achieved was essential to an ultimate Allied victory, which was based on the reduction of Germany's three armament centers in the Ruhr, the Saar, and Silesia. Patton had almost neutralized the Saar. On December 16, when the first word, ominous and vague, of von Rundstedt's attack came down to Third Army headquarters, still in Nancy, Patton was about to burst through the Siegfried Line itself and march deep into Germany.

This was the purpose of those strange attacks across the Saar River. To us who were there, they looked like isolated suicide battles, nibbling away at the Siegfried Line. We could now see they were part of a characteristically Patton plan, which was calculated to burst through the Line in two widely separated places, then to plunge ahead through the breaches, and join up in a vast semicircle right behind the Saar region.

One of these holes was being punched by the 90th at Dillingen; the other was being made by the 35th at Sarreguemines some thirty miles to the south. A third hole was being driven by the 95th Division in the center at Fraulautern.

By December 16, the holes had been widened almost enough to pass the tanks through. We were expecting a Patton blitz.

The reason was Patton's manner of positioning his armor. His favorite blitz force, the 4th Armored, was ready where it could move north, to exploit the 90th Infantry's Dillingen bridgehead or the 35th's penetration at Sarreguemines. The 6th Armored, the 5th Infantry, and the 10th Armored were all being held in reserve for a typical Patton punch thrown at the enemy where he was uncovered.

Instead, the Allies left themselves not merely uncovered, but really wide open. This was in the First Army sector, right along the German-Luxemburg border. This was the sector the German High Command had accurately assessed as the weakest link in the chain of our Armies from the extreme north to the extreme south. From von Rundstedt's point of view the opportunity to hit here, splitting the Allied western Armies, must have seemed a heaven-sent one. For while our troops outnumbered and "outweighed" the Germans along the entire front, and while our pressure was becoming sharply dangerous in the Ruhr and Saar, we had left only shadow defenses along sixty miles of our western line; and we had left these shadow defenses in the very sector where invading armies had crossed from central to western Europe for centuries. In brief, there was an open door through a wall of guns and men which extended for over 500 miles along the Reich's frontier.

The "Luxemburg Door" was, without doubt, the worst mistake committed by the Allied Supreme Command in the

Battle of Europe. It was a flagrant mistake for two obvious enough reasons: first, it was left in a sector which connected the northern and southern Army Groups, and in a sector which covered our most vital rear installations, where the supplies for five armies had been built up; secondly, even though the terrain was ideal for defense, it was left quite inadequately defended.

During the spell of explanations and heart-searching which followed the Ardennes break-through, a period when animosities rose high and the conduct of the war took on a most dangerous political complexion, the chief blame was laid at the door of General Bradley, then commanding the 12th Army Group, of which the First Army, under General Hodges, was the army in whose sector the break-through had occurred. General Bradley certainly was responsible for the reverse. So, in a measure, was Eisenhower, as Commander-in-Chief, and Hodges as commander of the defeated army. Later, we were told by our Intelligence: (1) that many Panzer divisions were out of contact and were thought to be refitting and reforming somewhere along the Luxemburg border; and (2) that an attack was expected in the Ardennes sector.

I will add another fact which I believe was not publicized at the time. A day before von Rundstedt struck with his 10th and 11th Panzer Armies, a Polish deserter crossed to the American lines and told our Intelligence that the attack was definitely coming. The Pole could not state specifically in what strength, but he claimed to know when, where, and how it was coming. His warning is said to have been disregarded as unreliable.

It is fairly clear that the blame extended all the way down through the American staff and armies concerned.

SHAEF, if it knew of the mysterious concentrations behind the German-Luxemburg frontier, if it had rightly assessed the meaning of the absence of some ten elite German divisions from the active front, should have adapted its overall strategy accordingly.

Eisenhower, therefore enters into the picture, but only as the director of a mining venture enters into a disaster in his mine. Bradley was much more involved. The responsibility, which he never denied, was directly his, as Group Commander.

General Hodges, commander of the First Army, was even more responsible. It is true his attention was concerned with the bitter struggle in the Julich-Duren sector; but he erred dangerously in neglecting his southern flank—and subsequent events were to show how dangerously.

But most direct blame must be apportioned to the Corps commander and staff which was responsible for covering the Ardennes. I do not mention names or make specific allegations, because I was not in this sector until the von Rundstedt drive had begun—and in any case I have no access to the secret reports which were, in the course of things, submitted to the proper authorities. But I was informed that this Corps was slack and neglectful. And the facts speak for themselves. The facts, plainly, were that the Corps and divisions covering this Ardennes sector were overrun and practically annihilated by von Rundstedt's Panzers, although many units fought with heroism and fought until they died.

I heard Bradley, on January 9, 1945, make his "Apologia" for the success of the von Rundstedt offensive, and his words are on record. The gist of his statement was that he and the Allied Supreme Commanders knew of the potential German threat, but had considered it a justifiable risk to concentrate their striking force elsewhere along the long front.

Patton, as the commander of a separate army, was in no way implicated in either the politics or the strategy of the Ardennes. Not at first. But he was to be involved immediately. And his role in the matter was characteristic indeed and was expressed characteristically.

2

We learned at a conference on a gray Sunday, December 17, that the German offensive in the Ardennes was not a localized prod at our lines, but an attack on a huge but still unestimated scale. The news which began to filter in was vague and disturbing, and the gist of it was that the Germans were coming out of the rain mists which covered the Luxemburg hills in large and even terrifying formations. On the war maps, which for two months now had shown a stabilized line to the north of Patton's army, ominous red arrows, representing the German spearheads, suddenly thrust deep into Luxemburg and Belgium; and within three days, fantastic changes showed on the maps, indicating that German Panzers were here, there, and everywhere, perhaps as far to the west as the Meuse River.

Officers and correspondents came down to our headquarters at Nancy with incredibly bad news, all jumbled up with unpleasant rumors and tales of horror. Massacres were spoken of. Break-throughs were hinted at. And, worst of all, frightening stories of Germans dressed in American uniforms and riding in American vehicles, and dropping by parachute behind our lines, spread up and down the front, creating an atmosphere of tension and danger.

Almost immediately General Patton was ordered by Supreme Allied Headquarters to discontinue his Saar offensive, and come to the aid of the First Army. This was serious news for every Third Army soldier. It was bitter news to those infantrymen who had reduced, after days of house-to-house fighting and pillbox smashing (which they called mouseholing), the Siegfried fortress towns of Dillingen, Fraulautern, and Sarreguemines. It was disturbing to Patton's staff, who were suddenly ordered to switch the entire Third Army from a direction facing east to a direction facing north.

Patton himself, the one who might have been expected to be most disturbed and disappointed by the upsetting of his careful two-month-old offensive, was the least excited of anybody I saw on the Western Front in those grim December days, and the most confident. At a conference he told us why. He pointed out that he had always advocated the best place to fight and defeat the Germans was in the field and under the sky, and not in an endless line of concrete pillboxes and blockhouses. If the German Army had decided to come out in the open and fight a showdown battle, he for one was glad of the opportunity to meet the challenge. He had, he said, ordered almost his entire army to change direction and move north, to hit von Rundstedt on the flank. He was not going to "piddle about" with a spare division. He was going to hit the Hun with everything he had.

Privately, and not for publication, as they used to say in those days, he expressed his opinion in one of those pithy, violent similes he specialized in. He is reported to have said: "If von Rundstedt wants to stick his —— into a meat grinder, I'll be only too happy to turn the handle."

This was exactly how Patton felt about the von Rundstedt drive, when every other Allied Commander on the Western Front was inclined—with sound reason—to view the break-through as a major disaster. They say—they said it cynically—that the desk officers and correspondents back at SHAEF in Paris were beginning to pack their bags.

And the Germans said in various Orders of the Day and propaganda utterances that this was their Victory Drive. The Nazi propagandists gave the objectives of the drive. Their time-table called for taking Antwerp on December 31; and the German High Command had certainly planned an airborne "drop" to be synchronized with a cross-country attack coming up from the south. Liége, Brussels, and Paris were all within the German plans, and the propaganda objective seemed to have been to drive west along the Channel coast to link up with the defenders of Dunkirk.

Militarily, neither side was concerned with propaganda. The German High Command was concerned with two objectives: The first was to split the northern and southern Allied armies and outflank the entire northern groups. The second, and equally vital objective, was to seize our oil dumps and war supplies, piled stories high in assembly points behind the line, and centering in Liége and Antwerp.

The scale of the von Rundstedt plan can be gauged from the two subsidiary offensives which were planned to coincide with the main Ardennes attack. One had been mentioned—the airborne landing around Antwerp. The second was a full-scale assault against the Seventh Army, calculated to retake Hagenau and break through between the Third and Seventh U. S. Armies.

It is clear, then, that the Germans hoped, by massing their last reserves and by brilliant strategy, to eliminate our entire Western Front, by first breaking through and then outflanking the independent armies.

There were many staff conferences during the mid-December days, and many urgent decisions were made. Some of those decisions concerned the use of our air forces, which were now asked to fly in the worst weather we had had on the Western Front up to that time. Von Rundstedt's meteorologists had predicted the weather accurately. It was a time of rain, low clouds, fogs, and zero visibility. Notwithstanding, our airmen were asked to fly—and they flew.

Another conference of the commanders of the four American armies on the Western Front: Simpson of the Ninth; Hodges of the First; Patton of the Third; and Patch of the Seventh, with the two American Army group commanders, namely, Bradley of the 12th Army Group and Devers of the 6th Army Group. General Eisenhower presided at this conference of the generals and their chiefs of staff. The story has it that Eisenhower outlined our Ardennes defensive strategy about as follows: Bradley, with Hodges and the First Army, was to hold von Rundstedt's northern flank, with Simpson and his Ninth Army side-slipping to cover the sectors uncovered by the switching of First Army Divisions. "Montgomery will move round to hold von Rundstedt on the west, or open end of his thrust, along the Meuse," Eisenhower said. "You, Patton, are to move divisions north to hold von Rundstedt on the south, while Patch covers up what you have to leave open on the Saar front."

"Me hold von Rundstedt?" said Patton. "I'll take von Rundstedt and shove him down Montgomery's throat."

Only he did not use the word "throat," but an expression referring rather to the other extreme of the digestive system.

The story may be apocryphal, but it has an authentic semblance, and could well illustrate Patton's constitutional aversion to any form of war associated with defense or holding.

3

Patton's contribution to the defeat of von Rundstedt's plan cannot be over-emphasized. Whereas Eisenhower allowed Patton a full week to organize the switch in the Third Army from its Saar front, which faced east, to the Ardennes front, which faced north, more than a hundred miles away, Patton actually effected the switch in three days. And he effected it not with his reserve divisions, such as the 4th Armored, which was waiting to exploit any Siegfried breakthrough, but with almost his entire army. In fact, Patton pulled out of the line seven divisions, abandoning such bitterly contested beaches in the West Wall as Dillingen, and combining his whole force into one gigantic javelin hurled into von Rundstedt's flank from the south.

The mere business of reorganizing such a switch was thought to be impossible in any period less than a week. At least, a week was considered necessary, not only to pull needed divisions back from an active front, but to entruck them, to move them along over a hundred miles of poor roads in wintertime, to re-deploy them, and to draw up a new order of battle and a new battle plan. What Patton did was again characteristic of a general who was too dynamic to abide by the rules as laid down in the textbooks. He did not wait for organization or plans. He told his field commanders to grab trucks where they could and to go north, expecting their orders en route. He worked out his plans for the new battle order and disposition of troops as his army moved.

He actually achieved the impossible. An army never

moved like this before. The 101st Airborne Division, for instance, was rushed into Bastogne 150 miles from the west from a pre-Christmas football game. Some of the men did not even have their helmets. The 4th Armored Division came up from the south nearly a hundred miles in a day and a night. The 10th Regiment of the 5th Infantry went from Sarreguemines to Arlon—sixty-nine miles along secondary roads—in a night. The 90th Division was withdrawn from Dillingen in a single night, without the loss of a man or a vehicle, and trucked fifty miles to the north within two days, when its forward elements were dug in in the snow-covered hills. A 10th Armored Division task force marched over seventy-five miles to cover Bastogne, while the 101st paratroopers were rushed in. It began like this, and during the six weeks that followed, Patton made forty-two divisional moves of an average of one hundred miles each. It was an astonishing performance—an impossible performance in the first three days—but there it was, it happened; the spectacle of a general hurling an entire army about as a divisional commander moves his regiments.

There can really be little doubt that Patton's achievement was the main factor in the defeat of von Rundstedt. If Patton had not moved so fast to threaten the German's flank, two dangerous developments could have taken place. Von Rundstedt could have swung his Panzer armies north to reach for Antwerp and outflank the entire Allied northern group of armies; or he could have split his forces and let them run back and forth *behind* all of our western forces, including Patton's Third Army. Admittedly, such German forces would have been small and isolated; but the very fact that they would have been behind our armies would have made them a sword in our backs. The effect of hostile units, however small, behind an army had already been demonstrated by Patton's forces which dashed along behind the rear of the Germans the previous summer, trapping and disorganizing the German Seventh Army.

4

Patton, hurtling north, had two decisive effects on the Ardennes campaign. The first was the relief of Bastogne, without whose sevenfold road network the Germans were unable to implement their spearhead thrusts many miles to the west. The second effect was the obvious one of bringing cracking pressure on the cylinder walls through which von Rundstedt was trying to drive his Panzers. The Germans themselves had suddenly to turn their faces from the west and the northwest to the south. The moment they did so— and that moment in time was two days before Christmas, 1944—the whole purpose of the Ardennes offensive was invalidated. For the moment they did so, their tactics changed from offense to defense. And they were bound to lose a defensive war.

So they lost the Battle of the Ardennes, though they maneuvered skilfully and the Allies maneuvered without skill, falling back on the safe tactics of shocked and frightened men who preferred to rely on known weight to unknown maneuverings. Patton enunciated the sound enough theory that we could now go back into Germany through the door by which the Germans had come out; but as December moved slowly into January, and the snows fell heavier, giving place to rain, the Germans withdrew through the door and made a fair attempt at shutting it fast in our faces. They were defeated morally and damaged materially, of course. But it was the moral shock which brought home to them the hopelessness of their cause, because the Ardennes offensive was the culmination of that national spiritual resurgence they began to experience in October, when our victorious armies stopped oil-less on the threshhold of their country; they realized they were still not unconditionally defeated, and allowed the realization to raise new hopes of which von Rundstedt's offensive was the fine Nazi flower.

The Ardennes campaign was the hardest our soldiers ever had to fight, not because of the intensity of battle, but because of the inclemency of the weather in Europe's last primeval region. Here, in the Ardennes, wild boar and deer still find sanctuary in the virgin forests from the hunter and the more dangerous adversary armed only with the road engineer's theodolyte or the merchant's scales. The snowfall and the freeze that December and January turned the Ardennes into a very still and white landscape, like a strangely unreal photograph. Every soldier who was in the Ardennes will recall the unreality of that coldness, because after a little time riding in a jeep or lying on the ground, not only the limbs but the senses were numbed, and you went about in a coma. This weather and this whole campaign came upon the American army unprepared. The men were not properly clad. They had inadequate clothing for the freezing temperature and dazzling white background against which they fought. Our equipment was not snow-camouflaged, so that the black hulks of our tanks, guns, and trucks could be seen for miles huddled on the snow-covered hills.

We began to see some strange sights. After men had clad themselves in as many suits of G.I. underwear as they could pull on, they wore anything else they could find to keep warm. Women's dresses were draped round their shoulders, scarves round their heads. Pixie caps of curious shape and design covered their ears and necks, and only the eyes were visible. Infantrymen made little sapling bowers in their foxholes, chipped from the frozen hillsides with axes. They slept in two's, in each other's arms. Since I had to ride four or five hours in an open jeep from the city of Luxemburg to the front fifty miles away, I wore everything I had, and emerged in the morning dressed, from the skin outwards as follows: a layer of woolen underwear, two pair of woolen socks, boots, and cloth snow-overshoes; regulation G.I. uniform, with my dress blouse over the light zipper jacket; over the dress blouse a short leather and fur coat taken from a German Wehrmacht warehouse in Verdun; over the fur jacket my army raincoat, with the wool lining; on my head a wool balaclava helmet, with garrison cap on the top of this; long scarf round my neck. It was difficult to move under this weight of clothing, but one simply wedged oneself in the back of a jeep with a similarly clad colleague, and sat there in a half coma until the end of the journey. In the command posts in a farmhouse, where a stove was burning, we discarded some of these clothes by layers. It was always a problem to get at a pencil and paper.

Conditions such as these, which tried the endurance of every man in the army, were a personal challenge to Patton and his creed of physical toughness. As an army commander, he could have directed operations from some warm nook at his headquarters, now situated in Luxemburg city, where the Army staff had moved into the many fine and even luxurious hotels. But now Patton, whose reputation in the Third Army was based on his ubiquity along the Front itself, drove himself beyond the endurance of ordinary men of his age. Every day he sallied forth in his jeep, well-bedecked with stars; and in this open vehicle he sat himself stiffly in the front seat beside his driver, folded his arms across his bemedalled chest, and whizzed along the ice-bound roads, shouting at military policemen to keep the convoys moving, personally challenging guards to discover if they knew the password for the day, inspecting isolated groups of men, stamping into command posts, and studying the course of the battle from forward observation posts. He would return to his headquarters at the end of the day, and walk into the evening briefing, a very tired and old-looking man. The cold was no respecter of Patton's big stature or harsh voice, and it lined his face with stiff wrinkles, watered his blue eyes, and gripped his vocal cords, so that his voice was as mild as an old woman's when he spoke to his staff.

There was a change in General Patton in those days. I believe he was undergoing a religious spell, brought on by the imminent danger to his fellow Americans, the generals who were his personal friends, and the officers and men who had died in great numbers during von Rundstedt's first onslaught; and who continued to fight and die through Christmastide. That Christmas of 1944 had been the gloomiest any American could have experienced. There were no celebrations; and there was nothing for us to do but fight and wait. It was a time when the longing for home became most acute. I don't know what Patton did to celebrate the birthday of the Prince of Peace; but most of the time he was in the field, visiting combat units. Everybody went about their daily routine and ate cold storage turkey in the evening for the sake of the tradition. Patton, one supposes, thought of home, as the rest of us did. The lovely, nostalgic music of the carols issuing from the radios affected his quick emotions, and one can visualize this big soldier whose poetic yearnings are so strong, sitting at his desk composing one of those pieces with their confused imagery which so sharply demarcates the dualism of his nature—the man who weeps over one injured soldier and pommels another.

Patton's seasonal association with the Almighty was typified in what vaguely resembles an Order of the Day to God from General George S. Patton, Jr., Third Army, Commanding. The Order took the conventional form of a Christmas card, which was neatly printed and circulated throughout the entire Army. The tone of this prayer is respectful, as befits a subordinate general addressing the Supreme Commander of the Universe. In it, General Patton is asking for some consideration for his army, as a good commander asks for replacements of men or equipment. But God is no quartermaster, and seldom intervenes in this department of war, concerning himself, as the Old Testament shows, primarily with climatic and geographic matters. Thus, he once parted a river for the Israelites to make a dry crossing; and on another occasion kept the sun in the western heavens long enough to enable a victorious battle to continue until the enemy were annihilated.

Customarily, then, God is only appealed to by warlike men nowadays on matters pertaining to meteorology, and Patton is a traditionalist in this respect. His prayer, it will be noted, is couched in the diplomatic language of a West Pointer, and this is what it says:

"Almighty and most merciful Father, we humbly beseech Thee, of Thy great goodness, to restrain these immoderate rains with which we have had to contend. Grant us fair weather for battle. Graciously hearken to us as soldiers who call upon Thee that, armed with Thy power, we may advance from victory to victory, and crush the oppression and wickedness of our enemies, and establish Thy justice among men and nations. Amen."

The prayerful Christmas card was received by the half million men of the Third Army without noticeable emotion. To the majority of them, the petitioner and the Petitioned were both vague and remote personalities who somehow governed their immediate destinies from high places to which they had no access. Those destinies were now being lived out in fields and woods in a foreign land; and it was natural that the weary rifleman, crouched in his hole, should see and think only as far as the next range of hills or the next forested slope to which he had to advance on the morrow.

The rains did stop soon after the printing and distribution of Patton's request. Who of us can say whether the General's prayer was answered, or whether some unknown soldier's praying much more silently in his water-soaked slit trench was the one who was heard; or whether the prayers of millions of anxious wives and mothers made the rains to stop; or whether they discontinued in the cause of justice among men and nations; or whether a cold front moved down from the Arctic and changed the weather from wet and warm to dry and cold?

The rains did stop. And Patton was able to re-deploy his army. Our fighters and bombers took off from airfields near and distant. And after several weeks the High Command was able to report that the situation in the Ardennes was restored.

Patton now found himself facing the Siegfried Line again on a straightened front. His whole army, in the meantime, had moved north, and the place where he had to attack was still harder than it had been in Lorraine and the Saar.

This was the time of the lowest ebb in the fortunes and seeming future of Patton's army. The Allied High Command had reverted to its original plan of crushing Germany in the north. The northern groups of armies, Canadians and Poles and British under General Montgomery; the Ninth and First armies under the group command of General Bradley, were the forces chosen for the knockout blow against Hitler's Reich.

Patton's orders were simple. He was to continue a policy of "active defense." What this meant in terms of the Supreme Headquarters Allied Expeditionary Force was that the Third Army was again low on priorities. Looking at the maps and looking at the numbers and conditions of the Third Army troops, it seemed as if Patton had played his part, and would be heard of no more.

In what sounded like a valedictory address, Patton told correspondents at a staff meeting about his orders, and the implication behind them. But "active defense," he said blandly, is an elastic term. We knew then that he had no intention of defending anything. He says he is sorry the word "defense" was ever invented.

In the coming months he demonstrated what he meant. "Active defense" was to be interpreted by Patton as meaning a forced march from the Saar River to Czechoslovakia in four months.

CHAPTER XVIII

"WHERE IS 'BLOODY' PATTON?"

I

BY the end of January, the Ardennes offensive was over; and so were various inter-Allied skirmishes, which threatened to mar Anglo-American good will. Thus the grim period ended, with the pinning of medals on sundry generals, with claims of victory, accounts of heroic episodes, such as the defense of Bastogne, and the return of the Allied armies to their assigned sectors on the Western Front. The frontal assault on the entire length of the Siegfried Line was resumed, and there was no doubt this time that we would crack through the Line, reach the Rhine, cross this formidable water barrier, and end the war in 1945. Although newspaper claims as to the extent of the destruction inflicted on the Wehrmacht were exaggerated, the best of the German reserves, constituted into the 5th and 6th Panzer Armies, had been mangled; and the blow delivered to German hopes and morale had been heavy enough to break their spirit and their capacity for prolonged resistance.

Of all the Allied generals and of all the Allied armies, General Patton and his Third Army emerged from the Ardennes trial the most resolute and the most assured. The battle had proved to this commander and this army the simple thesis that they were the best soldiers in Europe. All in the Third Army, from the Commander-in-Chief down to the veteran rifleman, believed this to be so. Patton's

"WHERE IS 'BLOODY' PATTON?" 245

invincibility was now almost legendary. His conduct had been exemplary. He was now held by his soldiers in esteem and affection; and there was no more criticism of his manner or his methods.

This time, his victory speech did not sound ludicrous, although it was couched in the same grandiose language.

"Neither heat, nor dust, nor floods, nor snow have stayed your progress," said Patton in his first General Order addressed "to the Officers and Men of the Third Army and our comrades of the 19th Tactical Air Command." And he added: "Under the protection of Almighty God and the inspired leadership of our President and the High Command you will continue your victorious course to the end that tyranny and vice shall be eliminated, our dead comrades avenged, and peace restored to a war-weary world . . . I can find no fitter expression for my feelings than to apply the immortal words spoken by General Scott at Chapultepec when he said, 'Brave soldiers and veterans, you have been baptized in fire and blood and have come out steel.'"

One cannot suppose that the officers and men of the Third Army were greatly impressed by Patton's reference to an obscure General and an obscure occasion, and the reiteration of that word "blood" had an unpleasant association for them. But still, the man 50,000 soldiers had once wanted to shoot was now their leader and friend and spokesman, and he had matched his grandiose words with grandiose victories, and they were ready enough to continue their victorious course if it brought peace to a war-weary world.

The Third Army's new sector now lay east of the Luxemburg border, stretching some hundred miles from Pruem in the Middle Rhineland to Saarbrücken, center of the Saarland. Patton's offensive was geared to the southern group of armies, the U. S. Seventh on his southern flank, and to the French First, south of the Seventh.

Of this unspectacular front, Patton's sector, with its mountains, rivers, fortifications, and lack of roads, looked like being the least spectacular. Our main blow was obviously coming further north, along the First and Ninth Army fronts. But Patton, with his usual confidence, started forthwith to attack, though there was some gloom even in the commander's own headquarters, due to his low priority for replacements and supplies, and due to the difficult terrain ahead of his army. We counted the rivers: the Pruem, the Our, the Saur, the Moselle, the Saar, the Kyll. These were rivers coursing along gorges through the mountain and hill ranges which stood between us and the Rhine.

So Patton got his elite infantry divisions into place, the 4th Infantry on the north, then the 90th Infantry, next the new 17th Airborne, then the 5th, and so on down the line; and all began to move forward, slowly at first. The advances looked small, and centered round such obscure places as Pruem, Echternach, Brandscheid, and Bitburg, which were only mountain villages in this rude German frontier country. Soon they were significant enough to answer the question asked by a worried German radio: "Where is 'bloody' Patton?" It was obvious soon enough that Patton was in position for another massive drive.

2

By the end of February, Patton had moved his entire army of twelve divisions onto German soil. The battered, broken cities of France, Luxemburg, and Belgium had been left behind; and now it was German villages and towns which were suddenly spouting columns of gray dust and tongues of flame. It was a moment of emotion for us all to step onto the soil of Germany, to see the German frontier villages broken and smoldering, to see American—and German— shells ripping chunks out of the Fatherland, to see German soldiers prisoners of war in their own land. All these sights of desolation symbolized a collapse, complete and final. For what German resistance now continued, as Patton suddenly broke away with his armor in the center, was desperate and disorganized. Units of the Wehrmacht cut off in the Saar-Moselle triangle fought fiercely for every inch of ground around the ancient city of Trier, while other units, far behind them, surrendered without firing a shot. It was significant.

It was significant, and soon it began to bear a remarkable resemblance to the Normandy front in July of the preceding year. We saw now that the strategic situation was almost the same. Again, as in Normandy, the Germans had massed their main forces at the northern end of the line, against the British and the American First and Ninth armies. Again they had ignored Patton. Again Patton was pouring his armor through a hole torn in the German defensive positions by infantry. Even the exploiting armor he suddenly hurled forward was the same—the 4th Armored Division, which suddenly disappeared from the War Room maps at Army Headquarters, because they were "out of contact."

Curiously, it was another German Seventh Army which Patton was about to destroy. The first Seventh Army had been trapped in Normandy. This second Seventh Army was newly reconstituted for the defense of the Middle Rhine.

It was a remarkable resemblance, with all the old signs

of a German collapse—disorganization, demoralization, mass surrenders, routs, and the motions of resistance, with the customary references to the Führer and fighting to the last man. Behind this hysteria which suddenly overwhelmed the German Seventh Army—behind and causing it—was the same 4th Armored Division, which had suddenly blitzed sixty-five miles in fifty-eight hours, right across the mountains and rivers of the Middle Rhineland, from Bitburg almost to Coblenz and the Rhine. A spearhead of this immortal 4th, Combat Command B, commanded by that legendary tankman, Lieutenant-Colonel Creighton W. Abrams, of West Newton, Massachusetts, had overrun so many towns and villages, taken so many prisoners, including a German Corps Commander, Major-General Graf Rothkirch, that no one at headquarters knew for a time what exactly was happening, except that a major breakthrough had been achieved and the Rhine had been reached.

They say Patton received a telegram soon after from a rival general with this message: "Congratulations on being the last to reach the Rhine." It was true that the Third Army was the last army on the Western Front to reach the great river; but what Patton lost in time, he compensated for in style. His drive to Coblenz represented now the deepest penetration into Germany. It had been made unexpectedly and dramatically and dangerously. One night Patton had been fighting in the Siegfried Line; the next he was on the Rhine, sixty-five miles to the east. His tanks had just gone. They roared along the mountain roads in one of those terrifying maneuvers when they disappear over some distant hilltop and are not heard of again for forty-eight hours. They had gone into the mountains and crossed rivers without benefit of infantry, supply columns, or supporting artillery. Now the head of this armored column was nearly a hundred miles in advance of the main infantry units. It stuck out on a long slender neck. On the maps, it looked impossible.

It was not only possible. It was brilliantly right, and it was a maneuver which had won great battles from the time the Germans had first used this armored spearhead tactic in France. The arrival of Patton's first tank on the Rhine in this manner finished the entire German Seventh Army, and sealed the fate of all German forces west of the Rhine from Coblenz south. What had happened in a matter of days was this: 5,230 square miles of Germany had been actually or potentially conquered; 4,225 towns had fallen; almost half a million German soldiers had been cut off from their armies elsewhere in the Reich; the Middle Rhineland and the Saar protectorate had been reduced; and the Allied armies now stood, on a solid front, right along the Rhine, from the Dutch to the Swiss borders. The blitz of the 4th Armored Division represented the greatest action in the war.

Consider the rivers Patton had crossed since he jumped off after the Ardennes offensive. The main ones were: the Moselle, the Saar, the Our, the Saur, the Pruem, the Kyll, the Simmern, and the Nahe. The crossing of each of them was a major military and engineering operation.

Consider the towns he had captured by the end of March: Trier, Coblenz, Gerolstein, Bad Kreuznach, Mainz, Worms, Ludwigshafen, Kaiserslautern, Witlich, Saarbrücken, with thousands of lesser places.

But still it was not rivers or towns which mattered. It was Patton's cutting and slicing tactics, which mattered—his masterly use of four full armored divisions, the 4th, 6th,

10th, and 11th, and ten infantry divisions. First, Patton swung north to make a junction with Hodges' First Army units on the Rhine, trapping thousands of Germans in a vast looping pocket. Then he swung south to join with Patch's Seventh Army, to enfold another 70,000 men in the Saar. It was a victory impossible to assess.

Yet his sense of the dramatic would not let Patton rest content with the cold facts and figures of victory. For at this time his were not the only successes to be front-paged on the newspapers of the world. Indeed, the events on the northern fronts tended to shadow his achievements, and the limelight was still on Montgomery, Simpson, and Hodges. Montgomery, commanding the British Second and the American Ninth Armies, had swept up to the Rhine, and was setting the stage for a crossing of the Rhine with so much fanfare in the press that about everything but the sale of tickets for ringside seats was being laid on. Further, the First Army had already crossed the Rhine at Remagen; and Patton was sorely disappointed that the first conqueror to cross the historic river since Caesar was not called George S. Patton, Jr. But Patton was not immediately concerned with the First Army's crossing, which had more of the element of luck than of strategy. He was concerned with Montgomery.

3

He knew that Montgomery was the first on the Allied time-table to cross the Rhine in force. It was true that Yankee enterprise had slipped a force across where the more sober conventions of British militarism demanded a long-prepared major assault. That this was the case was demonstrated by the caution of Montgomery in not making

"WHERE IS 'BLOODY' PATTON?"

a quick seizure of a bridgehead when his Ninth Army units suddenly burst out of the Roer-Rhine zone to the banks of the great river, which was inadequately defended in places between Wesel and Dusseldorf. But the Montgomery plan called for a tremendous, crushing blow, combining everything in the Allied complement of armaments—artillery barrages, airborne troops, bombers, fighter bombers, gliders, infantry, tanks, and naval weapons and personnel. It was the cautious and safe strategy of weight, like that used in Sicily. Zero hour for Montgomery's offensive was midnight, Friday, March 23.

Patton knew of Montgomery's plan and timing. He had himself no orders to cross the Rhine in any specific manner or at any specifiic time. But he had made his plans and decided on a time; and, characteristically, he decided to beat Montgomery and the Allied High Command across the river; and to do so in a manner calculated to steal his rival's thunder.

What Patton did was to cross the Rhine quietly, calmly, without firing a preparatory shot. Suddenly, a few hours before Montgomery loosed the greatest weight of Allied power since D Day, leaping the water barrier with thousands of planes, thousands of gliders, tons of bombs, massed artillery, airborne troops, several infantry divisions, amphibious tanks, naval craft, rubber boats, ducks, crocodiles, pontoon bridges, and all the paraphernalia of a seaborne expedition, Patton casually ordered elements of the 5th Infantry Division to paddle across the Rhine ten miles south of Mainz, at Oppenheim, without benefit of an artillery preparation, without even machine gun or rifle fire; in fact, in complete silence. To Patton, customarily so noisy in what he did and said, the hush of this historic moment, an hour and a half before midnight on Thursday, March 22, 1945, was a sweeter and louder music than the symphony of battle itself.

You can judge what the occasion meant to the General from the fact that his crossing of the Rhine was announced to the astonished world a few hours after it had been made. Normally, such a surprise operation as this is blacked out in a security silence. In this case, what had happened was this: Elements of the 5th Infantry had paddled across the Rhine in the darkness, without the customary artillery and air bombardments which are considered essential before an operation of this importance and difficulty. The skilful infantrymen had crossed so silently, however, that it was a full twenty minutes *after* they had landed on the eastern bank before the enemy were aware of the crossing, and started their tardy and inaccurate resistance with small arms. It was a full two hours before they had even accurately located the bridgehead site, and commenced shelling it with heavy cannon. This kind of resistance is no resistance at all. In that time almost the entire complement of the 5th Infantry was across the river. They had fanned out, secured their perimetral defenses for a counterattack, located the enemy batteries, silenced them, and begun moving inland, followed by a normal flow of supplies, ferried across the river almost without opposition.

Normally, I repeat, the advantages of such a surprise attack would be exploited behind a security silence, because though the enemy immediately engaged obviously knows where the attackers are, he does not know in what strength or to what extent; and he may not have the means of informing his headquarters. It is the first principle of military security that you never tell the enemy where you are or what you are doing until you are sure, through your counter-intelligence, that he knows.

Patton's Intelligence officers wished not to announce the crossing of the Rhine for a period of at least forty-eight hours, and persuaded the General to keep silent. But it was not difficult for the press to make him talk. Said a correspondent at the conference where the crossing was announced:

"Don't you think, General, this achievement should be reported as soon as possible—for the sake of the record?"

Patton could find a hundred reasons in his heart for answering "Yes," and the principal reason was that two hundred miles to the north, other armies, commanded by Field Marshal Sir Bernard Montgomery, were to cross the river, in the orthodox manner, in a matter of a few hours.

Thus Patton's Third Army crossed their twentieth and largest river.

CHAPTER XIX

DEATH OF A NATION

I

PATTON was not only across the Rhine, but his army was the nearest to Berlin. The capital was 226 miles to the northeast; and there was nothing between the Third Army and Berlin, but isolated units of the Wehrmacht and hurriedly erected roadblocks. As we passed these log and cement obstacles which had been piled between the ancient houses of German villages, I was reminded of the similar pitifully useless roadblocks the British had constructed as anti-invasion defenses. Such puny barriers are an utter waste of effort against mechanized armies. The method of reducing them is simple. A tank approaches cautiously, probing for antitank guns, and outflanking the position. With its cannon and machine guns it drives away the defenders, while a squad of infantry moves into the village from the adjacent fields, and clears out snipers. Then a tank or bulldozer moves up the road, and with a few heavy shoves pushes down the trees, and the roadblock is gone. Within an hour or so military police supervise German civilians in clearing away the rubble. Such roadblocks never held up our advance for more than a few minutes.

Now the war again took on that almost hilarious holiday aspect which had characterized the Third Army's race across France. In the vanguard went the 4th Armored Division, closely supported by the 5th and 90th Infantry. Among them, they so effectively chopped up the German forces they found that organized resistance collapsed all around. The 4th Armored kept leaping ahead and made new records for speed. It traveled forty miles in eighteen hours, once across the Rhine. The Infantry in trucks captured great cities like Darmstadt and Frankfurt with less than a score of casualties. So Patton's army bowled along the fine German highways in fine holiday mood, enjoying the scenery, the hidden stocks of German food, the cellars of looted French wine, and acquiring an astonishing variety of "souvenirs," from Leica cameras to accordions.

The greatest difficulty attending such an advance was no longer the opposition of the enemy or the obstacles of the terrain; it was the difficulty of knowing what friendly unit was where. There was never any time for divisional command posts to set up headquarters, and even the Corps were living on the roads. Patton himself was seldom seen at headquarters, which gradually got left miles behind the front. The commander was chasing back and forth in his jeep, with his attention directed not so much to military as to supply problems. These supply problems were partially solved by the drivers of the trucks. These drivers simply went at top speed along the Reichsautobahns and concrete highways as though they were on maneuvers in Louisiana. Certainly the German civilians were no more hostile than the citizens of small towns in America. It was only when a lone jeep had to pass through a pine forest that the riders were suddenly aware that they were in the heart of Germany; and that in war, death can await you round the next bend in the road.

In those days we feared only the guerilla bands of SS troops and the Hitler Jugend. Of the two, the latter were the more sinister. It seemed to us that every thin-faced, long-legged German boy was capable of turning a hidden weapon on us; and for correspondents, who rode unarmed through German villages where there was no American garrison, the little groups of these silent and expressionless youths were a constant ordeal which made an otherwise pleasant ride a tense experience. It was strange how unreal the war became, with the farmers ploughing their fields as before, the housewives cleaning their houses, the little children playing in the streets, groups of German soldiers marching unattended down the roads, with their hands on their heads—all of this vaguely sad and charming, until you heard a rifle shot or the ping of a bullet fly by your head as you stood talking in the street. Actually, there were extremely few incidents of terrorism such as that advocated by the werewolves; but I personally never felt safe so long as there was one German youth under eighteen in the vicinity.

While the newspapers at home exploited the public's obsession with the names of big towns and distances from Berlin, both the Allied and German High Commands were watching Patton as the commander of the most significant of the American armies. For the Third Army had become even more important in our strategy of these last days of the war than the Ninth, which was advancing frontally on Berlin with lightning speed. At this period, General Eisenhower and his advisers gave considerable credence to the National Redoubt theory, whereby the flower of all the German armies, navy and air force, withdrew to a redoubt area in the Bavarian Alps, there to create a kind of warrior state determined to resist to the end in a thousand mountain fastnesses. Detailed reports based on the information of agents, prisoners of war, and aerial reconnaissance undertook to show that the Nazis and the German High Command had prepared such a redoubt area in a *Götterdämmerung* frame of mind which was certainly in keeping with the Nazi creed of nihilistic melodrama. The National Redoubt was said to include Bavaria, the northern Italian Alps, and the western tip of Czechoslovakia. Into this vast and lofty land of mountains and clouds, the entire Nazi hierarchy, headed by the Führer and accompanied by those Junker generals most loyal to Naziism, were supposed to retire when everything else was lost. Plans were said to have been made for the gradual folding in of twenty to thirty elite SS and Wehrmacht divisions. In brief, a half a million of the true-blue Germans were expected to withdraw to the peaks, crags, and caves of the redoubt to resist the Allies until the end of time, if need be. The reports claimed the redoubt was well stocked with food, and had every facility for the production and repair of armaments.

2

The National Redoubt theory was indeed a curious phase of the war, and one with so many ramifications that it is hard to explain. It was certainly—and rightly—taken quite seriously by our High Command. Yet I heard no commander in the field give it much credence, and I remember General Gay, Patton's chief-of-staff, saying that it was militarily unfeasible. I never discovered where the idea of a redoubt originated, though I assume it was from the reports of our agents. I saw a number of extremely detailed official reports describing the redoubt, even to an assessment of the amount of coal available down there. Yet when we talked to General Kurt Dittmar, who fled to our lines in May with the express intention of turning "King's evidence" in the hope of saving himself, this best-informed of Nazi observers dismissed the redoubt theory as foolishness. And Dittmar, of course, was right. There was never anything even approximating such a military state within Germany, which was itself *the* redoubt, encircled by rivers, defense walls, and great armies.

Nonetheless, either some over-zealous agent or some too-imaginative staff officer sold our High Command with the redoubt theory, which actually shaped our strategy to some extent, though that strategy coincided with our obvious intention of covering the whole of Germany with armies from the Baltic to the Alps. As far as Patton was concerned, he was the field commander our High Command looked to, first, because his army lay along the northern frontier of the demarcated redoubt zone; secondly, because he was in a position now to cut Germany in two, thus denying the northern forces access to the fortress area; and thirdly, he was the type of commander best fitted for a showdown battle of the kind anticipated.

The extent to which the redoubt theory shaped Allied strategy can be seen from the direction Patton's army now took. It did not take the main highway from Frankfurt to Berlin, but suddenly swung south and east, down through Wurzburg to Nuremberg. In addition, it was the Third Army which now began to receive first priorities in replacements and new divisions. Before the campaign was to end, Patton was commanding the most powerful army in American military history—an army of eighteen divisions, six of them complete armored divisions.

The Germans feared Patton now more than ever. With surprising candor, they admitted on their radio that they "had now entered the last and decisive round" of the war.

Patton's drive east to Nuremberg was the Allied drive, out of all the multiple thrusts into Germany, which most alarmed them. They said that "while the Ruhr and the north German plain against which Montgomery and Bradley were driving was Eisenhower's ultimate objective, this is not danger point number one." Danger point number one was the "extremely critical situation" developing from Patton's Nuremberg spearhead, which threatened to cut the Reich in two and brought American armies 280 miles from the Russian armies operating in Czechoslovakia under Marshal Koniev.

By the end of March, 1945, the war had reached a fantastic stage on all fronts, and the world began to see not just the collapse of armies, but the death of a nation in its swiftest and most ghastly form. Germany was being hammered and ground into that same rubble and dust usually associated with a battlefield where armies attempt to annihilate each other and all the fields and trees and houses beneath which they bivouac. Because of the insane determination of Hitler and Himmler, every German inhabited place was a miniature battlefield; and while hundreds of villages were spared in the swift advance of the Allied armies, thousands of them were destroyed because a handful of blindly obedient SS men or Hitler Youths accepted their Führer's injunction to die in a truly Nazi total manner. During this period almost every large city in Germany was razed because a handful of SS men wanted to live a few days longer at the expense of the destruction of a city.

When Patton was able to pause long enough to take stock and issue an Order of the Day to his troops of the Third Army and the 19th Tactical Air Command, he was able to give some figures which spoke louder than any vaunting phrases. Between January 29, when the Third Army began its offensive, and March 22—that is in less than two months—the Third Army had captured 6,484 square miles of enemy territory and 3,072 cities, including Trier, Coblenz, Bingen, Worms, Mainz, Kaiserslautern, and Ludwigshafen. They had captured 140,112 soldiers, killed or wounded nearly 100,000 more, and practically eliminated two entire German armies, the Seventh and the First.

"History records no greater achievement in so limited a time," added the General.

3

But even such tremendous figures and facts no longer gave a picture of what was happening in Germany. What was happening, indeed, was no longer war. The war had gone beyond the personalities of generals or the prowess of armies, and had become a vast cataclysm in which half of Europe was being engulfed. The movements of our armies, though spectacular beyond belief, were nothing compared with the sudden wanderings of millions of people across the face of central Europe. Hundreds of thousands of German soldiers, some as prisoners of war, some as would-be prisoners, others as deserters in civilian clothes, still others as disciplined soldiers in search of an organization which could reform their lines, wandered about, avoiding the main roads and trekking through the fields and woods at night. Almost as numerous as the German soldiers were the released or escaped Allied prisoners of war who now poured from the Stalags—Americans, Britons, French, Russians, Yugoslavs, still in their uniforms for the most part, and all traveling westward towards our lines. They came in bands or singly, on foot, on bicycles, on farm carts, on requisitioned farm tractors. I recall an English sergeant who arrived with a German frau and her two children, with the story that she had protected him halfway across Germany. They had traveled in trains and buses, the Tommy still in his uniform. I recall emaciated American prisoners leaping from the bushes onto our jeep, calling out that they were Americans, then seizing our hands in a long grip, while the tears ran down their faces, because they were free. I recall a whole company of Mongolian Soviet troops, all in the gray-green German field uniforms, marching in military style along the road. There were tens of thousands on the move.

There were millions of liberated slaves on the move. These slaves—men and women, French, Russian, Hungarian, Jews, every nationality—streamed from the fields, the farms, the factories, and the wired camps where they lived, and with wild cries they marched and looted their way westward in the largest migration of people in history.

So, along the roads and across the fields and through the woods, came millions of people, until the whole world seemed chaotic and mad, except for the small American military units which alone, in these times, were living an orderly, civilized existence.

We could see then that the war was almost ended, and we could see that it was ending in an indescribable chaos, as though, of a sudden, the very foundations of western civilization had been torn away, and the structure of society was collapsing. As it collapsed, as the house which Hitler had built caved in, the true horror of that mansion of death gaped open. For there in the midst of this lush and prosperous German countryside, suddenly exposed to view were the concentration camps, the extermination centers, the slave pens, the prisons, the torture chambers of the Nazi inner sancta, the secret cells around which the whole great German edifice had been built.

You could never tell the effect of the concentration camps on the American armies in the field. It was not simply an effect of utter and desolate horror, which left the talkative American soldier so silent that you could hear his silence. It was something else. Really, it was a sudden spiritual awakening, which had never been accomplished by the oratory of his leaders, whether politicians or generals, or by appeals to patriotism, loyalty, duty, or whatever brave new world somebody somewhere had promised. For until the zone of the concentration camps was reached, not one in a hundred thousand American soldiers knew what was the faith for which he was asked to die, so that he fought and died as General Patton had exhorted him to do, for discipline and out of necessity. He had killed Germans out of a sense of duty and self-preservation, removing them from his path as stones in a wall which shut him out from his own home.

Then, after two and a half years of war, the Americans suddenly saw the real face of their enemy. During this month of April, Allied armies from the far north to the Alps overran fifty concentration camps, large and small—Belsen, Buchenwald, Langenstein, Flessenberg, Ohrdruf, Neunberg —and they realized they were not fighting simply because the Japanese had attacked Pearl Harbor, and Germany had declared war on the United States, and they had been drafted and trained and sent to Europe, but because hundreds of thousands of human beings had been tortured, starved, and mutilated, in fifty Nazi-created charnel houses. All over central Germany now, thousands of American soldiers were standing as we stood in the concentration camp at Langenstein, watching tight-skinned skeletons tottering about with the aid of wooden staves, or lying gasping on rags, waiting to die. We watched such a skeleton wobble up to a water cart in Langenstein, place his bony fingers below a dripping spout, and wipe his body; and somehow that figure and the motions he was making were more symbolic of the horror and cruelty of Germany than even the frail corpses the Red Cross men were carrying from the barracks of the concentration camps—so frail and bloodless that bones had broken through their skins without the bodies even bleeding.

Silent, we looked in at the windows of such a hospital hut, and saw gibbering men whispering for cigarettes and water, while their comrades croaked away the last of their lives on the wooden shelves where they lay.

After what we saw in the concentration camps and barns, such as Gardelegen where nearly a thousand men were burned alive, we looked out on the lush and fat German countryside and people with different eyes; and we knew, if nothing else, that the chaos which had fallen over Germany and the misery which was to follow its indescribable defeat, was a proper retribution; and every G.I. was glad that he had helped to destroy Germany and Germans and the creed they had sought to thrust upon the whole world.

In those days a tremendous bond was felt between all Americans, and the bond was a feeling of a holy duty well performed.

The Third Army overran its quota of concentration camps, and Third Army soldiers saw their share of the starved and mutilated men who had lived or died in them. General Patton acted instinctively and swiftly, rounded up the German civilians in the neighborhoods, and took them on conducted tours of the charnel houses they had lived alongside with studied ignorance or indifference. At the camp near Ohrdruf, nine miles south of the city of Gotha, 4,000 prisoners had been starved, clubbed, or burned to death, and their heads, arms, and trunks lay only partially covered with earth in the nearby woods. Patton had twenty-eight German civilians complete the interment of these mutilated corpses.

At Neunberg, elderly burghers, their wives, and children were given the task of burying 361 murdered Polish and Rumanian Jews, who had died from blows or bullets on a forced march from one concentration camp to another. From the vast shallow pits which lay scattered all over the area, it was apparent the Germans had controlled thousands of helpless lives until the advance of the Third Army made it advisable to beat or kick these human beings to death, as a Sykes would kick the entrails out of a dying dog. The many assemblages of shining-pated Germans and their wives and children now stood at a thousand graves, stoical, dry-eyed, and inwardly indignant, under the guns of a thousand silent Americans.

German civilians always protested they were ignorant of these concentration camps and their terrible inmates—even those Germans who lived in neat houses a hundred yards away. Yet every day, for ten years, they had seen a procession of bloodless ghosts, crawling along the road with staves, clad in a nightmare costume of stripes, proceeding to holes in the mountainsides, where they were digging caves for German underground industry. They had seen, too, these German civilians, the long trek of slaves and prisoners of war, who were always moving back and forth across the countryside, and they had not asked themselves who were these suffering people, where they came from, or whence they were going. The only protests were when the stench of the dead and dying, and the fumes from the crematories, filled the air with poisonous vapors.

4

That was about how the war ended—in the country of the concentration camps. Eleven months before, Patton and his army had sailed from England and landed on the beaches of Normandy. In 318 days, he had marched over 600 miles, crossing twenty-four rivers, capturing some 5,000 towns and villages, and liberating or occupying a broad swath right across Europe, from Normandy to Czechoslovakia.

Patton had accomplished great things, and perhaps the greatest thing he had done was to gain the loyalty of some half a million American soldiers, whose regard and affection for "Old Georgie" spoke louder than the hate of those 50,000 G.I.s who, two years before, down in Sicily, muttered their threats against "Old Blood and Guts."

So this was the odyssey of the General who began by commanding two and a half divisions of untried American troops and who now commanded eighteen divisions of superlatively trained and ripely experienced soldiers, who were ready to go wherever he ordered.

This personal loyalty to Patton was astonishing, and even extended to a jealous regard for the man's personal fame and success. At war's end we find a *New York Times* correspondent protesting the disappointments which had befallen Patton.

"The United States Third Army swung south yesterday

and moved towards the Germans' Alpine redoubt and away from a purported rendezvous with the Russians," said the *New York Times* on April 23. "This marked the third time that Lieutenant-General George S. Patton had been shunted from a looming major objective."

The two other objectives which had "loomed" for General Patton, according to this writer, were Paris, which his army had only skirted after expecting to enter it; and Berlin, which, as far back as the apple orchards of Normandy, had been the assumed goal of the Third Army.

The disappointment of the *New York Times* writer that Patton could never now call himself "Liberator of Paris," or "Conqueror of Berlin," or "Greeter of the Red Army," was indicative of the personal loyalty now general throughout the Third Army to their Commander. Officers and men were jealous of his prestige, and tended to suspect "politics" every time the Army had to change direction away from some famous city whose fall would mean headline publicity for "General Patton's Third Army."

However, when all the other Allied armies on the Western Front were ordered to cease their advances—with General Simpson's Ninth Army only a matter of hours from Berlin—Patton still had "carte blanche" from the Supreme Command to drive on as far as he could. With his eighteen divisions, he bore down on the redoubt area, which was now proved to exist only in the minds of over-imaginative Intelligence officers. On Patton's southern flank, the Seventh Army swept right through the redoubt to the North Italian border, without noteworthy resistance. By the first week of May, Patch's Seventh had also accomplished its mission, and only Patton was still fighting along the entire Western Front. Right up to the "Cease Fire" order, and even after it, Patton's armor was dashing about right in the middle of Europe, making forced marches to Pilsen and then on to Prague, where the Nazis had concentrated their last resistance against the revolting Czechs, in a typical Nazi manner, whereby they had the effrontery, even at this stage of the war, to try and give a "subject people" a lesson in German methods. The methods were to turn on the city, which had decided to liberate itself, with the last of the SS and the Luftwaffe, in an orgy of massacre and fury which was no longer war but the last chance for well-trained sadists to murder women and children. The SS did this by actually lashing children to their persons, as they advanced along the streets of Prague against the roadblocks thrown up by the Czechs. The SS also shot all men, of whatever age, they took from houses along the streets they had cleared.

Patton's was the nearest Allied army to Prague, and it was his armor which raced to the aid of the city when those dramatic calls came from the Prague radio, pleading for help. The SS had no desire to fight any longer with Patton, and as his tanks rolled up the road from Pilsen, they began to withdraw from the capital and march down the roads to our prison cages. Thousands of them, jack-booted and well-armed, marched stoically past our columns; and within a few hours, Patton's armor had burst into the city and ended the week's bitter events, which had been a struggle to the death between the last of the German army and the first of the people they had conquered. And so the war of the West ended.

The last day of the long campaign for the Third Army was a monument to its achievements; for on that day Patton took 50,000 prisoners, making a total of over half a million. Counting estimated killed and wounded, Patton had accounted for a million German soldiers.

As soldiers all over Europe laid down their arms, as peace came to half the world, as all men's minds turned to home, Patton stood for a moment alone, still thinking of war, still talking of war. In a message to his troops, the commander of the Third Army bluntly stated: "We have ahead of us a hard, bitter campaign against the Japanese. The same invincible fighting spirit displayed in Europe will be carried to the Pacific and will hasten the day of victory in the Pacific War."

Amid the ringing of bells and the prayers of thanksgiving and the sighs of relief, Patton's words went unheard. He was still, of course, the commander of the largest army in U. S. history, and it was true there was still a Pacific war to finish. But the time was coming when the world would no longer listen to warlike words or esteem warlike men. Even in his own army, which had followed him with increasing personal loyalty, American soldiers were no longer interested in an "invincible fighting spirit." Appeals to their "guts" now fell faintly on their ears. Five hundred thousand men in uniform were surely reverting to five hundred thousand normal civilians, in whose minds and hearts the long year of battle was becoming only a faint memory.

Soon the hundreds of battles they had fought, the scores of rivers and mountains they had crossed, the long marches right across Europe, the victories, the dangers, the hardships, the misery, and the beauty of all this, were to become vague and unreal. Soon the soldier himself, struggling to tell his experiences to the civilian world, would accept the attitude of that world that what he had done in the war was no longer very important. The events of yesterday, however great, are never so stirring as the expectations of tomorrow. So with gratitude because they had survived three years of battle, and with memories of their fallen comrades, a million American soldiers turned their faces and their thoughts homewards. For three years they had been soldiers and heroes. Now all they wanted was to be civilians and ordinary citizens in the towns and villages from whence they came. They sailed away from Europe, and took trains and buses from the American ports of debarkation, to arrive without fanfare in their communities, large and small, and to be welcomed home as sons, husbands, and lovers, not as soldiers and heroes any longer.

The heroes' welcome was left to the generals, in public ceremonies symbolizing not only the people's appreciation of their services, but the closing chapter of their career.

So General George S. Patton, Jr., now sixty years old, came home to his last victory, before disappearing from the front pages of the newspapers to the footnotes of the history books.

CHAPTER XX

TO VALHALLA VIA SUNSET BOULEVARD

I

GENERAL PATTON had told his wife two and a half years previously, when he set out on the Casablanca expedition, that he did not expect to come home again. And where, in the average man, such a pronouncement would amount to nothing more than a morbid groping after sympathy, it was, in Patton, the final expression of the heroic. He had envisaged for himself a special kind of homecoming, a triumphant entry into some Valhalla, with the distant plaudits of mortals echoing faintly in his no longer mortal ears; he, the Victor, erect, bemedalled, and helmeted, striding past ranks of dead warriors to join the immortals in some martial heaven.

But it became increasingly difficult for Patton to die on a battlefield as he progressed from commander of a small task force to commanding general of the largest army in American history; and so it came about that he returned home, not to Valhalla but to Boston, leaving the scene of his triumphs, not in a clap of thunder but in the roar of an airplane's engines.

But though it was America, and not Olympus, where Patton touched ground after a non-stop flight from Paris, he was to receive a welcome which the sad gods could not have staged. And the General could not have been disappointed in his intimations of immortality.

As his flotilla of four-motored transport planes approached America, squadrons of flying fortresses and fighter planes took off from air fields to escort the Conquering Hero home. As he landed, a salute from seventeen guns was fired for the first time in the war. The State and Military Governors, generals, military police, civic delegations, bands, clergymen, an estimated million people, and Patton's wife and three children, were waiting to welcome him home. America, with its flair for pageantry, was about to compensate Patton for the disappointment of not having died.

In fact, Boston on that day of June 8, 1945, vied with Imperial Rome in honoring the Conqueror of the far Germanic tribes. There were escorts of airplanes, the salute of cannon, the cheering of crowds, the martial music of bands, with sundry typical American refinements, such as the wailing of fire sirens. It was all on a grandiose and superhuman scale; and what was human in it, like the Conqueror's wife fondly patting the Conqueror's cheek, was lost in that hot June day of bread and circuses.

2

In return for such a welcome—even though it was the cheering of a Boston crowd and not the plaudits of the immortals which fell on his ears—Patton acted the role of the great warrior about to pass into history. He came splendidly dressed for the part. He was, indeed, in full buskin. On his fine head balanced the lacquered helmet, with its four stars, and three army insignia. On his chest was a tailored tunic, with four stars on each shoulder, thirty brightly-hued decorations on the left breast, five horizontal and four diagonal gold stripes on the sleeve. Beneath the tunic he wore a shirt with four stars on each lapel, making a total of twenty stars. The rest of his costume consisted of a gold-buckled belt, with a pistol thrust into it, riding breeches, pack-boots, and a riding crop. Four more stars embossed on the pistol brought the grand total to twenty-four stars.

The twenty-four star general also responded in his bearing and manner. On this occasion more than any other, it was necessary to stand stiff and erect, to hold the head back, the chest out, and the belly in. Thus he appeared in the doorway of the plane. Thus he leaped across to the gangplank before it was wheeled into place. So he descended to the ground, walked across the airfield, saluted the generals and army officers, shook hands with the civilians, kissed his wife and children, and waved his riding crop to the spectators.

Carried along in a red fire department car, the Conquering Hero stood proud and soldierly, like Caesar passing down the Via Sacra in a chariot. On that day Patton was Caesar to the American populace. He was all they expected of a victorious general. As he passed by they could see the shining helmet reflecting the rays of its four stars and the afternoon sun. They cheered the helmet, the stars, the decorations, and the black-handled pistol. "Women even scampered out of beauty parlors," says one historian, "and so thick was the throng, girls leaned forward and touched the General's arms."

In the evening, Patton was given a state reception in Boston at the first official state dinner given by the Commonwealth of Massachusetts since Marshal Foch was welcomed there, in 1919. The General, say the historians, was in a jovial mood. "He snapped peanuts at people he knew, blew kisses at his daughters, jumped up and down, and kissed a rose a pretty lady handed him. He also made a speech; his voice became hoarse with emotion and he whispered, "I can't say any more," and wept quietly with a handkerchief to his eyes.

So, on the eighth day of June, 1945, General George Smith Patton, Jr., came home to America. The commander who had killed, wounded, or captured nearly a million Germans came home to weep into a handkerchief at a Boston dinner party. The soldier who had hoped to die on a foreign field was banqueting, not in the halls of Valhalla, but in the ballroom of the Copley-Plaza Hotel.

3

General Patton had one last rite to perform. Like generations of conquerors before him, he wished to give dutiful thanks to the God of Battle.

"There is a little church out there in Los Angeles," he said, "where I was baptized and confirmed. God has been very good to me, and I'd like to go there and give thanks to Him."

In Los Angeles, where he went from Boston, he was duly welcomed by "the greatest constellation of stars ever assembled." When the tumult and the cheering had ended, Patton remembered his vow. On Sunday, accompanied by his wife and sister, he set out for the Episcopal Church of Our Saviour at San Gabriel, preceded by an escort of motorcyclist police. Amid the shrieking of sirens, he came back to "the little church." Here he was welcomed by the Rev. Franklin L. Gibson, and here he placed a wreath of roses at the monument to his friend and aide, Major Richard Jensen, who had died at his side in Africa.

And here, too, he stood in the presence of a hundred awed and uncomprehending children, and told them:

"In my opinion there will be another war, because there have always been wars . . . You are the soldiers, sailors, and nurses of the next war, if we don't stop wars."

And he told this little company of boys in their dark Sunday suits and girls with bows in their hair that he had found much comfort in religion during battle, and urged them to cultivate their religious life.

"For if the day of war does come again, you will find strong support in religion."

Standing before them, erect, bestarred, bemedalled, his head gray, his eyes a little uncertain, his riding crop clutched in his hands, he led the Sunday-school in singing "Onward Christian Soldiers, marching as to war."

And so General George S. Patton, Jr., came home, came back to the church where he had been baptized and confirmed, to give thanks to the God of Battles.

>"Great God, who through the ages
> Has braced the bloodstained hand,
> As Saturn, Jove, or Woden,
> Has lead our warrior band,
>
> Again we seek Thy counsel
> But not in cringing guise,
> We whine not for Thy mercy—
> To slay, God make us wise."

"To slay, God make us wise." General George S. Patton, Jr., has written, in one line, the sum of his philosophy, the history of his life, and the epitaph by which those who come after will remember him.

EPILOGUE

AFTER his hero's welcome in the United States in the spring of 1945, Patton returned to Germany, resuming command of his Third Army, then stationed in Bavaria with headquarters at Bad Tölz. As the civil administrator of a sizeable section of a nation conquered in an ideological war, Patton was bound to be exposed to controversy. Characteristically considering the Germans as good soldiers who had manfully lost in a fair fight and brushing aside the subtleties of politics, Patton proceeded with the denazification of Bavaria slowly, thereby bringing down upon his head the recriminations of politically-minded observers and commentators. Lashing out angrily against his critics, he stated on September twenty-second in one of his ill-timed and untactful remarks that too much fuss was being made over Nazism; that the Nazis could be compared to the losers in an election contest between Republicans and Democrats in the United States. General Eisenhower called Patton to Frankfurt to rebuke him for his remarks, and on September twenty-fifth Patton gave an interview in which he retracted many of his assertions.

On October second, ten days after the furor concerning the denazification of Bavaria, Patton was relieved from command of his beloved Third Army. He bore the blow in soldierly silence. His new assignment was the command of the Fifteenth Army, an army without weapons engaged in studying the tactics of the recently completed war for the light they might give on future conflicts and in compiling a detailed history. The transfer was widely interpreted as a demotion, since to place an eminent fighting man in command of a paper organization appeared almost an insult, but observers who emphasized this neglected the fact that the Third Army's actual combat was over and that Patton's favorite avocation since the age of seven had been reading military history and studying tactics. Patton was as much in his element as if he had been in a tank.

On December ninth, shortly before he was scheduled to go home for a long leave, the General set out one afternoon to shoot pheasant. The army sedan in which he was riding collided with a two and a half ton truck just north of Mannheim. Patton, who at first appeared slightly injured, was the only one hurt. The following day he was paralyzed from the neck down, a condition resulting from a broken neck and spinal injuries. During the next few days, especially after the arrival of Mrs. Patton, his condition improved until by the fourteenth it was pronounced "excellent" and plans were made to move him to the United States. The progress continued under expert care in the Seventh Army Headquarters Hospital at Heidelberg until the afternoon of December nineteenth. Patton was cheerful and confident and had regained some movement in his body. Hopes of bringing him to America within a week or ten days were high.

On the nineteenth a blood clot appeared in his lung, and this, aggravated by the paralysis, proved too great a strain on his heart. On December 21, 1945, General Patton, who had expected and hoped to die in a tank in combat, died peacefully in his sleep in a plaster cast, yet he went down in a gallant fight against his injuries and in a place symbolic of his success—a hospital which had been a barracks for enemy cavalry. Mrs. Patton was at his side. It was just a year after his swift thrusts had brought relief to the encircled defenders of Bastogne.

Immediately messages of condolence and praise began to pour into Heidelberg from all over the world. President Truman, Prime Minister Attlee, the royal families of Belgium and Luxembourg, the government of France—all expressed to Mrs. Patton grief and admiration. General Eisenhower and General Bradley, Patton's superiors in his most colorful days, added their words. And Lieutenant-General Joseph T. McNarney, Chief of Staff of the United States Forces in the European Theatre, terming him "a great fighter and a great man," said: "He went down fighting. General Patton would have died in no other way."

George S. Patton, Jr., 02605, with no other designation on his white wooden cross than this name and this army serial number, lies buried with thirty thousand other American soldiers in the military cemetery at Hamm, a few miles from the City of Luxembourg. He lies in a country which he and they liberated and which saw the greatest battles of a fighting man. He was buried by the Third Army among the men who had fought with him.

Printed in the United States
134138LV00008B/144/A